This book is an extraordinary gift to those who are ~~~~~~~~~ with the challenges and complexities of being ~~~~~~~~~~~~~ and non-violently active at the dark e~  arry Bury's wisdom and courageous ~ and inspiration for living on the front~ ~gle. Harry is one of the most interesting ~ and his book is no less intriguing. A must read!

~ **Sister Judith Cauley**

Maverick Priest is the story of a remarkable Man of God who, in a very real sense, devoted his life to living the life of a true Christian. A remarkable book of self-sacrifice.

~ **Arun Gandhi,** Founder/President,
Gandhi Worldwide Education Institute,
Rochester, New York, www.arungandhi.org

It has been my privilege to know Harry Bury since I was in grade school. He has been a major force in my life, for my entire life. One of the many wonders of this man is the force he is to all who meet him. He carries with him pure kindness and compassion. His life has been lived with an utter determination to make the world a place of peace and nonviolence. He never stops believing that it will happen and working to make it so. *Maverick Priest* opens the doors Harry has traveled through in the world, and in his conscience, one experience more remarkable than the next, ever hopeful and uplifting. This *Maverick Priest,* I am certain, will become a force in the lives of all who read him. God Bless his gentle soul.

~ **Nancy Nelson,** Television News Anchor,
Stage and Film Actress, Radio Host,
Named by CBS Sunday Morning as the "Infomercial Queen"

Maverick Priest by Father Harry J. Bury is an extraordinary book by an extraordinary Catholic priest. Fr. Bury has been a warrior for peace in our violent world for most of his 90 years. He has waged peace in Vietnam, India, Africa, Palestine, Israel, and elsewhere. He has led demonstrations for peace everywhere and served at the side of Mother Teresa in India. In Gaza, he pleaded, "For God's sake, for humanity's sake, stop the killing!" His relentless peacemaking efforts offended some governmental, political, and church authorities, and he has been arrested and jailed everywhere, and once kidnapped at gunpoint. But nothing could dissuade him from taking seriously and acting on Jesus' command to "love." "Forgiveness dominates Jesus' life and teaching," he writes. This is no ordinary pastor. Peacemakers run the risk of being jailed, abused, and even crucified. But it was Jesus who said, "Blessed are the peacemakers for they shall be called the sons of God." (Matthew 5:9)

~ **Cal Samra,** Editor of *The Joyful Noiseletter,*
Author of *The Pursuit of Health and Longevity*

Maverick Priest: A Life on the Edge is an inspirational book about Fr. Harry Bury, and it is a much-awaited companion to his previous book, *An Invitation to Think and Feel Different in the New Millennium*, in which he expressed his ideas about a wide range of topics.

We first came to know Fr. Harry at the Newman Student Association at the University of Minnesota in 1966. He breathed life into the Mass and showed how the liturgy could be both a joyful community and a call to action. He officiated at our marriage and sent us off to the Peace Corps.

His life has continued to be an inspiration. Most recently, we called him from Florida where we were visiting Sandy's mother, Retta, who turns 97 in July. He answered the phone with his upbeat trademark greeting, "Happy Thursday!" His exuberance takes you a little off guard as he crosses the boundary that separates people. He sent his love to Retta.

On the political and social scene, he said he was angrier than ever. In answer to the question of what we should do, he said that you must have faith. It is this call to action, joy in people, and faith in God that make him such a great man and make his life a great read.

~ **Sandy and Dr. Charlie Slater,** Professor,
California State University Long Beach

Maverick Priest by Father Harry Bury, who lives up to the title of his remarkable and honest autobiography, offers us a deep and profound insight into the good intentions and flaws of "the church" and of ourselves.

He bares his soul in his writing as he gives us a glimpse into the minds and hearts of religious and secular leaders—including Mother Teresa, who was a special friend and inspiration to him.

His commitment and dedication to helping the people of Vietnam is commendable as is his commitment for us to understand the unjustified atrocities eventuated by wars.

A major theme of Bury's book is we must stop using war as a means of international policy and make every effort to build bridges of understanding between countries—and each other. He emphasizes this can only happen if we are willing to put major efforts into understanding ourselves as individuals in order to better understand others. His book will inspire you to open your mind and heart to the most important three words in all literature: *God is Love.*

~ **Paddy S. Welles,** Ph.D., co-author of *LOVE AND WAR:*
Human Nature in Crisis

Maverick
Pries✝

A STORY OF LIFE ON THE EDGE

Father **Harry J. Bury,** Ph.D.

Robert D. Reed Publishers

Robert D. Reed Publishers . Bandon, OR

Robert D. Reed Publishers
P.O. Box 1992
Bandon, OR 97411
Phone: 541-347-9882; Fax: -9883
E-mail: 4bobreed@msn.com
Website: www.rdrpublishers.com

Cover Designer: Cleone Reed
Book Designer: Amy Cole
Editor: Connie Anderson, Words & Deeds, Inc.

Soft-cover ISBN: 978-1-944297-32-9
Kindle ISBN: 978-1-944297-33-6

Library of Congress Number: 2018939288

Designed and Formatted in the United States of America

Note: Once a priest has been named, like Fr. Bob Willis, thereafter most often he will just be called by his last name, i.e., Willis.

Dedication

Written in honor of my deceased parents,
Leona Commers and Harold Bury;
my sister Louise, a Discalced Carmelite Nun
who continues to inspire me;
and my brother Frederick,
from whom I never cease to learn.

And to all peace activists,
especially from 1965 through to the present,
who I know have my back.

Father Harry J. Bury, Ph.D.
Priest, Professor, Political Activist, Warrior for Peace

About the Author

Harry J. Bury is an American Roman Catholic priest and Professor Emeritus of Organizational Behavior and Administration from Case Western Reserve University. He taught at Baldwin Wallace University from 1980–2010, and consulted not only in the U.S., but also numerous other countries.

Bury's activism started as a new priest serving at the University's Newman Center in the '60s when young Catholic men asked him to write a letter for them as a conscientious objector for the Vietnam War. In 1971, at the request of some Vietnamese, he and three others chained themselves to the U.S. Embassy gate in Saigon to protest the Vietnam War. In 2005, Harry was abducted in Gaza while serving as a human shield between Israeli soldiers and Palestinian citizens.

Bury believes in dialogue and compromise between people in the community and around the world. In his 88 years, he's never hesitated to "risk the worst in order to achieve the best."

Acknowledgments

For a long time I was stuck. I wanted to write this memoir, but just couldn't get started. Voicing my frustration, Carol Masters suggested and offered to listen to me tell my story into a tape recorder from which she would type it into book form. Her generous idea pieced my mental and emotional blockages—and this memoir was born. I am forever grateful. It would not have happened without her.

Several other women read the entire manuscript contributing to its final edition. I'm most grateful for their spirited suggestions, critical analysis, and loving inspiration that contributed to the manuscript's birth.

Lee Orcutt, Poet Lee, as she is known, worked her words of magic in making my life experiences come alive.

Anne O'Tremba corrected my lapses in grammar and spelling. She acted as my agent as well, encouraging me in the process.

Nancy Nelson, long-time friend, has been invaluable along every step of this process, and I always appreciate her insights.

Connie Anderson had the horrendous task of editing the final manuscript down to a reasonable number of words. Her loving inspiration, along with her supreme competence, made a marvelous difference in the final document.

Cleone Reed deserves my gratitude for her editorial collaboration during the final phases of this text.

Writing a book can take over one's life for a while. I found that it invited me to relive many of the experiences, especially the ones in Vietnam. During this time, I needed support. I'm deeply grateful for my many friends who were here for me.

Prologue

A short time ago I met with Frank Kroncke, who had been a Program Director at the Newman Center from 1969 to part of 1970. He asked me if a central question for Harry and for the book might be "Why has Harry Bury remained a priest?" through all the turmoil, world events, and emotional challenges of the last half of the twentieth century.

There are 41,500 Diocesan and Religious priests in the United States today. During the past 60 years 25,000 priests have left the priesthood in the United States, and worldwide over 120,000 priests have left. http://www.leavingthepriesthood.com.

Among my friends are several priests who decided to leave, whether it was to be married or for some other reasons, mostly because the church was too slow to implement the reforms of Vatican II. In the turbulent Sixties, many young people, not only the draftees for a questionable war, were wondering about the directions their lives would take in a society that seemed to be coming apart. Dropping out, turning on, or turning around were endemic to the culture.

Harry had been serving in diocesan ministry for about a decade during the Sixties, and he speaks of periods of "restlessness" that, despite his sense that he was doing well in his ministries, tormented him. What forced many young priests to leave was not ministerial difficulties, but the inability to live their lives in the manner to which they felt called. It was clear that Harry felt called to serve others, whether it was because he himself had experienced being marginalized, or because his heart went out to people that he understood as oppressed, but beloved of God.

Looking back at Harry's time at the Newman Center, Darrell Fasching, a Catholic student at the University of Minnesota, commented that "Father Bury's special gift was to touch the hearts of people. He was a healing listener who exuded the love of God in Christ for each and every individual. He helped students see their responsibility to be healing presences in a world torn apart both by racism and the issues of civil rights, and by the Vietnam War."

I am not Catholic, but Lutheran. When we began to work together on this memoir, Harry asked, "Are you a devout Lutheran?" I laughed; I hadn't heard those two descriptors linked. I wasn't sure my devotion had much to do with church. But as we talked over the months and years that followed, I found many consonances (harmony or agreements) in the expressions of our faith stories.

I'd been active in the Minnesota peace movement, demonstrating, with others—at the doors of weapons makers and in government offices—over U.S. military incursions in Central America and later Iraq; I'd been arrested and had served time in jail. My faith was a motivator for these actions, specifically the faith that the force behind and within creation was a force for good, a loving power, and that I was called to act in a way that held up love and nonviolence.

Later, I asked Frank Kroncke what Harry's emphasis was in his sermons and counseling at Newman. "Love," Frank said, "it was always love." As Harry explains, "I'm not a do-gooder working out my own personal challenges under the guise of helping others, but rather I'm more like a reformed alcoholic who has experienced the liberation power of God's justice and mercy... I have come to believe the Christ in me needs to look out for and love Christ in others." In another word, as Lutherans have a habit of expressing it, grace.

– Carol Masters

Preface

This is a story of my effort to be faithful to the Gospel, a radical follower of Christ. It reflects my present recollections of my experiences over a period of decades. Dialogues and events have been recreated from memory and, in some cases, have been compressed to convey the substance of what was said or what occurred.

My life and this book reflect a philosophy of life that has been developing to include four basic conscious assumptions:

1. Although truth exists, I assume no one can be absolutely sure about anything because total reality cannot be comprehended by the finite human mind. If I only know a part of reality, and do not comprehend the whole, all my knowledge is partial, not the whole truth. Hence, it is senseless to kill each other over who is absolutely correct and who is off-target.

2. I assume nothing is perfect on earth. Both the positive and the negative exist in every person, in everything, in every situation. It makes sense then to look for what is good, and direct our energy to make it better, to focus on challenges and opportunities, not problems.

3. Our separation from each other is an assumption. I assume, instead, *that we are all one*. What's good for others needs to be good for me, and vice-versa, or it is not beneficial at all.

4. I assume that no evil people exist—only good people who do bad things out of ignorance, believing it is in their own self-interest—a question of values. Our goal, then, is not to punish, but to educate.

5. The reader will notice I often write my life's story in the present tense because some descriptions are present reflections of the past and others are intended to make my past experiences interesting, experiences with which you, the reader, can identify.

6. This is my story of a radical change of mind and heart leading to revolutionary behavior. I have many regrets. If I could live my life over again in some situations, I would act differently. But, it is what it is. Thanks for sharing my journey.

"Nothing ever goes away
until it has taught us what we need to know."

—Pema Chodron, author;
also an American Tibetan Buddhist in Nova Scotia, Canada

Introduction

My mother, Leona Commers, and my father, Harold Bury, started me off on an unbelievable life journey, guided more by their example than by words and admonitions—wisdom that sadly I too often ignored. My parents' behavior motivated me to rank *social justice among the highest of values.* By their actions, my concern for social justice drove me to live a life quite different from the average Roman Catholic priest. It was not a lark. My behavior, conscience-driven, has had consequences not always in agreement with civil and church authorities.

Seeking social justice became for me the emblem of a follower of Jesus Christ in the twentieth and twenty-first centuries.

My first experience of war resistance was as a letter writer for University of Minnesota students who were applying for conscientious objector status.

My first trip to Vietnam was in June 1971 as a researcher seeking to understand how the Vietnamese people felt about the presence of American troops in their country. My second trip was at the request of the Vietnamese to protest the war. Then years later in 1987, I taught in liberated and united Vietnam until just a few years ago. I firmly believe that diplomacy is more effective than fighting.

Justice is not retribution or punishment. Theoretically well intentioned, in practice, punishment is, under the guise of justice, often a strategy for seeking vengeance. Nor is punishment Christlike. As I read the sacred scriptures, forgiveness dominates Jesus' life and teaching. And Pope Francis wrote, "To work for social justice is to promote equal opportunity for everyone. No one is excluded. All are included. Working for social justice means appreciating differences in gender, race, and nationality."

It is my *faith* that enables me to trust we are all family, children of a creator God.

It is my *hope* that enables me to persist in seeking social justice against significant odds. This is despite friends and others who continue to try to persuade me that I will not make much of a difference that's worth the effort or the risk.

Recently, when I explain my new mission to create an environment in which the Twin Cities of Minnesota can become free from violence, friends try to contain a laugh and say, "Good luck!" I perceive their message to be that I'm unrealistic. "You live in la-la-land," one friend told me. A few others have joined me, which I have found encouraging and increased my hope.

It is unconditional *love*, love of God, love of every human being, and love of myself as well as creation, that drives me to seek social justice.

This faith, hope, and love are a gift from God. Now in the autumn of my life, to be able to share my story fills my heart with deep gratitude.

Table of Contents

Dedication vii

About the Author.. ix

Acknowledgments.. xi

Prologue xiii

Preface.. xv

Introduction.. xvii

Chapter 1: Unchained: My Conscience Was Calling (1971) 1

Chapter 2: Being Arrested...and All That Followed (1971)................ 7

    More Expected 9

    A Return to the United States Embassy..11

    Empty Voting Places 13

    Willis' Meeting with the Buddhists 15

    No Concelebration! 16

    Arrested Again... 18

    Vientiane, Laos's Capital City – October 4, 1971 21

    Heading to Rome... 24

    A Special Delivery.. 25

**Chapter 3:From the Beginning...Looking Forward,
Looking Back (1930–1945)** 29

    Standing Tall... 29

    Growing-Up Years in Minneapolis, Minnesota 30

    Our Parents Played Fair.. 31

    Love and Affection 31

    Dad Was My Silent Partner 33

Chapter 4: Off to the Seminary to Start My Training (1945–1955).... 37

    Why Be a Priest? 37

Minor Seminary 38
Nazareth Hall's New Rector "Sets Me Straight"........................... 42
Major Seminary–the Road to Becoming a Priest – 1949 44
Doubts About Becoming a Priest 47

Chapter 5: Early Priesthood—Unaware and Restless (1955–1965) ... 51
St. Frances Cabrini Parish 51
Confessor.. 52
Preacher... 52
Hospital Ministry.. 53
St. Helena's Parish.. 57
The University of Notre Dame and the Second Vatican Council..... 59
Meeting and Working With Mother Teresa 61
Mother Teresa's "Beatification" – 2004 64

Chapter 6: Newman Apostolate: In the Beginning (1965–1967) 67
Newman Center.. 67
Disoriented and Disconnected... 68
Father George Garrelts 70
Discovering the Campus 71
Changes and the Hope of More 72
Music, Music, Music... 74

**Chapter 7: Newman Apostolate: The Beginning of the End
(1967–1970)**.. 77
The Hippie Movement: Summer of Love 77
The Thinking of Abraham Maslow 79
Christ's Resurrection 80
The Wonder of Berkeley... 81
Joan Baez Gives a Concert... 81
Returning to Newman in Minnesota 85
Minnesota-born Daniel Berrigan: Jesuit Priest, Poet, Teacher,
    Dramatist, Peacemaker, War Resister, and Truth-teller 86
Before the Trial.. 88
Conscientious Objection... 89
Eugene McCarthy Was a Friend... 90
The Milwaukee Fourteen.. 91
Participating in a Sensitivity Group 92
New Structure at Newman 93

Mass at the Pentagon 94
Nonviolence 97
Frank Kroncke's Invitation 99
My Second Arrest 100
Case Western Reserve University 102
Kent State Tragedy – May 4, 1970 104
The Paris Peace Talks – June 1970 106
John Denver Gives a Concert 107
On My Way 109

Chapter 8: Graduate School Beginnings (Fall of 1970) 111
On Leaving Newman 111
Homebody 113
Challenges 114
New Community 116
Gestalt Institute of Cleveland 116

Chapter 9: My First Trip to Vietnam (1971) 119
Research—Summer 1971 119
Reporter Tom Fox Approaches Me 120
Paris Mission 120
Relief and Disappointment 121
North Vietnamese Priests 122
Rome…but Not a Holiday 123
Protest in Rome 124
Stopover in Israel 125
Lost in Calcutta 127
Following Mother Teresa 128
Bangladesh Refugee Camp 131
In Thailand, Disbelief 134

Chapter 10: An Invitation to Return to Saigon 137
Strangers in Saigon – First Visit, October 1971 137
Ngo Cong Duc and Tin Sang 140
Visit to Quang Ngãi 140
My Lai Village Tragedy 142
Setting the Stage 143
Ten Priests and a Bishop, Please 144
A History Lesson 145

The Catholic Third Force 146
Pentagon Papers 148
The Hunt Is On 149
On Our Own 151

Chapter 11: Hanoi: Another Invitation (September 1972) 155
Coming Home 155
Another Invitation to Return to Vietnam 157
Arrival in Hanoi 160
Captured American Pilots 161
The Catholic Committee in Hanoi 162
Freedom of the Church 164
Traveling by Night 167
The Decoys 175
Meeting with the Cardinal Archbishop of Hanoi 178
Celebrating the Eucharist in Hanoi 180
Enlightenment 183
Returning Home 185

Chapter 12: A Catalyst for My Personal Development (1972) 187
PhD Candidate 187
Maturity at 40? 188
Friendship and Maturity 189
Aspects of Friendship 190
PhD Dissertation 192
Characteristics of Mature Priests 194
Double Bind 195

Chapter 13: Various Positions I Applied for... and Those I Held .. 201
Archdiocese of Saint Paul 201
Psychotherapy: Beech Brook 204
Teaching and Learning at Baldwin Wallace 205
Conversant in Costa Rica 206
Experiencing Liberation Theology in Nicaragua 207
Surprises in Guatemala 208
Professor-in-Residence: Hong Kong 210

Chapter 14: May I Return to Vietnam? (June 1987) 213
A Hospitable Hanoi 214

Polaroids for Peace 216
Why Does the U.S. Still Punish Us? 218
After Many Years, Back to Ho Chi Minh City 222
Patriot: Doan Van Toai 226
Ho Chi Minh City – 1992 229

Chapter 15: Holy Week in Vietnam (March/April 1994) 231

Chapter 16: Teaching Opportunity in Thailand (2002) 245
Assumption University 245
Burapha University 249
Moving On 251
Thailand's Political Turmoil 251
What Would I Do if Asked to Help Thailand? 257

Chapter 17: Responding to a World Under Threat (2005) 263
Heading to Palestine in July 2005 263
At Ecce Homo 264
Entering Gaza 265
The Wall of Rafah 267
Visualizing the Future 269
Holy Family Church 272
Muwasse 275
Demolished Homes 279
A Hallowed Site: Remembering Rachel 280
The Future of Palestine 281
The Governor of Rafah 284
Unsafe to Stay in Gaza 285
Appreciative Inquiry Approach: Discover, Dream, Design, Deliver .. 286
Time to Reflect 288
Abducted! 291
Must We Leave? 298
Visiting Bethlehem 300
On a Bus to Hebron 302
Conclusion 303

Chapter 18: Vietnam Revisited (2014) 307
Prison Reform 307
Ho Chi Minh City (HCMC) 308

Vietnamese Women and the Church 310
Third Force Once Again 313
An English Newspaper in Vietnam 314

Chapter 19: Another Mission: Twin Cities Nonviolent 317
Living in Minnesota – Byrne Residence 317
The Association of US Catholic Priests (AUSCP) 318
Twin Cities Nonviolent 319
Asking the Archbishop 319
Meeting Father Rutton 322
Announcing…Our Upcoming Twin Cities Nonviolent Event
  (TCNV) – September 21–30, 2018 323
The United States Bishops Annual Meeting 325
Washington, D.C. 326
April 4, 2017 327

Chapter 20: The End is the Beginning 329
Transformative Change 329
1) Physical Discoveries 330
2) Intellectual Discoveries 332
Socialization 333
• First Assumption 334
• Second Assumption 336
• Third Assumption 337
• Fourth Assumption 338
3) Emotional Discoveries 340
4) Spiritual Discoveries 344
Working for Social Justice 347
Coming Forth 351

Index 353

This photo shows it clearly: four human beings bound together physically, emotionally, and spiritually, crying out with one voice:

**"For God's sake, for humanity's sake,
stop the killing!"**

*Shown are (left to right): Bob Willis, John Dee, Harry Bury,
and Len Hirsch*

CHAPTER 1

Unchained: My Conscience Was Calling (1971)

Saigon, Vietnam – October 2, 1971

"Friend Bob Dalton always told me it is different when *you have boots on the ground*."

—Harry Bury

I'm not locked down, not immobilized. In my forty-one years, I resisted anyone trying to immobilize me. The chain is merely looped over my left foot, snaking behind my right ankle as it coils through the gate of the United States' Embassy in Saigon. Owing to a glitch in plans, I only pretended to be chained to the iron bars. My three colleagues were not pretending. Father Bob Willis, Father John Dee, and my Ph.D. schoolmate Leonard Hirsch were padlocked to the gate—and none of us carried a key.

Moments before, we had stopped our taxi fifty yards past the U.S. Embassy entrance. Since the Tet offensive in 1968, no one had been allowed to stop a vehicle in front of the embassy. It was shortly after 9:00 a.m., but already we were drenched in sweat and squinting in the hot October sun.

As we started to walk casually toward the entrance, a crowd of reporters and photographers came out of nowhere and charged at us. Quickening our pace, making every effort to ignore them, we reached and slipped through the personnel gate. We approached the U.S. Marine guard seated just inside, perched high behind a desk as he peered down at us like a judge.

"Pardon me," I began calmly, trying to hide my feelings of excitement, "I wonder if you would help us. We would like to see Ambassador Bunker today, if possible."

The Marine grabbed a phone and turned toward the embassy building, gazing up at the windows as though he could see the ambassador in his office. He kept his back to us while making the call.

That was our moment. Quickly, my fellow peacemakers moved back and to the left, reaching the embassy's automobile entrance gate. Energized and motivated, they threw open Father Dee's guitar case which secretly hid padlocks and chain. Wrapping the chain around their ankles and the bars, they secured themselves with padlocks.

"Sorry, Father," the Marine said, lying to us, we learned later, "The Ambassador's out of the city. Can anyone else help you?"

"No, thank you very much," I said and rushed over to join my colleagues, twelve paces to my left. I found them already securely fastened. To my dismay they had used too much chain, leaving nothing for me to fasten my ankle to the iron bars. I wished we had practiced beforehand.

"Slide over!" I huffed, trying hard not to elbow Leonard as I wedged myself between him and Father Dee. "There's not enough chain, and I can't get it around my ankle!"

"Fake it!" Dee whispered. Obediently, I tucked my left shoe beneath the heavy links and stepped over the chain, pushing it back with my right ankle. No one could tell I was not actually chained. And who would check?

We were breaking U.S. law, going against the policies of our government by protesting this war, and doing it in the very country the war was devastating. I was in turmoil because I respected the law, but my conscience demanded more. I love my country with all my heart, and that's why I was seeking to make it better. Our values told us that our nation was making not only a terrible mistake, but going against the will of God by attacking the small nation which was seeking unification and liberation in its civil war. We waited for the authorities to respond.

Members of the press on the outside pushed against the embassy gate, yelled questions at us in Vietnamese and English while cameras flashed incessantly. Eager hands grabbed at our prepared statement written in both Vietnamese and English that explained our behavior.

Our written statement emphasized that "Jesus died for Communists as well as Catholic Christians, for North Vietnamese as well as South Vietnamese people. No one is an enemy. If we kill each other, no one wins."

Within minutes, a tall middle-aged embassy security officer approached from behind the four of us. Assuming I was the spokesperson, he asked almost politely, "How long, Father, do you intend to remain here?"

Taken aback by his question and his apparent calm, I blurted out, "Until the war is over! Until the killing of Vietnamese and Americans stops!"

The officer paused, perhaps surprised by my words and my passion. Recovering quickly, he asked, "Would you like some chairs to sit on?"

I believe now he was making fun of us rather than being kind. "No!" I shouted, "Not necessary!" and continued to hand our position paper through the bars to eager hands. The officer neither asked for a copy nor did I think to hand him one. He disappeared while noise and commotion raged on in front of us.

I wonder what we would have done had the embassy officer taken us at our word and left the four of us there for hours or days. My brothers could not free themselves had they wanted to; our Vietnamese friends, as planned, had the keys to the padlocks. What would we do when we needed to urinate? True, cassocks cover a multitude of sins, but....

Later people asked me, "What did it feel like? Were you afraid?" Never having learned to be aware of my feelings, I was too taken up in the moment to realize my emotional state. Afraid? If I were, I was unaware of it. My heart seemed to be pounding within me.

I do remember that Leonard, an agnostic, just moments before we set forth, saying, "This is easy for you guys; you believe in an afterlife." At the time, I gave a thoughtless laugh and agreed. Now, I seriously agree. A strong faith in a life beyond this one gives me courage. At the same time, we all need to confront the fact that we will die: knowing that leads us to evaluate our purpose and meaning of each day.

In addition, I assumed that, besides my three compatriots, the Catholic Church community and the Organizational Behavior Department at Case Western Reserve University had our backs. And, of course, I could always depend on my family.

There was not one word of support, however, from my priest friends back in the Archdiocese of St. Paul, Minnesota. Many years later, I pointedly asked a classmate, Father Jim Remes, "Why didn't you support me in my efforts to resist the war in Vietnam?"

After a moment he said, "I didn't think what you were doing would do any good."

I shot back an objection, "How would anyone know that unless they tried?" I wish I would have quoted Mother Teresa who said, "God does not call us to be successful but to be faithful."

Similarly, the man Bob Willis reported to, another Jesuit, asked him angrily, "What did you think you were going to do, stop the war?" Willis confided he never had that as a thought, let alone a goal. He was simply following his conscience.

I view my actions as a bit part, hardly a prophet. My intent was to raise the awareness of the American public to other and maybe new information about the Vietnam War. I assumed I was acting in accordance with Gospel values. At least, I wanted to act boldly according to the Gospels, and my intent was to be a good priest.

Less than forty-five minutes later, more embassy security guards appeared, armed with a huge bolt cutter. With quick snaps, they sliced through the heavy chains like cutting paper. Once unleashed, we were ushered out through the gate we originally entered; guitar case, chains, and padlocks were tossed after us as if pitched in disdain. Outside, we were no longer protected by embassy territory. From the outset, we planned that U.S. authorities would deal with us, not Vietnamese, because tiger cages were not all that appealing. We had seen photos of other South Vietnamese captives.

The crowd physically pushed against us, continuing their barrage of questions. At a loss as to what to do next, and to maintain our balance, the four of us hung onto the bars of the same gate, but on the outside this time, almost in desperation. Ironically, the South Vietnamese police arrived before we could catch our breath. "Inviting" us to go with them, they cleared a path through the noisy crowd to waiting patrol cars, which whisked us away to the nearest police station. What next, I thought? Were we being removed to somewhere we did not wish to go? I didn't think to pray.

All these years later, I continue to treasure a few links of our chains—given to me by my Vietnamese friends—as relics of our experience. Still deeply connected to these comrades in peacemaking, I imagine what it would be like if today we were chained to the U.S. Embassy in Kabul, Afghanistan. I can hear us urgently shouting much the same message: "Muslims, Christians, Jews, Afghans, Americans, Israelis, Iranians, all of us are God's children, one family for whom Jesus gave his life.

FOR THE LOVE OF ALLAH!
FOR THE LOVE OF GOD!
STOP KILLING EACH OTHER!
START LOVING EACH OTHER!

The words from Pete Seeger's song, "Where Have All the Flowers Gone?" still have a hold on me: *"When will they ever learn?"*

CHAPTER 2

Being Arrested...and All That Followed (1971)

**"Like many other peace workers,
I never hesitated to risk 'the worst' in order
to achieve something better."**

—Harry Bury

Within minutes, the four of us were transported to the nearby Vietnamese police station. Screams from the chaotic crowd at the U.S. Embassy continued to ring in our ears. We were led into a large, bright room with busy clerks dashing about on this Saturday morning. The sun shining through the many windows created an atmosphere far different from the dungeon I had been expecting.

We were directed to a table in the center of the room and ordered in English to "Sit down and wait!" We had hardly a moment to speak to each other before a police official approached, waving in our faces the statement in Vietnamese we had been distributing while chained to the embassy gate.

"Who wrote this?" he asked sternly, shoving the paper closer to us. Clearly, the authorities wanted to get their hands on our Vietnamese friends responsible for the demonstration.

"He called himself Mr. Ngoc," I offered, which is a name as common as Johnson in Minnesota. We would not betray our friend, Tran Ngoc Bau, a Catholic employed as a social worker for Lutheran Family Services. (In Vietnam the surname is listed first and the first name last. Being a close friend, we called him by his first name, Bau.)

"Where did you meet him?" the official shot back. "Who is he?"

"At our hotel. That's all we know about him. We only met him once," we lied.

Unable to get any other information out of us, he appeared frustrated and walked away. We were surprised and grateful we had been questioned as a group, able to collaborate and not contradict one another in our story.

Not long afterward, two officials from the U.S. Embassy entered and approached us. Jerry, the smaller fellow, did the talking while his partner, Peter, surveyed the scene. Although business-like, Jerry was friendly. He appeared to sincerely want to help us. A troubleshooter for the embassy, his job apparently was to come to the rescue of American citizens who lost their passports, or drank too much and became a public nuisance. Peter was aloof, surveying the scene. He could have been Jerry's partner, bodyguard, or supervisor making sure that Jerry did his job correctly.

Jerry admitted he didn't know what he could do for us, suggesting our behavior was out of the ordinary. However, he assured us he would try his best. I think he was in *over his head*.

Shortly, the two returned, obviously pleased at having achieved their objective.

"The Vietnamese authorities are willing to let you go," Jerry said, "if you all promise not to do any more demonstrations." Almost as one, and with little thought, the four of us gave our word. I believe we were sincere. We had no further plans to cause trouble. In my mind, we had done what we were asked to do, and had done enough. Our determination to chain ourselves to the inside of the embassy gate made us U.S., not Vietnamese, lawbreakers, and the Americans threw us out without pressing charges; this freed the Vietnamese of responsibility for our behavior. Wise on our part!

Jerry and his partner Peter once more went off to report our promise of "No more demonstrations" to the Vietnamese authorities.

On returning, Jerry motioned us to follow them as he and his silent partner headed for the door. I had no trouble obeying when it is perceived to be in my own self-interest. Quickly, we jumped to our feet in our eagerness to be free.

Once outside, we could not believe our good fortune. Jerry warned us, "Don't do anything else!" Then added, "If you do, I probably won't be able to help you again." I heard it as, "I'll not be able to save you again." We assured him we would keep our promise.

Jerry then mentioned that he learned we had requested to see the United States Ambassador, Ellsworth Bunker, asking, "Do you still want to talk to the ambassador?"

"Absolutely!" we all chimed in. Willis wondered, "But we understood he isn't in Saigon." Jerry explained that his presence was not to be public knowledge during the election weekend.

Jerry promised to do what he could to arrange a meeting that afternoon, offering to call us at our hotel. Expecting nothing to come of it, we headed for our hotel. To our surprise, Jerry did manage to get us an appointment with Ambassador Bunker at 3:30 that afternoon.

More Expected

Bau, among others, was waiting for us when we arrived at the hotel. He invited us to accompany him and his colleagues to a special meeting. Without question, we went. We were there to serve.

Traveling on the back of motorbikes, we weaved through heavy traffic with the utmost of ease. My mind was too occupied for me to be scared, although I did hang on tight. We finally arrived at Father Can's Young Christian Workers (YCW) headquarters. We entered a large room occupied by some hundred Vietnamese young people, and to our surprise, we were greeted by deafening applause. They were manifestly grateful for what the four of us had done to support their cause.

After many expressions of thanks, our friends got down to business. What to do about tomorrow, Sunday, October 3, the day of the election? According to the newspapers, President Thieu was expected to vote about noon at the main voting place in the center of Saigon.

Our Vietnamese friends then suggested that the four of us knock over an American truck and set it on fire at the exact time President Thieu arrived to vote. I was dumbfounded. I hadn't been mentally or emotionally prepared for acting violently. Thankfully, Leonard spoke up in all seriousness.

"All over America, our nonviolent action is appearing on TV, showing us protesting the immorality of this war being perpetrated against the Vietnamese people. Our protest has given second thoughts to many Americans about U.S policy. It has a positive effect toward questioning the violence our military is doing in your country. But if tomorrow, the four of us perform a violent act, as you suggest, it will destroy much of the goodwill we achieved today among the American public!"

Our Vietnamese friends "got it." They understood and agreed. I was relieved. More discussion was followed by a new suggestion.

"How about the four of you doing something to distract the crowd's attention—then some of the Vietnamese young men will tip over a truck and set it on fire?"

"Oh my goodness," I thought, quoting my mother when she was disturbed. "What could we do?"

It didn't seem that there was any way to get out of this plan, so we reluctantly agreed. My conscience imagined the truck being empty, and no one being injured.

Second plan. Sunday evening at 7 p.m. we were to go to the church most frequented by Catholic military personnel and their families. We would ask the American priest and pastor if we could concelebrate (say it together) Mass with him. Once he agreed to that idea, I intended to ask if I could give the homily or sermon. If he refused, our Vietnamese friends would print copies of my sermon beforehand in both languages, and we would then pass out our written message of Christ's peace to the assembled congregation.

It would state that this message would have been my homily, had I not been forbidden to give it.

A Return to the United States Embassy

My job that Saturday night was to write the homily. First, however, was a trip once more to the U.S. Embassy to visit with the Ambassador. We moved through the now-familiar gate, passed a different Marine on his perch, and entered what appeared to be a six-story building with a roof large enough for helicopters to land—which they did four years later during the evacuation in 1975.

Ambassador Bunker, a gray-haired man in his late seventies, greeted us politely as if we were normal American citizens just stopping by to say "Hello." Once we were seated, the Ambassador spoke to us about the American mission in Vietnam as if we were uninformed students. It seemed like a classroom with our teacher giving us a lecture on how things really were, lest we be mistaken. We were able to ask questions but not to supply answers. As I listened, I was reminded of what President Nixon was saying back in the States. I'd hoped Bunker would have a different view, informed by being in Vietnam. I'd hoped he had mixed with people of Vietnam and at least heard their point of view. If he did, he was not sharing it with us. Actually, I found it hard to listen.

When Willis asked the Ambassador what he had learned from his stay in Vietnam, the Ambassador asked, "What do you mean?"

"From the people?"

"Which ones?"

"The people down below, the people rioting in the streets," Willis said, motioning with his arm.

"We are not here for them," the Ambassador answered. I was startled. "Certainly, if we were, we would have to change our policies. But, that isn't why we're here."

In the eyes of the U.S. Government, we inferred, the people of Vietnam were simply pawns on the chessboard. The more

11

important pieces in U.S. policy strategy were Russia and China. We were killing Vietnamese to warn Russia and China we would do anything to stop the spread of Communism. "Back off!" was our government's threat.

Dee asked what the Ambassador thought about the morality of the destruction and deaths that were taking place in this country on both sides. To his credit, Ambassador Bunker understood. Looking away, he spoke less authoritatively, "What you are implying is that we must cease using war as a means of international policy. Why that would be a major policy change."

We departed less enlightened but more convinced that U.S. policies and actions in Vietnam were mistaken and unethical.

Later, Willis shared his view of what he learned. "In Ambassador Bunker, I just heard President Nixon and our conservative bishops. Our so-called leaders are protective of U.S. economic and social privileges. None of them hesitates to use others to preserve his position."

Dee said, "He did address our question about war as a social policy...."

Willis shook his head in disgust, continuing his point: "They don't care about moral values like just distribution of the world's resources. They don't comprehend talk about a community of sharing. They brush aside any implication that people have the right to govern themselves, without interference and manipulation of the Big Powers."

I would have preferred that Ambassador Bunker ask us questions such as, "What motivated you to travel to the other side of the world and chain yourself to the embassy gate?" At least we could have enlightened the Ambassador rather than be lectured. But that would have required more listening on his part.

Empty Voting Places

Sunday morning after we feasted on a delicious breakfast, Bau and his companions drove us by motorbike to three different voting places. Our mission was simply to observe voters. In all three locations, very few people voted. Those who did were dressed in western clothes, indicating that likely they were employed by the South Vietnamese or the U.S. government. The next day's newspapers claimed that 94 percent voted for President Thieu—in a one-man election—hardly a demonstration of democracy in action.

Just before noon, we proceeded to the center of Saigon. Every day, we had experienced these same streets crammed with people, even on Sunday. I had imagined throngs of people going about their business, some voting, others waiting to get a peek at the president when he appeared.

What we found were empty, deserted streets, a ghost town with no cars, no trucks, and few people. As we slowly walked in the direction of the voting booth, it was clear our plan wasn't going to work. Then, members of the press, hungry for another story, spotted us, ran toward us and surrounded us, pumping out questions: "Why are you here? What did the police do to you yesterday?"

Trying to keep our promise to distract people so the youths could fulfill their plan, I addressed the eager reporters, as Leonard, who came up with the idea, had coached me:

"We are instituting a People's American Embassy. After our protest yesterday, and our visit with Ambassador Bunker, we're convinced that the present U.S. Embassy doesn't faithfully represent the desires and intentions of United States people. Therefore, we are establishing this People's American Embassy."

Reporters quickly captured our message, writing eagerly. I learned that my statement appeared in U.S. newspapers the next day. Before I could finish, however, we were interrupted. A squadron of Vietnamese soldiers bore down on us. The leading officer screamed at us, intent on breaking up the gathering, which had attracted thirty-some press people.

Leonard spotted a sign for the offices of United Press International (UPI). He yelled, "Come on, this way!" Obediently, we followed Leonard, bounding up the stairs, and burst into a room filled with press corps. Close behind came the Vietnamese army captain with his men. The UPI manager, recognizing us from yesterday, met the captain at the door. Holding up his hand to stop, he said sternly, "This is the headquarters of United Press International. Stop right there, unless you want your actions seen on TV all over the world." The captain peered at all of us in the room, thought better of it, and led his troops down the stairs and back onto the now-empty street.

During the ensuing conversation, I mentioned we would like to go to Hanoi because we were interested in understanding what the Vietnamese people in the North thought about the U.S. presence in their country. Although I didn't mention it, I was also eager to find out whether a viable Catholic Church existed in the North—or had the Communists, as many feared, been successful in destroying it?

A cameraman volunteered an easy way to reach the capital of Laos where a North Vietnamese Embassy was located. "If you go to Bangkok, all you have to do when you arrive at the airport is walk across the street to a train station; the train will take you north to the border. There you can cross the Mekong Delta River and into Laos. Within walking distance is Vientiane, the capital of Laos." He went on, "It's kind of like Istanbul was in the First World War because it is neutral. All the embassies from the warring parties are there. The North Vietnamese have an embassy and, of course, so does the U.S. The North Vietnamese Embassy can arrange a visit for you to Hanoi."

The photographer suggested we stay at the Continental Hotel, which was the best and cleanest, owned by a French-Vietnamese sympathizer. He cautioned, "The hotel is also a nest of spies, so be careful about your table conversation." Good information that came in handy later.

Over tea at UPI headquarters, some discussion arose about the war, along with words of gratitude for what we had done the day before. The manager said, "Until your protest yesterday, we were beginning to think the anti-war movement in the United States had run out of steam." Hearing his words, we were pleased that at least some Americans in Vietnam shared our perceptions of the war. Once the Vietnamese soldiers no longer huddled around the UPI entrance downstairs, we were able to sneak out the back way and return safely to our hotel.

Willis' Meeting with the Buddhists

Willis wanted to meet with a Buddhist monk from the An Quan Pagoda Monastery located in Saigon. To protest the war, two of their monks, at different times, doused their bodies with gasoline, lit themselves on fire, and experienced terrifying deaths. Our efforts paled in the light of their sacrifice. What had motivated the monks to take their own lives were the deaths of so many innocent Vietnamese people, and the desire for the nation to be liberated from foreign influence, and then unified with their brothers in the North, forming one country.

One of Bau's friends arranged for Willis to meet that evening with the Venerable Thich Thieu Hoa, the Elder, head monk of the monastery. They discussed the war and together prayed for peace.

Then this friend took Willis to a meeting with a community of Buddhist sisters at a pagoda. Six sisters and their leader were joined by another six laywomen who were being given sanctuary in the monastery. Willis received an earful. Their words came out through their tears as they told of the personal and family suffering the war had caused. For nearly two hours, Willis sat and listened, saying very little except to express his sorrow for the carnage our government was perpetrating on the people of Vietnam simply because of our fear of communism.

15

For the Vietnamese woman, the American presence has meant murder and rape. For long centuries
Vietnam has been known for two beautiful qualities,
her gentleness and her virtue. Contact with this war
and its warriors have destroyed both. Many have
become dissolute playthings of American passion.
Out of shame, and out of fear, women dare not, and
will not, look an American man directly in the face.
(Willis, Robert, *Breaking the Chains, a Catholic
Memoir*, iUniverse, Inc, New York, Lincoln,
Shanghai, 2005).

Willis told us that these women did more than cry. They were a
strong force, threatening the government in their efforts for prison
reform, in their demands for some protection for family life, in
their quest for rehabilitation at the government's expense for their
injured husbands and sons, and in their pressure of exemption from
army service for their young teenagers. It was an evening that
would haunt Willis' dreams for the rest of his life.

No Concelebration!

While Willis was meeting with our Buddhist friends, we other three
arrived at the parish church about 6:30 that evening. Leonard, Dee,
and I walked through the church, past the communion rail and the
sanctuary, where I dutifully genuflected and entered the sacristy
where we found the priest, an American missionary, preparing to
celebrate the Eucharist.

After introducing ourselves, I asked whether Father John and
I could offer Mass with him. He seemed to hesitate; then he consented but without showing any enthusiasm. To his credit, he probably hadn't had much experience concelebrating at mass because
this was a new development in the liturgy of the church, instituted
by the Second Vatican Council some six years earlier.

16

I then broached the major question. "Father, would it be okay if I gave the homily?" Again he hesitated as if in deep thought. Obviously, this offer was new for him. He was accustomed to being a one-man show.

Finally, he asked, somewhat suspiciously, "What are you going to speak about?"

"Peace," I replied as simply as I could. I wish now I had said, "Gospel Values."

"Peace!" he roared, sounding as if attacked, "I've been a priest here for 30 years. I understand these people. You've only been here a short time." Hearing his protest, I wondered if he knew what we had done at the embassy the day before. *"You don't know what you're talking ab*out."

"Vietnamese priests have informed us," I said, almost apologetically. I hoped my demeanor would soften him.

"Who?" he questioned in a raised voice.

I quickly rattled off the names of our Vietnamese priest friends.

"Oh," he said shrugging, "they were educated in Paris. They are a bunch of Communists!"

This was a common American accusation when a person questions U.S. policy.

His dismissive tone was typical of those who wrote off Vietnamese nationalists who were working for reunification. He went on, "I know this country. It's much better now, much safer, since the U.S. invasion of Cambodia."

Another pause, then he continued. "I've changed my mind. No concelebration. You can say mass at the altars along the side." He pointed to the door. Conversation closed.

Amazing how there is no room at the table of the Lord for people who think differently politically.

Surprised at the Father's certainty and vehemence, slowly we departed back through the sanctuary, past the communion rail, forgetting to genuflect, down the side aisle without so much as glancing at the side altars. People were beginning to straggle in. We, in turn, began to hand out my sermon to the worshippers, who were only Vietnamese. We later learned that the American soldiers and their families had been confined to base for the duration of election weekend.

Within minutes, the priest approached us, now clearly agitated. "You can't do that here. You must leave."

Without objection, we moved to the outside gate and continued to distribute our statement to the people who came for mass. It was now a few minutes after seven. We returned to the vestibule of the church and watched Father begin mass with his back to the people. He prayed softly so I could not hear whether he prayed in Latin or Vietnamese.

After reading the scriptures, Father began to preach in English about our Guardian Angels. If we had stayed, perhaps we might have heard how our guardian angels were here protecting us during this dangerous time of war. His sweet guardian angel description, however, so disappointed me I could not remain. Perceiving we were unwanted, we missed mass.

Arrested Again

We suspect that Father called the police. As my two companions and I reached the entrance gate, it seemed like the world had stopped still. The crowded street of a moment ago was silent and empty. Nothing moved. An eerie feeling crept over me; then a sense of urgency.

At the end of the block, a taxi stood some 50 yards from us. "Look, a taxi; let's run for it!" We started to run and got as far as the corner. Whistles blew, four armored cars screeched to a stop, surrounding us on all sides. At least forty soldiers held us in their gun sights. The captain yelled at us in English, "Give me your passports!" Instantly, Leonard and I dug deep into our pockets, produced our passports, and handed them over. Father John took his out but kept clutching it tightly with both hands, refusing to give it up. The captain, already out of patience, threatened us. Leonard then barked at Dee, "For God's sake, give him the passport. It's his country." Quickly, Dee handed it to the captain. I'm not aware of feeling afraid.

The police station near the church was decidedly different from the one near the embassy of the day before. Dark and dismal, it looked like a dungeon. We were placed together in a large dimly lit room. No iron bars, I realized gratefully. Immediately, we planned our story, so if we were questioned separately, our answers would be consistent. Once we were satisfied that "we had it all altogether," what should we do? Dee had brought his guitar in hopes of playing and singing at the Mass. Out it came from its case, which had held the chains the day before. He quietly began to serenade us with anti-war and religious songs. I joined in when I knew the words. Len listened, his head in his hands.

By 10:30 p.m. Dee had been through his repertoire and gave in to his need for rest. The three of us became silent. I meditated. About midnight, Jerry and Peter came through the door. Embarrassed, my face turned red. It was not like me to go back on my word. *Oh, if I could just disappear or become invisible!*

Jerry looked forlorn. "I don't know if I can help you this time," he said, speaking kindly as he surveyed the three of us clothed in the same garb as yesterday.

What could we say? No excuses. No explanations. I managed, "It's nice to see you two." Jerry said he would see what he could do for us and left, with silent Peter following. Ten or fifteen minutes later, the three of us were separated so they could question us individually. I was taken to a small, sparse, windowless room with three chairs and a wooden table barely large enough to hold a typewriter. Behind it crouched a Vietnamese soldier, a colonel who introduced himself, and I did the same. We both ignored the corporal behind his antiquated typewriter.

"Please sit down, Father," the colonel said in English as he motioned me to the chair in front of the table. I relaxed instantly upon hearing him address me as "Father." I assumed he was Catholic. In his hands, he held my homily in Vietnamese. It is a mystery to me how he obtained it.

"I can read Vietnamese, of course," he explained in clear English, "but tell me in brief what this statement is saying."

After a moment's reflection, I said, "The statement is about peace. It says war is evil. It says Jesus does not want us to kill each other. Jesus wants us to love each other even if we disagree or do not like each other. It says that American soldiers need to go home because there's been enough killing, and the South Vietnamese people are fully capable of making peace with their brothers and sisters in the North. Vietnam is one country and God wants this civil war to end."

The colonel's face lit up with pleasure. "You mean you believe the Vietnamese can run their own country, and the American soldiers should go home?"

"Yes, definitely."

Turning toward the corporal, the colonel began to dictate in Vietnamese while the soldier typed diligently. It didn't take long, maybe five minutes, and the colonel sent me back to the large dungeon room. The other two soon joined me. Apparently, we had passed. Another officer approached, accompanied by four others in order to communicate the seriousness of his message. He would allow us to go, on the condition we fly out of Saigon first thing the next morning. We expressed our gratitude and hurried for the exit. It was past midnight, but we had no difficulty finding a taxi to our hotel. Willis had returned earlier from his visit with the Buddhists. We told him about the necessity of our early Monday morning departure. Fine with him. We were all happy to leave.

"We feel free when we escape," even if it be but from the frying pan into the fire."

—Eric Hoffer

Sadly, we never saw Jerry or Peter again. Years later, I tried to contact them. Since I couldn't remember their last names, my attempts were unsuccessful. The Department of Diplomacy in Washington D.C., which supplied the diplomatic staff for the U.S Embassies throughout the world, was unable or unwilling to disclose their names. I was deeply disappointed. I so wanted to thank Jerry for his help and kindness. It would be enlightening, too, to know in retrospect what he thought about our actions, and his perception then and now about the war.

We still had a mission to fulfill. The Vietnamese priests had given us a package filled with letters to the World's Synod of Catholic bishops who were about to meet in Rome. The priests asked that we return to the United States by way of Rome and deliver the letters in hopes the bishops would discuss the immorality of the Vietnam conflict at their meeting.

Leonard said, "I can't stay. I've promised I'd be back at Cleveland State to teach." He needed to make money for his continuing education; he regretted dropping out, but he really had to leave.

Vientiane, Laos's Capital City – October 4, 1971

The three of us had a whole week before the bishops were to gather in Rome. I suggested to Willis and Dee we try to get to Hanoi with news of what we had done in Saigon. I hoped that the religious nature of our action would have a positive influence on leaders of North Vietnam, who in their Communistic mental model were purported to be anti-god and anti-religion. The two agreed. Willis said he could not go on to Rome, however, as he was due back in San Diego for a class with Carl Rogers, a humanistic psychologist. Big Carl, as he was affectionately known to his students, supported Willis' venture politically, and even financially, giving him a few hundred dollars for expenses.

Our Air Vietnam plane flew to Bangkok, Thailand, at 7 a.m. on Monday morning, October 4. Len had left us at the airport, catching another plane for the States. After exiting the Bangkok airport, the three of us crossed the asphalt road, found the station, and learned the train for the border didn't come until 6 p.m. Time to reflect, meditate, and be grateful we were still alive.

The adrenalin from our adventures had long since drained, but the train provided no relief from our fatigue. The 12-hour train ride was an unforgettable experience. The train stopped so many times I lost count. Peasant families with goats, chickens, and children climbed on and off throughout the journey. The hard wooden seats, too narrow for westerners to lie on, even three rather skinny priests, made the trip and the night seem endless. We arrived bleary-eyed and made our way down to the river's edge. There we found a boatman willing to transport us for a small fee to Laos on the other side of the Mekong River.

Our U.S. passports easily got us through the soldier checkpoint and on to the capital of Laos, Vientiane. With its dirt streets, Vientiane spoke of the absence of modern trappings. A city of a few hundred thousand people (a large enclave really) in a country I hardly knew existed, suddenly became the center of my universe.

The Continental Hotel, the largest building in town, had single rooms for the three of us. After lunch and a shower, we took a taxi to the North Vietnamese Embassy on the edge of town. Dressed in our priestly robes, we were received in a small waiting room near the entrance. We explained to the official that we wished to visit Hanoi. We showed him dozens of photos and newspaper articles in Vietnamese describing what we had done in Saigon. The official left, and we waited. When he returned, he told us we would need to speak to a Mr. Tran, who was not in. "Could you come back tomorrow at three in the afternoon?" We agreed and left for our hotel.

In the meantime, the train experience had taken its toll on Willis. He fell terribly ill and went immediately to his room. The next morning, he could barely make it down for breakfast. He had a blinding headache, sore throat, upset stomach, and diarrhea. He instinctively vetoed our idea that he might seek medical aid through the American embassy: we wanted to keep a low profile, he insisted. Nonetheless, he did manage to leave his bed to travel to the Vietnamese embassy for our 3 p.m. meeting.

Mr. Tran, a pleasant, well-groomed man of about forty, having reviewed our documents, was very impressed by what we had done in Saigon. He promised to send our documents with our request to Hanoi by diplomatic pouch.

"Thank you, in the name of my people," he said gravely, "for your courage and effort in coming to protest American involvement." He asked us to wait in town for the response, and told us the diplomatic pouch was the direct, most efficient means, but "it could take several days." In fact, it took until Saturday to receive our answer.

On our ride back to the hotel, we commented on Mr. Tran's astuteness in separating the American people from the actions of our government. We were reminded that people of Vietnam understood that many Americans were outraged that our country used other nations to maintain our high standard of living. Back at the hotel, Willis fell once more into bed and remained there until Saturday. Room service brought him food.

What should we do while we waited? We'd heard about an American military airbase nearby, which Dee and I visited, taking advantage of the PX canteen to buy some American chocolates and other goodies. We came and went throughout the base without difficulty or questions. Since we were obviously Americans, people apparently assumed we were there contributing to the war effort. After all, Laos was hardly an attractive spot in those times for American tourists.

At a park, we chanced upon Pat, an American, and a number of Laotian teenagers playing basketball. Invited to participate, Dee then impressed me with his agility. However, neither of us had the staying power of Pat and the Laotian kids. Pat had been a student at San Diego State University. Four months previously, he and three others came to Vietnam in hopes of exchanging themselves for four captured U.S. pilots. I don't recall this news ever making our papers. Unsuccessful, the other three had returned to the United

States. Pat stayed on, living with a Laotian girlfriend in Vientiane. My guess is that Pat was another of the U.S. spies gathering what information he could. He was a student; I can't think how else he got his money. Unknown to the American people, a civil war was going on in Laos with the North Vietnamese supporting the Communists on one side, and the U.S.-backed Royalists on the other. Pat knew people on all sides of the conflict and had traveled numerous times out of the city into enemy territory. At the time I had no knowledge of the Specter AC–130 modified aircraft flying out of Ubon Retchathani, Thailand, attacking North Vietnamese trucks traveling down the Ho Chi Minh Trail in Laos in order to fortify the Vietcong in the South.

Our lives were an open book, so we told him everything.

Saturday morning, we received word at our hotel to come to the North Vietnamese Embassy. Willis was better, and the three of us took a taxi to our meeting. Mr. Tran greeted us warmly. Then he expressed regret that the two priests who would be our hosts, and whom I had met previously in Paris, were currently in Prague at an International Conference of Christians and Marxists. He added that the foreign ministry asked us to put off our visit for the time being. An invitation would be sent when it was possible to receive us in Hanoi. I had mixed feelings about not being able to go to Hanoi—so this was disappointment mixed with relief.

Heading to Rome

Willis immediately made plans to fly back to school in California. In those days it was easy to change airline reservations at the last moment with no extra cost. Dee and I changed our return tickets to first fly to Rome via Bombay (now Mumbai). During the flight, I became so ill (probably the same infection Father Bob suffered) that when the plane landed in Bombay, I was incapable of leaving the plane with the other passengers. I urged Dee to leave with the others, and I promptly collapsed on the floor. The cleaners vacuumed around me, as though a passenger on the floor was a common occurrence. No one said a word to me. On takeoff, I managed to crawl back into my seat for the rest of the flight, which was a complete blur.

Once in Rome, somehow, with Dee's help, I made it to a hotel and into bed; I hardly moved for twelve hours. Dee did what he could, securing aspirin to ease my headache. He then attended the beatification ceremony of Father Maximilian Kolbe at the Vatican.

Maximilian was and is my kind of man. A World War II-era Franciscan friar, he gave up his life so that a family man would not be killed. During the war, the Nazis had a rule that if someone escaped from Auschwitz concentration camp, they would kill ten people there. One of the ten picked to die was the father of a family. Kolbe asked if they would take him instead, and the Germans agreed. The priest was Beatified as a martyr that day, October 15, 1971, and later canonized in 1982 as a saint in heaven. The father and his family whom Kolbe saved attended the Canonization ceremony.

After the ceremony, Dee lunched at the North American College and sought to talk with bishops, to interest them in what we had done to call attention to the immorality of the Vietnam War. He was able to obtain the telephone number of the flat where my Archbishop Leo Binz of St. Paul was staying.

A Special Delivery

The next day I felt stronger and called the Archbishop. When I finally got through, I informed him I had a message from the Vietnamese Church to the bishops at the meeting. He said he was terribly busy, but if I could come to his apartment at 6:30 that evening, he could greet me before attending a study group meeting.

It was quite dark when my taxi arrived at the Archbishop's flat. I groped to find the buzzer. When he opened the door and took one look at me, he jokingly remarked, "I see you're out of your chains!" I was in no mood to laugh because I did not experience our Saigon protest as a laughing matter. Nor did I have the energy to disagree. The Archbishop's comment is an example of how we clergy tend to trivialize attempts to be faithful. Later, I learned he was quite upset when informed of our action and arrest. Angry at me for what I had done, and at the same time, so concerned for my wellbeing, he had called Senator Eugene McCarthy's office requesting help for me.

I presented the letters from the Church in Vietnam, which gave significant information about the situation on the ground. When I pleaded the need for the bishops to address the immorality of the war, the Archbishop seemed sincere when he said he was sorry, but the meeting's agenda was set and could not be changed.

What was I to do with all these letters, which seemed to be written in blood that was a cry for help from the Vietnamese Church? I begged him, "Please, Archbishop, give these letters to someone in the Vatican who might be able to show them to the Pope." He took them from me and placed them in his briefcase, saying he would do so. I suppose he didn't want to disappoint me again. I never heard what happened to the letters. I wish I had asked him to tell me when I saw him at home later in Minnesota.

At my departure, the Archbishop offered to drop me at my hotel. Still wobbly from my illness and reluctant to search for a taxi out in the night, I agreed. During the ride, he didn't ask any questions about my experience of the last two and a half weeks in Southeast Asia. He probably had no knowledge of our week in Laos and our request to visit Hanoi. I assumed his failure to ask questions represented his disapproval. Our conversation was of no consequence.

As I exited the taxi, the Archbishop kindly asked if I needed any money. Too proud to admit it, I answered, "No, thank you." Two years later at a meeting in his office in St. Paul, he asked me, "After you receive your Ph.D., having traveled so much of the world, do you think you'll be able to be happy back here in the Archdiocese?" He quoted lyrics from a song from the First World War, "How You Going to Keep Them Happy Down on the Farm after They've Seen Paree?" Why not, I thought, and said yes without fully realizing the depth of his question. I guess he doubted I would; otherwise, why did he ask the question?

Once I completed the Ph.D. in Organizational Behavior, I came to understand what he meant. I had no desire to go back to being a parish priest. Lacking humility, I thought: with God's grace, I can still be a "good" priest even though not a parish priest.

Shortly after my encounter with the Archbishop, Dee and I flew back to the United States—he to his Winona Diocese in Minnesota, and I to classes at the University in Cleveland, Ohio.

Little did I know that our experiences in Southeast Asia were only the beginning. And I came to know full well what the English poet and priest Gerard Manley Hopkins wrote:

"God shall o'er-brim the measures you have spent with oil of gladness, for sackcloth and frieze...

Your scarce-sheathed bones are weary of being bent: Lo, God shall strengthen all the feeble knees."

CHAPTER 3

From the Beginning... Looking Forward, Looking Back (1930–1945)

Standing Tall

I was fifteen years old in 1945 when I declared my intention to be a priest. My mother said, "Your father and I are pleased you want to be a priest. But don't become one to please us; become a priest to please God. And if you become a priest, be a good priest. We have enough bad ones." It was the only time I heard my mother say anything negative about a priest or priests. Respect for the clergy was paramount in my parents' lives. Yet my mother was an aware woman, and little got past her.

What does it mean to be "a good priest?" What do people mean when they say, "She's a good woman" or, "He's a good guy?" In my opinion, the pronouncement is given judgmentally as though the world were black and white. The opposite statement is also given with certainty. "He's no good!" Today, people associate "goodness" with values they share, behaviors they admire or desire, and "badness" with values and behaviors they despise or fear. Sadly, judgments are biases, for total truth is unknowable.

When my mother told me to be a good priest, I wasn't thinking about piety, temperance, obedience, and avoiding scandal. If she had specifically mentioned these things, I would have thought, "Obviously."

What I assumed she meant by such a demand was that I should be effective, stand out, and stand tall.

I thought (and still think in part) that a good priest was one able to speak like Father Charles E. Coughlin, the "Radio Priest" from Royal Oak, Michigan, well known during the depression era. He spoke passionately for social justice. My parents listened with rapt attention. My dad discussed and argued the priest's political views over many a meal with our guests. It was as if he invited friends for dinner to enlighten them, so convinced was Dad of the importance of Father Coughlin's message. It was clear to me as a little boy that Father Coughlin stood tall in my father and mother's mind. In addition, both my parents grew in their faith by listening to Monsignor Fulton J. Sheen. My parents believed we could all benefit from this intelligent and humorous leader.

Now nearer the end of my life, I think to be a good priest means to seek to be authentic, and a man of conscience. It is the story I want to tell in this book.

I see my journey through life as a mission. While I do not claim intimacy with God, I believe God was with me as I confronted and continue to confront authorities, whether in government or the Church. I have been stimulated to threaten the status quo. Often rejected, my spirit still rejoices. Facing what seems impossible, I embrace the fullness of conscience among my family, friends, and associates.

Growing-Up Years in Minneapolis, Minnesota

I wanted to be very good at something. I was competitive, not so much with others, mostly with myself. I enjoyed winning at games, but I viewed my winning as good fortune rather than talent. I assumed I lacked talent, so I was determined to work extra hard to be good at anything, especially in sports.

Our Parents Played Fair

Mother and Dad went out of their way to treat all of us children fairly. It was simply the right thing to do. We never experienced our parents loving any one of us more than any other.

Mother's love for Jesus and the Church was intense. Understanding that motivation years later, I thought I was following her example—a Christ-like example that others could imitate—when I protested U.S. military intervention in Vietnam. At that time, though, neither Mother nor Dad had advanced that far and were unable to defend themselves in their political beliefs. They were hassled by family and friends about my anti-war actions.

Love and Affection

I grew up in the pre-sixties American culture in which tough guys didn't think or talk about love. I wanted to be tough. Mother hugged and kissed us when we were little; I have no memory of my father ever doing so. Not having received such affection himself as a youngster, he did not know how to give it.

None of the men I admired were famous for expressing affection.

The older I became, the more I resisted any such affection. I viewed it as contrary to how "real men" were depicted in the movies, on the radio, and even at church. Superman, the Lone Ranger, the Green Hornet, Batman—none of these heroes had wives and children. Not even Jesus or bishops and priests did. In films, Humphrey Bogart, Errol Flynn, James Cagney, and other stars heroically saved women and children. Rarely, if ever, did they display a vulnerable side, which would have been considered weakness, not strength. These behaviors were reinforced when we were told upon getting hurt, "Big boys don't cry." So, I didn't—until I learned to become aware of my feelings in the 1960s.

> **Finally I understood. I came to learn that
> to be a good priest was to be an effective lover,
> not afraid to express gratitude, love, and affection.
> Loving is the attribute of the strong. Loving is
> standing tall. It's being a good priest.**

Being human and finite, I am dependent on others, not only physically, but emotionally, intellectually, and spiritually. We all need others in order to be fulfilled, just as we needed a mother and father to be born. We all desperately need to be loved and to love. But as a young student, a son, a brother, I didn't get it.

My parents never gave me the impression that in their eyes or in God's eyes I didn't measure up. They never flew into a rage telling me, "You'll never amount to anything because you don't study or because you're lazy." They loved me not only because they were good lovers but also because I was lovable in their eyes and in the eyes of God. When Mother became exasperated with the stupid things I did, the worst she would say is, "You ought to be ashamed of yourself!" I didn't know what that word meant, but I knew whatever I was doing had best not be done again. Consequently, my self-esteem and self-image were not terribly damaged.

I've eventually come to understand that threats and punishments do not effectively change human behavior, but they do help to make sneaks out of many of us. Incentives in the form of rewards are far better tactics for encouraging children and others to develop acceptable family and societal behaviors.

When I misbehaved, it wasn't because I enjoyed causing my parents grief, or to anger the nuns at school; my motivation was to have fun. I thought it would be exciting. My objective was not to do evil. My parents understood it made no sense to shout at me that I was "a bad boy." It was far more effective to enlighten me and help me to see the error of my behavior.

When I grew to manhood and "misbehaved" in terms of the conventional norms of society and the rules of the church, I was motivated by my conscience, not by fear or out of mere curiosity. The threat of punishment was not relevant.

Losses were valuable learning experiences, preparing me for more serious defeats in sports as a teenager, and for tragedies such as the deaths of my parents as an adult. Losing empowered me to stand up and act in accordance with my conscience, not fearful of losing, being put down or being rejected. That said, winning, too, had its benefits. Either way, I discovered that participation *is the key*.

Dad Was My Silent Partner

Dad, strong in character and conscientious, was nevertheless not inclined to give advice. According to Mother he "was not raised very Catholic," although he and his siblings were baptized in the Catholic faith.

Only Dad and his youngest brother Joe remained Catholics, probably influenced by their Catholic wives. This difference in the family also added to the fire of conflict when Dad referred to Father Coughlin as his source of information and proof of his arguments, which were completely unacceptable to some, especially to one of his brothers.

As a youngster, I found it intriguing and enjoyed seeing the adults fiercely disputing. Somehow, it gave me permission to disagree, to question a point of view. Nobody had the absolute truth. Opinions ruled. Ideas and questions reigned over acceptance and obedience. Opportunity to debate became for me a motivator to study. Unfortunately, school offered few opportunities to debate.

Dad was a great dad. He provided a moral compass by focusing on the big picture. His knowledge came from Father Coughlin's radio broadcasts and newspaper. Over many a meal with us children present, the adults would discuss Coughlin's beliefs about social justice. I paid rapt attention. It struck me that what they were earnestly discussing had great importance. From my parents, I learned that empathy and compassion were integral to a vision of fairness and justice. They heard such values from Coughlin, who influenced people like my parents to provide a bed, food, and shelter to many over the years, and without complaint. They didn't blame the victim for his or her poverty.

My dad, in belonging to the Redmen Organization, an association of men similar to the Rotary Club, had an intuitive sense of the atrocities perpetrated by European Christian Nations based on the Doctrine of Discovery. The doctrine decreed by Pope Nicholas V's Papal Bull in 1452 provided a legal cover to invade and destroy Indigenous Peoples around the world. Growing up, lacking knowledge of the State of Minnesota's history, I had no idea of the genocide, ethnic cleansing, and colonization of the Dakota People.

I'm embarrassed to have recently learned that Fort Snelling, which housed a concentration camp of the Dakota People from 1862–63, still stands as an honored symbol of American Imperialism. I was completely ignorant of the roles Governors Alexander Ramsey and Henry Sibley played—and are still honored today for their crimes against humanity.

The fort needs to be torn down in a process of educating the public as to the actual history of Minnesota.

My parents had no knowledge of the Jewish Holocaust, horrible beyond words. Without this information, they were opposed to our nation entering the war against Germany. They assumed President Roosevelt was motivated to save the British Empire, as we did in World War I. My parents didn't believe such an obligation would be worth the heavy cost of young American lives. Dad was quite explicit about where he stood, and at eleven, I stood with my dad.

Once the Japanese attacked Pearl Harbor on Sunday, December 7, 1941, Dad ceased his opposition to the war. I remember radio news broadcaster Walter Winchell declaring we would lick the "Japs" in two weeks. We followed the news on the radio, praying daily for an end to the killing. We especially prayed for Uncle Joe, who became a bombardier flying out of England over Germany in daylight—while the British bombed at night, which I thought was enormously unfair. We also prayed for Uncle Dick's son Arthur, who volunteered for the Navy, as well as for all the American servicemen.

Only later did I learn of the behavior of clergy on both sides, blessing Christian soldiers as they went into battle to kill each other. I wondered, *but not until age 42*, what would have happened if, refusing to follow their leaders, Christians simply put down their arms and refused to kill their brothers and sisters and their children on the other side. For both the Germans and the Allies, God was believed to be on their side and not on the other. At my young age, *I didn't realize the irony of such thinking.*

With the exception of gas rationing, our family's life was not much affected by the war. When the United States dropped atomic bombs on Hiroshima and Nagasaki, August 6 and August 9, 1945, there was no celebration in the Bury home. Despite the propaganda, we had empathy for the Japanese people. The reason given for the mass killing of Japanese civilians was to save American lives that would most assuredly perish with an invasion of Japan.

I have learned recently through the Freedom of Information Act that U.S. intelligence reports revealed that if Japan had been blockaded by sea, the island nation would have been forced to surrender in six months. The motivation to drop the atomic bombs was not simply to end the war, but to send a strong signal to the Communists in the Soviet Union: "Don't step on our toes. You, too, might get the Japanese genocide treatment."

In 1952, the United States had tested a nuclear bomb that was 450 times more powerful than the two that massacred thousands of Japanese citizens. General Omar Bradley observed: "The world has achieved brilliance without wisdom, power without conscience. Ours is a world of nuclear giants and ethical infants. We know more about war than we know about peace, more about killing than living."

I couldn't agree more.

CHAPTER 4

Off to the Seminary to Start My Training (1945–1955)

Why Be a Priest?

My call to serve in the priesthood was both ordinary and serendipitous. One day in the spring of tenth grade, a young priest celebrated his first mass at St. Anne's, my parish church. The joy of the celebration for so many people impressed me. Afterward, my friend Don said, "A guy wants to take us out to Nazareth Hall where you learn to be a priest. Do you want to go?"

"Sure," I said. It sounded like something different and fun.

On that Sunday afternoon in May, I watched students on the Nazareth Hall's baseball field and saw them dropping balls. I thought: I can play as well as they can. My size wouldn't keep me out of the sports activities I loved. Besides, it could be exciting to live away from home and be on my own. Nazareth Hall was a minor seminary and boarding school not far from home in the countryside and located on beautiful Lake Johanna.

Don told me he wanted to study to be a priest. He was going to be a high school freshman, two years behind me. I thought about the idea, too. However, it wasn't the first sense of a call to serve that I'd experienced.

I felt something was missing. What was I going to do with my life? Going to movies and parties didn't seem to be really living.

It occurred to me that happiness was to be found in contributing to life in a meaningful way, being on a mission. What might that be?

I played with the thought of becoming a doctor and curing the ill. I mentally argued with myself. But I could help only a few people, and eventually they would die anyway. Next I thought that I could be a politician. Many people could benefit, especially poor people, like my dad and grandpa, who would be treated more fairly. But, alas, they too would eventually die. I wasn't thinking about generations to come. I then thought about being a priest like Father Coughlin. I could help people experience justice in this life and help people live forever in the next life. Nothing could be better than that. A sense of peace came over me, a load lifted.

"Nobody can get inside me until the angels get there first."

– Poet Joseph Ceravolo

Soon after the visit to Nazareth Hall, I asked my parents if I could attend the school to become a priest. They were not enthusiastic. They thought I wanted to go only because my friend Don had signed up. When I explained my reasoning, they gave in. We applied through the rector, and I was accepted. I don't know what my parents paid, but the rector worked it out so it was within their budget.

Minor Seminary

The minor seminary was a boarding school for boys in high school, and the first two years of college, who thought they were likely to be priest someday. After Labor Day, Don and I were off to study to be priests. I quickly deserted Don, the freshman, as I made every effort to become integrated with the junior class.

My first year was daunting. In the classroom and on the athletic field, I had a difficult time living up to my own expectations. Deep down I wanted to be as good and equal to everyone else, to fit in and possibly excel.

When my parents came on visiting Sundays, they got an earful of me feeling sorry for myself. As we sat in the car, I'd complain about my unhappiness. I had few friends, didn't make first-string quarterback on the football team, and was having trouble with Greek and Latin. They listened attentively, saying little but communicating their belief that I could do it. I was intelligent enough, they said; I just needed to give it time. God would help me. Soon I would make friends and gain confidence. They were correct. Over time, my discouragement ebbed. Their "having my back" every visiting Sunday made the difference. Because we weren't allowed to read newspapers at the seminary, Mother, in doing and delivering my laundry, wrapped "treats" in the Sunday sports section, enabling me to keep up with what was going on in the sports world. From the beginning, I learned not all rules are sacrosanct.

Other students supported me, too. I felt accepted and included by a number of them.

My classmate, Don Conroy, introduced me to Kenneth Roberts' historical novels, *Northwest Passage* and *Rabble in Arms,* among others. Roberts' treatment of General Benedict Arnold influenced me to question the accuracy of reports in history books and newspapers. For the most part, American history has nothing good to say about the "traitor." His name was denounced. When a person wanted to insult another in the Post-Revolutionary days, one would call him a "Benedict Arnold." Kenneth Roberts, however, describes him in *Rabble in Arms* as a remarkable human being, and a competent general who was committed to doing what was best for his country. I admired Benedict's dedication, writing dispatches in his tent late into the night as his troops slept. He thought the Continental Congress betrayed him in failing to supply the rifles, ammunition, and food that his army troops desperately needed. In the end, he concluded, the Revolution was hopeless. While he was mistaken, it seemed to me that he was well intentioned. It had a lasting effect on my thinking that the general public could be mistaken, deceived by government propaganda.

Some of my fellow students introduced me to and taught me many things that affected my entire life. Fred Fleming introduced me to poetry and classical music. I am forever grateful.

Quenton Kennedy became my sparring partner at meals as we argued vehemently over the war, politics, and economics. He didn't buy my Father Coughlin ideas or data from Charles Callan Tansil's book, *Back Door to War,* which supplied information that Roosevelt deliberately antagonized the Japanese into attacking our country. Author Tansil suggested Roosevelt had advanced knowledge of the sneak attack on Pearl Harbor—but didn't warn our military. Roosevelt's motivation was to solidify the American people's anger toward Japan so they would completely support the war. Kennedy didn't believe it. Having read more than I did, and possessing a logical mind with the ability to clearly articulate his ideas, he was able to argue his case well. I often found that I was not persuaded but lacked the appropriate words to counter his points. The result for me was greater motivation to read more and educate myself.

I hadn't yet learned it was okay to change my mind. Then my self-concept was not strong enough to allow me to admit I was wrong about something I cared deeply about.

Frank Kittock became a friend because of his interest and ability in sports. He intrigued me in his inclination to see the value of everything we were learning. Aware of the weaknesses of Church leaders, which he doesn't ignore to this day; he focuses on their strengths and works to increase their positive qualities. I respect him greatly for that.

I marveled at the older students who could get up and speak "off the cuff" with clarity and confidence, and with seemingly little preparation. Particular students were chosen to introduce visiting speakers. I so admired a student's ability to share detailed information about the speaker without notes. I wanted to be able *to do that*. Upperclassmen, who were outstanding, not only in sports, but also in public speaking and in the classroom, became my heroes.

An exception to the rule of primarily male speakers was Dorothy Day. Brought to our campus by our priest professor Marion Casey, Dorothy was the founder of the *Catholic Worker* newspaper, which still today sells at one cent a copy. She also founded Catholic Worker houses throughout our country. Catholic Worker staff traditionally have lived like the poor and fed the hungry. She called for a revolution, a complete reconstruction of society from the ground up. The employer who overworked and underpaid employees was unacceptable, church person or not. She revered priests but despised clericalism. She took seriously God's commandment not to kill and Jesus' exhortation to love our enemies. By word and example, she introduced me to active-nonviolence. Of all our speakers, Dorothy stood tallest and impressed me the most. Many consider her a saint.

After the first year, I found myself enjoying the minor seminary. I learned how to study. My grades and confidence improved.

When I graduated from Nazareth Hall in the spring of 1949, having completed my sophomore year in college, my grades were much better, though not great, because I'd been far behind my classmates from the outset. Without outstanding talent and help, it is impossible for the poor to "catch up." Understanding this dynamic motivated me later to work to improve opportunities for everyone.

The experience helped me understand how the poor have a difficult challenge in societies all around the world. They begin the 100-yard race 50 yards behind others who receive more opportunity.

If every child, not only in our nation but throughout the world, had educational opportunities similar to those members of the elite, I am convinced the achievements and contributions of many would be monumental. Our planet would have more skilled artists if more children had a chance to play a piano or a violin. How many kids in Africa and other parts of our global community perish from hunger and treatable illnesses, having never seen a piano or a violin, much less had a chance to play such an instrument? How many potential poets and novelists haven't used their God-given talents because they weren't able to go to school and learn to read and write? Too many, I realized.

Likely the Nazareth Hall faculty didn't consider me among their brightest and most accomplished.

Oftentimes, such low-level expectations by others become self-fulfilling prophecies. Expected to be average, the individual gets the message and performs in an average manner. Successful leaders in government, business, and the church expect their followers to reach their God-given potential and perform to their highest abilities. Many followers do, making both themselves and their leaders successful. Why don't we seek to see the best in everyone? I suspect a major reason we don't want to back another person is that, if the individual fails, we fear we'll look foolish.

Many of us are terribly afraid to admit we made a mistake, so we take few risks. If we have not gone out on a limb and made up our minds—we don't have to change our minds.

Nazareth Hall's New Rector "Sets Me Straight"

Just before our graduation from Nazareth Hall, the new rector summoned each sixth-year student to his office. It was the only time in four years I was privileged to enter the rector's office or speak to him personally. I was called to listen, I concluded afterward, not to share ideas. I was simply a college student, similar to an employee, who had little to contribute.

The rector received me standing, his baldhead looked haloed against the dark woodwork. His posture indicated that this was to be a short meeting, and that I should be grateful for his advice.

When he spoke, his words left me at a loss. "The trouble with you," he spoke authoritatively as if he really knew me, "is that you wear your feelings on your sleeve. One only needs to look at you to know what you're feeling." He further explained, "When you're happy, it's no secret; similarly, when you are upset."

The rector insisted this was not a good way for me to be. I took his words to heart. After all, he was my elder, a priest, and an administrator.

In the days to follow, I tried to develop a poker-faced personality. Over time I forgot his advice, until, in a T-Group training session (a.k.a. sensitivity training) in graduate school, I came to learn that being transparent was sometimes the preferable and more effective way to be. I can be disturbed or elated—and still be in control of my emotions. If that was what the rector intended to convey, at the time I certainly didn't understand what he was telling me. I heard his well-meaning advice as negative criticism. I heard *I was not good enough, that I didn't measure up, that I had a long way to go, if I were to be a good priest*. Okay, I had six more years in the major seminary to improve.

The question I wanted a positive answer to was: Is there anybody out there who would like me just because I was me, and not for what I could do for them? Then again, am I good enough to be accepted and valued by strangers? Why did I care about this issue? I wanted to leave a mark on this world, and I was wise enough to realize I couldn't do it alone or with just a few. I'd learned from earlier experiences that if I wanted to play football, I needed to organize others to make it happen. Change and revolution takes lots of strangers working together. Did I have the personality to attract others to work with me to change things? I deeply needed to know.

For me, and possibly for other classmates, the question lingered well into our adult lives. On the other hand, logic of worldly success rests on the fallacy: the strange error that our success depends on the thoughts, opinions, and applause of other men. A weird life it is, indeed, to be living always in somebody else's imagination, as if that were the only place in which *one could become real*.

> **Later, I came to act, not out of a need to be liked, nor do I fear being disliked. What I need and want now is the ability to attract people who share my values as we work for peace with justice.**

Major Seminary–the Road to Becoming a Priest – 1949

The major seminary encompasses the last two years of college and four years of theology.

In the fall at the age of nineteen, I arrived with an open mind, eager to learn to become an instrument of social justice and peace. I wanted to develop a global vision. I thought our Church needed to accommodate immigrants, show a sacramental respect for creation, and be meaningful liturgically. Although I had grown up with these values, I was incapable of articulating them. I lacked awareness and, of course, the skill to make them happen.

Unfortunately, our professors were not prepared to teach all this. They had little training in pedagogy/teaching because it was taken for granted that individuals with graduate degrees knew how to teach what they have been taught. Consequently, our professors lectured during our entire class period, with little tolerance for questions. Questioning, analyzing, and synthesizing were not encouraged. Memorization, and the ability to play back in exams exactly what was presented, ensured a passing grade.

Philosophy was new to me, and I was anxious to learn about it. I became convinced that the metaphysics and logic courses, which constituted our first two years, were a necessary foundation for theology. In the History of Philosophy, however, questions that had vexed human beings through the ages were answered without consideration of the contributions of non-Catholic philosophers who came after Aristotle. If they were mentioned at all, it was only to point out the errors of these philosophers. We were living in an intellectual ghetto where everyone thought the same, so therefore, how could we be wrong? Moreover, we were taught the Holy Spirit was guiding the Institutional Church, protecting it from error. *Seminary life was an insular existence.*

The courses were interesting enough to keep me engaged because I did understand that they were a means to an end, a life of not only service, but competent service, but not intensely personal. I was being prepared not to fail those coming to me, but to help them understand why and how to be a good Roman Catholic—as our professors understood it.

We were being prepared to argue the truths taught by the institutional church, not how to enable others to experience God, and not how to develop a personal relationship with Christ. Perhaps, our professors assumed that through our own prayer life we would develop the competence and commitment to be effective spiritual counselors. I thought I knew God and God's son, Jesus. I suspect I had ideas only about God, or what God is not, and some things about the life of Jesus. I was trained to do priestly things, with the major focus on saying mass and administering the sacraments.

Moral theology was taught to us from manuals dating back through the previous two centuries. The manuals set out to prove a proposition, totally rational with no empirical focus (sociology, economics, anthropology, etc.). They taught in the context of canon law, that is, by a canon lawyer, preparing us for the confessional, training us to correctly administer the sacrament of penance. The principle concern was the analysis of individuals' discrete acts resulting from deliberate choices.

The focus on individual acts and their evaluation in terms of Catholic teaching resulted in a sin-obsessed minimalism. Little emphasis was placed on building the kingdom of God on earth. I cannot remember our professors discussing, with the same seriousness as they discussed fornication, such moral issues as unfair labor practices, killing innocents in war, racism, or capital punishment.

John Riley, my classmate from Peoria, Illinois, became my closest friend then and for years afterward. Often during study periods, we would agree to meet in the library, and we'd battle over mysterious dogmatic questions that had no answers. For example, how can we be truly free and, therefore, responsible and accountable for our actions, if we cannot do even one good thing without God's efficacious grace, including getting that grace to begin with? Or how can we freely act, if God already knows what we are going to do, because God's reality sees past, present, and future all at the same time?

I took my studies seriously and struggled to understand and explain how the mysteries of God were neither contradictory nor unreasonable. I have my friend John to thank for what I learned.

Living at home during summer vacations, I found work. For three summers, I really liked being a counselor at the Catholic Order of Foresters Boys Camp. Another summer I worked at the Catholic Boys Orphanage in Minneapolis. During that period, two boys, at different times, needed more than the orphanage could give them. With my parents' approval, I brought them home. They stayed with our family or someone we knew until grown.

At the January break in my first year at the St. Paul Seminary, my grandfather got me a job at the lumberyard where he worked. Beyond the discomfort of working in the bitter cold, I gained an appreciation for how unions help the laboring man, as well as a valuable understanding of just how hard making a living is for the millions of people like my grandfather.

My mother used to complain that her father never saved a dime, having had no bank account, which for her bordered on the absurd.

However, we were forever grateful to Gramps, who gave me two dollars out of his paycheck each week for ten years, so I would have spending money once I went to the seminary.

Doubts About Becoming a Priest

In the spring of my second year at the major seminary, I considered quitting. I found the last year of philosophy a bore. From my youth I had craved excitement and enjoyed the unpredictability in life. At age twenty-one, I longed for engagement with the wider world. Four more years of theological study seemed like an eternity. On a particular spring day free from school, one of my seminary class-mates, Jim O'Toole, was experiencing similar feelings. The two of us visited a Navy recruiter's office in downtown Minneapolis to inquire about being Navy pilots. We imagined flying airplanes would be exciting, landing on aircraft carriers, testing our nerves and endurance, while serving our country in a time of crisis. The country was engaged in another war, this time in Korea. The two of us signed up to take the qualifying exam in the summer.

> **A month later, my parents came for Sunday visiting day, which they never missed once in my ten years of seminary life.**

"A Navy recruiter called the house," Mom said with a puzzled look. Surprised and embarrassed, I nearly choked. I had almost for-gotten about the recruiter's office visit because I was so focused on preparing for final exams. "Yes," I confessed sheepishly, "I was looking into it." I stared down at the floor.

"Well," Mom said, "when I told him you weren't home, that you were at the seminary studying to be a priest, the man said: 'Tell your son we need chaplains more than we need pilots.'" This startled me. Later I thought: Yes, maybe being a chaplain would fulfill my idea of helping people in this life, and also in the next. Maybe the military was a place where I could make a significant contribution.

What I heard from that recruiter was that "I was needed." Whenever during my lifetime a person has said those three small words to me, "I need you," I have done whatever I could to fulfill that need.

At the beginning and end of each academic year, the seminary scheduled a six-day silent retreat. As this second year came to an end, I chanced upon Thomas Merton's bestselling autobiography, *The Seven Storey Mountain*, published in 1946. It's the story of Merton's wild secular life, the fathering of a child without being married, almost committing suicide, converting to Catholicism in 1938, and then entering the Abbey of Our Lady of Gethsemane in Kentucky to become a Trappist Monk. The book is a page-turner; it awed me; I very much identified with this human being struggling to find himself. His spiritual journey reminded me of similar experiences Dorothy Day had faced and overcame. It was from Thomas Merton and his book that I relearned to pray for my own needs as well as for the needs of others. He wrote in the *Seven Storey Mountain*:

> "It is a kind of pride to insist that none of our prayers should ever be petitions for our own needs: for this is only another subtle way of trying to put ourselves on the same plane as God—acting as if we had no needs, as if we were not creatures, not dependent on Him and dependent, by His will, on material things too."

I asked the retreat master, "How can I know if God wants me to be a priest?"

His answer: "It would be nice if God sent an angel to tap you on the shoulder telling you God wants you to be a priest. But, alas, it doesn't work that way." I thought of the angel Gabriel visiting Mary and asking her to be the mother of Jesus; that clarity would be nice. The retreat master continued, "How it usually works is someday *you just know*." His remarks were not all that satisfying, but they appealed to my risk-taking nature. I was determined to give it a try and see what happens. Thoughts of being a pilot evaporated.

"You will know your vocation by the joy that it brings you. You will know, you will know when it is right."

– Dorothy Day

It happened as Dorothy Day and the retreat master priest said. Over time I took it for granted that God intended for me to be a priest. On May 30, 1955, I was ordained with eleven other classmates at the cathedral of the St. Paul Archdiocese. The next day I celebrated my first Mass at my home parish, St. Anne. Surprisingly, I was prepared to do it correctly that I felt little anxiety.

Two weeks before that, the Archbishop had interviewed the twelve of us to be ordained for the St. Paul Archdiocese. He asked us, "What do *you* want? What would we like to do after ordination?" We knew from others that it didn't matter what we said; the archbishop would assign the newly ordained where and how he pleased.

I was determined to simply speak the truth. I knew I was not yet prepared to be a leader that I wanted to be, similar to Bishop Sheen, Father Coughlin, or John A. Ryan, the social justice priest from the archdiocese. Thus to the Archbishop's question, I replied meekly, "I would like to attend the Catholic University in Washington D.C. and do graduate work in sociology." Earlier I had told my pastor that I would be pleased to be assigned to a Black parish. His immediate response was to try to persuade me that was a foolish idea.

I listened and concluded I needed further education to meet that challenge. On the day of ordination, each of us received our assignment. I was sent to St. Frances Cabrini parish in Minneapolis, as an assistant to the priest there. Few people of color lived in the area, and in the days ahead, my efforts to encourage them to come did not sit well with the pastor.

CHAPTER 5

Early Priesthood—Unaware and Restless (1955–1965)

St. Frances Cabrini Parish

Soon after we celebrated my ordination at my home parish of St. Anne, my parents and I drove to Littleton, Colorado, to visit my sister at her Carmelite Monastery. I presided at Mass with my sister and her community, and with my parents participating. Intimate and unforgettable—to place the Body of Christ on the tongues of my parents and sister was *a privilege beyond words*.

Two weeks later, on a Saturday morning in June 1955, I arrived at my first assigned parish, St. Frances Cabrini Church in southeast Minneapolis, near the University of Minnesota. The parishioners and, especially, the pastor, Henry Sledz, welcomed me with open arms.

Made up of mainly young families, of all sorts of income levels, blue collar and white collar, the parish was economically diverse. It included the University of Minnesota and its hospital, and a government-subsidized housing project teeming with children eager for activities to fill their time after school.

An enthusiastic beginner at twenty-five, brimming with physical and emotional energy, I was highly motivated to be the best priest I could be.

Confessor

That very afternoon, my first challenge was to administer the Sacrament of Reconciliation, hearing people's confession of sins. The seminary, of course, had prepared me for the task. Happily, there were no surprises.

As I listened to sins being confessed, I didn't lecture the parishioners. I praised them for coming and invited them to be grateful to God and the community for forgiving them. From my own experience in wrongdoing, I had punished myself more than enough with horrible guilt feelings. What I needed from my confessor was understanding and assurance that I was not an evil person and that God, and the Christian community, continued to love and accept me. I believed this was true of others as well, so I treated them accordingly. Simple projection.

Further, I was reluctant to give adults advice unless they requested it. Rather, I'd ask questions, confident that they knew what they needed to do to avoid repeating the same sins. My role was that of facilitator, not judge.

In my youth, priests asked me to say prayers for my penance, which I dutifully did. It did not, however, encourage me to pray. Just the opposite: As a child, I saw praying as a punishment. Now as a priest, I wanted people to fall in love with praying to God, not see praying as something onerous.

I wished I could do more and often felt ineffective. I needed to realize I was simply an instrument and needed to trust more in God. What I was missing was a competent person to guide me in my spiritual journey, someone who was mature and deeply committed to living like Jesus, someone who could help me be a more effective confessor. I needed help...but I didn't realize it.

Preacher

The difference was vast between what I said to people in the confessional and what I wanted to communicate in sermons. In the

confessional, the message was God loves and forgives us unconditionally; therefore one can be at peace in mind and heart. In sermons at Mass I tried to convey that all of us needed to be challenged, to hear not only that God loves and forgives us, but that we
are charged to do the same. Peace with justice is loving God back,
as in the Gospel of Matthew, where Jesus says, "When you did it to
the least of my brethren, you did it to me."

I'm afraid I never knew enough stories to illustrate the message,
though. My sermons in those early years were more admonitions
and advice than examples of living like Christ.

On the Sunday morning after my arrival, I had the privilege of
presiding at Mass and giving my first sermon. Teaching how to give
effective sermons was not a high priority at the seminary. Content
was more important than delivery.

For years, I wrote out my sermons and memorized or read them
to the congregation. I didn't know enough to get help. Attending
Toastmasters or a Dale Carnegie course would have been a huge
benefit but I had no knowledge of those resources. I spent hours
in preparation each week, which constituted my spiritual reading.
Such a practice didn't result in personal spiritual growth, although
I hope it contributed to the growth of others. I became proficient at
telling others to be more Christ-like without applying the lessons
to myself. I was not experiencing the joy of Christ, so how could I
share it with the congregation?

Hospital Ministry

The pastor had been badgering Archbishop Binz for an assistant
priest for at least a year or two. Although Cabrini was a small parish
of perhaps 200 families, the University of Minnesota Hospital was
within its boundaries. The various buildings in 1955 had more than
500 beds and drew the very ill from other hospitals in Minnesota
because of its fine reputation for heart surgery. Patients came from
all over the U.S. and even internationally. Sledz was responsible
for the spiritual wellbeing of Catholic patients, and he found the

task greater than he could handle by himself. His hospital ministry intruded on many of the things he tried to do in the parish.

Most incoming patients were terribly ill and many died. The chaplain was on call 24/7 to administer last rites, and quite often the call came in the middle of the night. After a few years of this service, and in failing health himself, Sledz was promised a priest from the ordination class of 1955.

Monday morning came quickly. Sledz drove me to the University Hospital once we were finished with our masses and breakfast. After introducing me to the hospital superintendent who received me graciously, Sledz took me on an hour's tour of the facility. I noticed he didn't introduce me to patients or even other staff. Upon conclusion of the tour, he simply said, "Take over!" From that moment, the hospital ministry was my responsibility. His message was clear: If possible, he would never enter the hospital again.

What a blessing! He couldn't have presented me with a better gift. He was entrusting me with the spiritual care of all the Catholics in this hospital. I was delighted and grateful, but unfortunately I never told him. The thought of having this important responsibility excited me beyond words. I would be in control of carrying out my duties as I saw best. Sledz didn't care how I managed, as long as I removed the burden from his shoulders.

The next morning, on entering the hospital, I froze with fear. No training at the seminary had prepared me for how to begin. I couldn't even remember the places he had showed me the day before. In my hospital mailbox were many diverse messages; for example, some patients wanted to see me before surgery. I was clueless as to how to find the stations where their rooms were. Then I remembered I'd experienced the same anxiety at fourteen on my first day of work at the stationery company. The manager loaded my arms with packages and sent me to deliver them to business offices throughout the Minneapolis loop. That experience instilled confidence in me that I could likewise master this hospital challenge. And so I did.

Every Monday I visited, blessed, and prayed with each Catholic patient in the hospital. I promised and brought Holy Communion to each one every week, and always on the surgery day. Every morning, except Sundays, I arrived at the hospital at 5:45 a.m. to distribute Communion and finished in time to begin mass at the church at 7:00 a.m. Each evening I went to visit whoever was scheduled for surgery the next day with the promise to bring them Communion, and to anoint those in need.

I didn't mind being called to anoint a dying patient in the middle of the night because I knew someone needed me. It was a privilege to administer to those who were ill, and especially to those who were dying. I viewed myself on a mission of utmost importance.

After a time, my confidence grew. I believed I was capable of the normal priestly responsibilities, as I understood them. I began looking for more challenges. From an enthusiastic beginner, I became a somewhat disillusioned priest who wanted to be more effective and influential. I wasn't unhappy; I was restless but didn't know why. This restlessness would persist. Today, I understand Thomas Merton's words:

"We must make the choices that enable us to fulfill the deepest capacities of our real selves."

Back then, few alternatives to do so were evident to me.

One day Sledz and I went to the park with the altar boys to play baseball. Out from the government projects adjacent to the park poured more youngsters eager to participate. Adopting the mission to coach youth sports was a slam-dunk for me. From that moment on, I began coaching all the kids—Catholic or not, and most from the projects, really poor kids—in baseball, football, and hockey. The kids responded with enthusiasm.

After a year or so, the older kids seemed to enjoy spending time with me; I was their elder, but as a newly ordained priest in his first parish, not that much older.

As far as my coaching went, I spent more time with the younger, elementary school children. We had a number of successes at sports, and even won the city championship in baseball. Nevertheless, the sports mission was not enough for me.

I assumed what I was doing, as an assistant pastor, was what every other priest could do just as well. Somehow, something was missing. I didn't know what.

What I learned in those years was that a "good priest," in the eyes of the Archbishop, was one who did not cause scandal, raised sufficient funds to pay the parish bills, and sent an annual assessment to the Archbishop's office, the Chancery. Sledz shared nothing with me about our budget, which was fine. I knew nothing about finances then nor had any reason to care. In 1955, my salary was $80 a month.

Since I was not accustomed in the seminary to reading newspapers, magazines, or watching TV (the pastor had the only TV set in the rectory), my political understanding was narrow and enclosed, and my knowledge of what was going on in the latter part of the 1950s was extremely limited.

I began over time to experience a common work-related affliction: disengagement, accompanied, I think now, by mediocrity, because I was doing the same things in the same ways. Some parishioners noticed from my behavior that something was wrong. They suspected that somehow Sledz might be an obstacle to my realizing my potential. Without my knowledge, they wrote the Archbishop, telling him I was being underutilized. They observed that I was struggling under paternalistic rule. The Archbishop, not in the habit of being told how to manage his priests, without consulting with these parishioners or with me, assigned me to the Church of St. Helena in the fall of 1959. It was a large lower middle-class parish in South Minneapolis ruled by Monsignor Owen J. Rowan. Surprised but happy, and ready for a new challenge, I understood it as the providence of God.

"Men and women have achieved the fullness of their humanity only by freely committing themselves to challenge."

– William J. O'Malley

St. Helena's Parish

The pastor of St. Helena's and his assistant, Father Don Schnitzius, received a letter from the Archbishop telling them I was their new assistant. The pastor, Monsignor Owen J. Rowan, was 90 years old; he was founder of the parish and had seen many assistants come and go. Erect and trim for an elderly man, he was beginning to slow down but still firmly held the reins of an active parish and school.

Neither Schnitzius nor Monsignor Rowan had known anything about me, although my reputation as a successful coach preceded me among the children and their parents. Unlike Cabrini, St. Helena's had a school from first through eighth grades, and almost immediately people had high hopes I would coach the boys, since they had no football team. Except for golf, the pastor had no interest in sports, and had never built a gymnasium.

Schnitzius and I started a youth group that met regularly on Sunday nights during the school year. Together with youth leaders, we designed programs that were so popular they drew teenagers from surrounding parishes.

Even though we drew from 75 to 100 young people on Sunday nights, I wondered whether we were having an effect on what the youth were thinking about, in terms of Christ and their own behavior in the world. It seemed that other variables—music, movies, their friends—were far more influential than our weekly efforts. I concluded that Schnitzius and I were glorified baby sitters

I wrote the Archbishop, requesting to go into the U.S. military as a chaplain. This was 1961. My request was denied. Not upset, I looked for other activities that would be significant and effective.

Most interesting and fruitful was the work that two of us assistants did engaging some 30 young couples in the Christian Family Movement (CFM). We met bi-weekly in homes with five or six couples. Together we read scripture, reflected on its meaning, and applied it to our daily lives, discussing actions that would make life better for ourselves and our community, and not just the parish. President John Kennedy had just been assassinated, the Civil Rights struggle was beginning to take center stage in our land, and racial justice was attracting people's attention. Having never traveled in the South, I was ignorant of separate drinking fountains, people of color not free to sleep or eat in the same establishments as whites, and not be able to vote or receive a quality education. Jim Crow was alive, and well, but I didn't know of him.

One Sunday, influenced by Martin Luther King, and without asking the pastor, I replaced the customary "movie pledge." Instead of having the congregation pledge not to attend sexually immoral movies (violent films were not considered immoral), I asked people to stand and pledge that they would be willing to sell their home to a family of color, or that they would not move if such a family moved into their neighborhood. I asked them to sign a pledge card to that effect, which I would mail to local real estate agents. That was the only time the Monsignor became visibly upset with me; he walked through the church, in his 94-year-old body, disposing of the cards.

I believe it was the neighborhood that influences whether people of color have a chance to become all that they can be. An integrated neighborhood seemed more effective than busing students long distances to schools. After-school programs in which children can get to know each other, fair better when students live near the school.

One of my biggest regrets is not going to Selma in 1965 when Martin Luther King invited ministers, rabbis, and priests to march with him. I didn't know of his invitation until the event took place. Only one priest of the archdiocese answered his call, Don Conroy.

The University of Notre Dame and the Second Vatican Council

In the summer of 1964, Rowan allowed me to go to the University of Notre Dame for summer school. The Vatican Ecumenical Council, which began in the fall of 1962, was into its third session.

It was my good fortune to study with outstanding visiting professors at Notre Dame, who opened my eyes to meaningful changes taking place in the church.

I learned the importance of being psychologically mature in order to become an effective Christian in the world. I began to think more about Jesus, who taught us how to live and die, inviting us to build the kingdom of God *on earth* as it is in heaven. I was just beginning to understand. It was a slow process.

> **I realized that Jesus was far ahead of our learning curve. His teaching was so outrageous, unconventional, and controversial that even His followers didn't get it.**

For example, when Jesus ordered Peter to "put up his sword," Jesus was teaching us to be nonviolent. Unfortunately, down through the centuries, Christians have been as ferocious as unbelievers in Jesus were in killing their enemies.

In addition, I came to understand that, instead of regarding scripture and tradition as two independent sources of our faith, the new theological thinking emerging from the Council spoke of these two divine sources as a cohesive whole: Scripture in written form, tradition in unwritten form. A major lesson for me was the Council Fathers' agreement that our understanding of Scripture could evolve and grow. Tradition captures this evolution and growth down through the ages.

> ## "Tradition is not traditional or the way we have always done it; tradition is the way for the people of God, which is the Church, to read the signs of the times and invent the future."
>
> —Christian Brother Louis DeThomasis

Thanks to the Vatican Council and later, Sister Judy Cauley, I came to believe that when God urged me "to love my neighbor as myself," God meant me to love my neighbor who *is* myself. My neighbor and I are one, although not the same. We all have the same Christ-life pulsating through us. Vietnamese and Americans are one. To fight with the Vietnamese is to fight with our very selves. It would be a long time before I understood the radical implications of this revelation, but a sense of this idea drove my conscience eventually to do whatever I could to end the killing of our very own selves.

> ## "A developed conscience is based on a developed consciousness."
>
> – Don Conroy

Slowly I was beginning to develop.

At St. Helena's I came to believe that what I was doing was mostly irrelevant in the parishioners' eyes. I had a deep longing to be a part of something larger than myself. I'd expected the priesthood would be the most powerful connection to God and to others. But it didn't seem to be happening. I didn't feel linked to what is highest in each of us. I longed to be deeply involved in demanding and fulfilling projects. Did I expect too much?

One day at lunch, Monsignor Rowan was lamenting that none of the eighth grade graduates were showing any desire to go to the minor seminary, Nazareth Hall. Thoughtlessly, I spoke my mind. "I believe I know why they are not interested in becoming priests."

Monsignor leaned toward me, frowning, his eyes fixed on mine. "Why?"

"Who would want to be like us?"

He shook his head, indicating a lack of understanding of my words. He didn't get it—nor did I completely get it.

Meeting and Working With Mother Teresa

As I learned more and was motivated to spread the wonderful news of Vatican II and live Gospel values, I initiated a spiritual book club with five doctors and their wives. Dr. Warren Kump had been a resident at University Hospitals when I was at Cabrini. His wife Patty was a fervent Catholic; Warren was a convert to Catholicism. The two of them contacted four other couples. Together we would pick a spiritual book relating to the work of the Council, read it in a month's time, and then come together sharing and learning from each other's insights.

Our prayer and study led us to desire more. Then Patty read an article about an obscure nun in Calcutta, India, who was working with the poor. She wrote to this nun—Mother Teresa—and told her about our group. She asked Mother Teresa if we could do something to help her with her work in Calcutta. Mother Teresa wrote back and asked us simply to pray for her nuns and their work with poor people. We agreed, but we wanted to do more. We boxed up used clothing and sent the packages to Mother Teresa. She responded, thanking us, but noting, diplomatically, that she could have purchased far more appropriate clothing for the needy with the amount of postage money necessary to get our packages to her. We got the message. The poor would hardly wear Western ties and sport coats.

We then began to send her small amounts of money. In addition, we began to engage others in assisting Mother's mission. She called us her "co-workers," and Patty became the connection among us. In just a few years the co-workers' group expanded into hundreds, with representatives in many countries besides the United States.

Mother Teresa began to make numerous trips to Catholic Relief Services in New York City. She would then fly to Minneapolis to visit with us and to counsel Patty, who was publishing a monthly newsletter and mailing it to Mother Teresa's co-workers. Mother would write a brief message, telling stories about the nuns' experiences as they went about their mission of being attentive to the needs of the poor and dying. She also thanked the co-workers for their prayers and urged them to pray more. She never asked for money.

As the news of Mother Teresa and her work spread, people began to send generous amounts to support the mission. Mother, in turn, wanted to expand her work beyond India. Some of the money that people were so generously sending her she wished to use for this purpose. India, however, had a law preventing substantial amounts of money from being taken out of the country. A developing country, India needed to have large amounts of money in circulation for its economy to sustain itself.

Mother Teresa would never break the law. Because I was the priest in the United States in 1964 whom she knew best, she asked me if I would open a bank account for her order (The Missionaries of Charity), from which she could withdraw funds and use them to establish missions for the poor in places like Moscow and Havana, Cuba, as well as in New York, Los Angeles, and other U.S. cities. The sisters in her community would feel better if they knew a priest was looking after the donated money.

Eager to help, I agreed to open the bank account and arranged for her to speak at St. Catherine's College in St. Paul on an upcoming Sunday afternoon. The Archbishop of St. Paul, Leo Binz, soon learned of the future bank account and Mother's talk. He summoned me to his office.

I had been a priest for eight years and had never spoken personally with the Archbishop, much less been a guest in his office. I arrived thinking that he wanted to talk to me about Mother Teresa. I was hardly seated when the Archbishop entered his office in a rush. Without a greeting, he sat down behind his desk. His face and body demeanor signaled he was not a happy man. Almost shouting, he conveyed intense anger at me for intending to open a bank account for "this Indian" (he didn't realize Mother Teresa was Albanian and not born in India), and for inviting her to speak in our archdiocese without consulting his office. He went on to complain that "Indians"—he meant Catholic missionaries from India—always tried to get more funds than everyone else, and that this "Indian nun" needed to go through the Office of the Propagation of the Faith, like every other missionary group, and not try to collect archdiocesan funds in other ways. His points were reasonable, if uninformed.

I was just trying to help the missions, and had no idea I was going against archdiocesan protocol.

As the Archbishop paused to catch his breath, I quickly asked, "What would you do if you were me?" He responded, "Don't open a bank account for this nun, and cancel her talk!" I nodded, assuring him I would do exactly as he said. Privately, I wondered how I was going to cancel the talk in time and in a way that would not disappoint people who saw the advertising and planned to attend. It was already Wednesday and Mother Teresa's talk was scheduled for the coming Sunday afternoon.

Almost as quickly as the meeting began, it ended. Father Bill Hunt, the Archbishop's secretary, led me to the door. As I opened the door to depart, he whispered, "The archbishop is not always like this. He really is a nice guy." I nodded, my mind far from the archbishop and his behavior. How was I to carry out his directive and communicate the cancellation so people wouldn't be inconvenienced?

By the time I arrived at St. Helena's rectory, I had a plan. I first called St. Catherine's College with the bad news. The St. Joseph nun there seemed to understand my dilemma and said she would take care of announcing the cancellation to the public. I sighed in relief. Then I phoned Mother Teresa in New York to let her know of the results of the meeting. Mother's response was predictable, "It's okay. Jesus doesn't want me to speak in St. Paul at this time. Jesus will provide other times in the future." Her voice suggested she was perfectly at peace with the Archbishop's demands. I was not surprised at her reaction. Had I thought about it, I could have expected it. As it was, feelings of relief flooded over me.

Unbeknownst to me, however, hidden behind Mother Teresa's peaceful response lurked her deep concern. She prayed and wrote letters, voicing her worry that I might leave the priesthood because of the Archbishop's behavior toward me, which, she observed, would not have happened were it not for her.

Mother Teresa's "Beatification" – 2004

Mother Teresa died in 1997 at the age of 87. Many years later, in preparation for her beatification, the Vatican collected all of Mother Teresa's correspondence. The purpose was to make certain nothing existed in her life that suggested she was not a saintly person. In the process, Mother Teresa's references of concern for me were found among her letters. I received an email from her nuns in Rome, inviting me to come for the ceremony and be one of 300 priests who would distribute Holy Communion at Mother Teresa's Beatification Mass celebrated by Pope John Paul II.

It was the summer of 2004 and I was free, an emeritus professor. I wrote that I would be honored to participate. Their response was that once I arrived in Rome for the celebration, I should come to Mother Teresa's convent. As advised, I went to the convent, and on giving my name, was ushered in to see "Sister Angela." Sitting behind her desk, Sister Angela reached down and produced a white envelope. She held it up above her head, shook it for emphasis, and said, "Cardinals and bishops wanted one of these, and you get it."

The "it" was an invitation to concelebrate the Beatification Mass for Mother Teresa with Pope John Paul II on the steps of St. Peter's Basilica. More than a million people stretching all the way to the Tiber River would participate. Indeed an honor—to be one of the 44 other priests, cardinals, and bishops joining with the Holy Father in this prayerful action. When the day came, I laughed internally at Mother Teresa's cosmic joke. Thirty-three years earlier, in 1971, the Swiss Guard had arrested me for saying a "Protest Mass" on those very same steps, when I was not able to visit Pope Paul VI and plead the Vietnamese cause. I was ordered to "leave Rome and never come back." Here I was, thanks to Mother Teresa, praying the Mass with our Holy Father, Pope John Paul II. Who can predict the strange ways of God?

Words of Thomas Merton come to mind:

"Every moment and every event of every man's life on earth plants something in his soul."

CHAPTER 6

Newman Apostolate: In the Beginning (1965–1967)

Newman Center

In June 1965, a letter arrived from Archbishop Leo Binz stating that I was transferred from Saint Helena Church to the Newman Center on the campus of the University of Minnesota. The two-story building stood front and center of campus life, beside "fraternity row," at 1701 University Avenue in Minneapolis. On football Saturday afternoons, the Minnesota Rouser resounded in brass and percussion as the university marching band pranced past the Center, heading for the stadium. On any day, University Avenue was lively with cars, bicycles, buses, and walkers, students, and professors going to and from classes and the adjacent retail hub of Dinkytown.

For students, Newman was the "go-to" place on the way from parking lots to campus, between classes, for classes, for liturgy, for food breaks, for meet and greet, and for study. Most knew about and visited the Newman Center, not only Catholics—a Baptist friend frequently visited the Center with one of her sorority sisters, confessing, "The positive energy permeated Newman and made it the place to be!"

In addition to the comfortable, open atmosphere, what some students found attractive about the Newman Center was a philosophical posture that one student said, "Was more vibrant and inquiring, and more committed to core ethical principles than I was used to in a neighborhood parish setting." At Newman we were reminded of John Cardinal Newman's comments describing faith as something that matures through challenge, and thought it was good to be educated in a secular setting where one would be called on to evaluate, refine, and defend one's faith.

Questioning, of course, is part of believing, and the young adults there as elsewhere were questioning their orthodoxies in the face of a violent culture and mental challenges of the Sixties. The Center drew many academics, sometimes called D3s, "Doubters of Dogmatic Detail." Politically and philosophically, professors and students asked one another, "What's the evidence?" "What biases might have colored this observation?" The environment was entirely supportive to young people beginning their spiritual journey, as it was to those questioners like me, whom the atmosphere both comforted and inspired.

Disoriented and Disconnected

I remained disoriented and disconnected, but with little awareness. I had grown in curiosity and knowledge but not in "holiness." If someone were to ask what is Bury like, "pious" would hardly come to mind. I wasn't irreverent, but I didn't spend hours before the Blessed Sacrament in deep prayer.

> I began to question traditional teachings of the Church, such as people condemned to hell. I was mixed up, and searching.

Was I not born into, reared, and live in a universe that had the answers? My mind was filled with wonder, but wracked with questions. I sought to assist others spiritually—but it was the blind leading the blind. Priests were expected to have answers; why else would one come to a priest for guidance? I had been taught for years what a priest was supposed to be, and I was moving away from the traditional conception. God commands us to love the Lord our God with our whole heart, soul, mind, and strength, and to love our neighbor as ourselves. I thought I was handling the latter fairly well; however, the former suffered. God wasn't the first thing on my mind when I woke up in the morning, or the last when I drifted off to sleep. I was taking God for granted while I thought I was doing what God wanted me to do, when I thought of it at all.

If one doesn't know what one lacks, one doesn't need to go through the pain to change. To change is fearful, and the fear was not so much of the unknown as it was fear of losing the known. I lived a life of denial—my restlessness was equivalent to the Prodigal Son's "eating husks meant for pigs," while convincing myself I was doing just fine, *even being a good priest.*

Every day out of habit I prayed the breviary in Latin—rote mumbling—as a duty, not a privilege. Meditation escaped me. Excusing myself, I asserted I was doing "the work of the Lord" in carrying out my priestly duties. Presiding at daily Mass and two masses on Sunday, I assumed was sufficient.

Where did the "zing" go that I experienced in the early days of my priesthood?

No lectures, sermons, or retreats awakened me. Like the Prodigal Son, to come to my senses, I needed to fall on my face to realize I was living like a pig. For Saint Paul, waking up happened in a flash, maybe because he was ready. For me, it has been a long, lingering process from which I still haven't fully emerged.

Father George Garrelts

Father George Garrelts, the director of Newman Center, and his associate, Don Conroy, had asked Archbishop Binz to assign me to Newman because "Harry was one priest who continued to read."

Shortly after my arrival at Newman, Garrelts made a startling request. He asked me to take two weeks and explore the University of Minnesota campus, suggesting I go wherever I was welcome. "Visit the Student Union, fraternity and sorority houses, the library, the *Minnesota Daily* student newspaper, the athletic department, students, professors, administrators, staff, including groundskeepers and janitors, and the Protestant and Jewish campus chaplains who also sit in classes. And then come back and tell me what *you think you can do* to contribute to the spiritual lives of the people at the university." This was startling—because in my adult life, I never had a manager communicate to me that *he thought I could think*.

For most of my 35 years I'd been told what to think, what to do, how to do it and, especially, what not to think and do. What I thought was of little account. Hence, I concluded, since neither pastors nor, certainly, the Archbishop ever asked my advice about anything—the only thing that ever counted was what my superiors thought.

To be invited rather than ordered also surprised me. Garrelts trusted I was capable of discovering how I could be most effective. Amazing!

The zing came back. I felt both challenged and fearful. If someone had asked me, at the time, though, "How do you feel about what Garrelts said?" I would have answered, "Good," without being able to name the feeling.

Could I measure up? Could I contribute in a meaningful way? In my mid-thirties, I still asked questions like a 15-year-old. I wanted to give the position all I had, especially since his request showed confidence in me.

However, my tour of the campus was interrupted when Garrelts suggested I attend the Newman Chaplains' annual convention being held that year at the University of Colorado in Boulder. Another eye-opener. I listened, observed, and learned from my experienced colleagues from many universities throughout the United States.

After nearly a week's time, I returned to the University of Minnesota Newman Center eager to introduce many of the innovative and creative ideas I had experienced. It convinced me to look at Catholicism in a different way in order to reach the younger generations.

Discovering the Campus

My continuing exploration of campus life met with the kindest of welcomes from administrators, professors, coaches, staff, other campus chaplains, and students. Everyone expressed, directly or indirectly, a need for my contribution. We were all on the same team, with the objective of creating an atmosphere in which students and all of us could learn. Campus life at the University of Minnesota was a far cry from the atheistic ghetto about which Catholics had been warned.

My initial suggestion to Garrelts was to build an office in the front of the building, at the entrance to the student lounge. My campus research taught me that students wanted to find a priest easily and quickly—a spiritual person who would be open (non-judgmental), friendly, cheerful, and skilled in listening. Many times, I thought, students weren't looking for advice or someone to tell them what to do, but someone who would give time and attention, and listen with empathy and compassion. I suspected they also wanted someone holy, someone who was close to God. Although that hadn't been mentioned, it may have been taken for granted since it was a priest seeking their thoughts and ideas.

Student counseling appeared to be a crucial issue on campus in the shadow of the Vietnam War. I knew I needed competence to responsibly fulfill that need. So I began to take classes in psychology on campus in hopes of better understanding others and myself. Moreover, attending class, writing papers, and taking exams enabled me to identify with students' challenges and, I assumed, gave them a window into the humanity of the priesthood. I likened it to Mother Teresa's missionaries who lived like the poor they were serving.

Daily supper with my colleagues was not only physically nourishing but a stimulating intellectual exercise. Many nights, remarkable guests, from professors to priests teaching or studying at the university, frequented our table. Conversations ranged between current events, novels, recent and ancient philosophy, theology, and liturgy. Noticeably absent was clerical gossip. I found these meals an utter delight, and I never missed one.

Changes and the Hope of More

The Vatican Council II of 1962 permeated everything we intended to do at Newman. It was a spiritual and intellectual stimulus that seemed to give us strength to take risks without realizing they were risks, in other words, to be free from fear.

Some priests resented losing what they perceived as their honored and prominent role *as the one in charge*. We at Newman, on the contrary, welcomed lay brothers and sisters as partners in the apostolate. If we were to bring Christ to campus, obviously we couldn't do it alone. And bringing Christ to campus didn't mean making converts to Catholicism, but making the campus a more human and humane place, bringing about the kingdom of God "on earth as it is in heaven."

One practical result of this vision manifested itself in our addressing each other by our first names. Many students and others gradually did the same. That practice may seem like a small change, but it made a huge difference in traditional behavior.

In the same spirit, to identify with students as someone not "above" them, I had substituted a black turtleneck sweater for the Roman collar. I didn't wear a necktie in order to send the same message to my business and professorial associates. Priests were not members of an elite. We looked to dismantle the hierarchy and work for an egalitarian structure. In fact, later on, even President Carter sometimes dressed in jeans.

The Vatican Council II was and is a story of hope. The Church moved from a fortress-on-the-hill mentality to that of a good neighbor, eager to work for the benefit of all. Pre-Council, the kind of God that people worshipped appeared to be an angry God. This idea led to fear of authority. After the Council, our *raison d'être* at Newman became to help create an environment in which church leaders and laity could raise questions openly and without fear, as together we sought to understand the complex, swiftly changing spiritual and secular issues of modernity.

Admittedly, we were not very good at it. Having been reared in an authoritarian climate ourselves, we learned as we stumbled along, sometimes ordering instead of inviting. Our vision was, however, to establish appropriate structures at Newman that would encourage wide participation.

Evidence of the change was the removal of many outdated rules and regulations which, prior to the Council, indicated mortal sins against God, such as eating meat on Fridays, eating food after midnight before receiving Holy Communion or, for the priest, failing to read a small portion of the Divine Office he was obligated to pray. Even the mortally sinful act of missing Mass on Sundays and Holidays was played down. Joy—and privilege of participating in the liturgy and receiving Christ, the Son of God, in Holy Communion—replaced the obligation to worship. Many people gradually came to realize they didn't "have to go" to Mass, but they "got to go." People appreciated the changes because they'd grown weary of hearing more about the laws of the Church than the love of Jesus. They were eager to learn how to manifest this love practically in the global community.

Music, Music, Music

At Newman the organ became silent, never to be heard there again. Aelred Tapals, a monk from St. John's Abbey in Collegeville, Minnesota, reminded us that back in the 16th century, when the organ was introduced into churches, it inspired people and was readily accepted. Religious authorities, however, condemned the organ because it played secular music in taverns. Similar objections came up when we replaced the organ with the piano and guitars at the Eucharist. To me, guitars, piano, and drums fit the spirit of the 20th century youth culture.

The liturgies were less rigidly formal, wherein students and community members experienced being participants rather than spectators. Folk music fostered that atmosphere of participation. This joyful singing reminded me of a hootenanny. This also imparted a celebratory flavor to the liturgy. According to an attendee, "This was something I hadn't experienced before. You would have a room with a couple hundred people in it, many having a certain amount of angst over the uncertainties of the nature of divinity and redemption, and the likelihood that what they had been taught was metaphor or oversimplification. Then someone like Cyril Paul would play music that shouted, 'There's a lot to celebrate here.'"

Cyril Paul from Trinidad and Tobago in the West Indies came via Saint John's with his Tumba drums (bongo drums) and served as catalyst for the new musical consciousness. Tutored and guided by Father Alfred Longley of the Archdiocese, Cyril led us in singing the Gelineau Psalms. With his group of musicians on piano, guitars, and bass, he made the psalms come alive at the 11:30 Sunday morning Eucharist, presenting: "How Lovely is Your Dwelling Place, O Lord, Our God," "We Shall Go Up with Joy to the House of Our God," and "Be Not Afraid, I Go Before You Always." He also introduced Negro spirituals. The melodic and responsorial nature of the compositions was highly engaging, drawing in the congregation. For all of us, the music held meaning and purpose.

Cyril, spiritually motivated and working from his heart, attempted to link the musical forms to the sacred readings. The music's clear joyousness drew students and people from miles away.

Cyril was an inspiration to me and to the students, who introduced largely secular songs that spoke indirectly of our redemption—written and performed by The Beatles, Simon and Garfunkel, Pete Seeger, Bob Dylan, among others—a message seldom heard prior to the Council. Folk music in general became part of the repertoire, integrating (versus compartmentalizing) religion with participants' daily lives. John Denver composed an "Our Father" for us. (Participants still sing his musical version at the Eucharist at Cabrini today.)

The experience of all these exciting changes and the joyful participation of students and educators convinced me that I belonged to a community where people mattered to each other.

Students who had drifted away from Sunday Eucharist started to return, and commuters began preferring Newman to their home parishes. Educated Catholics from the Twin Cities, hungering to understand the relevance of church renewal, appeared as well. When I arrived in 1965, we had four Sunday Eucharists, and that number had doubled by Christmas 1967 to accommodate the crowds. Participants were energized, engaged with the music (no concertizing choir), in union with their God and one another. We went forth from the chapel intent on living out the gospel—stopping first in the student lounge for donuts and conversation.

The Vietnam War was beginning to capture headlines, despite our government's efforts to keep its acts secret from the public.

In the 1960s, the Newman Center faced a time of political unrest. Disclosures about the lack of civil rights at home brought people's attention to weaknesses in our nation's internal affairs.

Dissent among university communities began to grow. Conroy realized the times were ripe for those in leadership positions to advance the Church's teaching on social justice—along with its application to civil rights and its tradition of nonviolent action central to the Gospel. He was instrumental in bringing to the campus African-American comic Dick Gregory, community organizer Saul Alinsky, and John Howard Griffin. Griffin authored *Black Like Me*, which depicts his experience of darkening his skin and journeying through Louisiana, Mississippi, Alabama, and Georgia to face segregation.

Conroy came to understand that teaching "belief" was empty if we did not act on what we were teaching. "It's one thing," he stated, "to proclaim the doctrine of the People of God on distributive justice and the equal rights of humans; however, as we read in Corinthians I, such words ring false, if not accompanied with love which is faith in action." Our faith in the Sixties needed not only lectures by outstanding, courageous activists in justice and civil rights, but also a call to action. Conroy's insights had a profound influence on my thinking and acting. They led him to Selma, at Martin Luther King's invitation to clergy to march across the Edmund Pettus Bridge, under the threat of police brutality. He took two carloads of students to Alabama and joined the Selma-to-Montgomery marchers. The experience ended in gratitude to God that the students under his leadership safely returned.

I regret I was not awake enough then to also answer Martin Luther King's call.

CHAPTER 7

Newman Apostolate: The Beginning of the End (1967–1970)

The Hippie Movement: Summer of Love

The accepted practice at Minnesota Newman was for each of the three chaplains to go away to study during alternate summers, while the other two priests remained to serve the needs of the summer-school students. My opportunity came the summer of 1967.

I was drawn to Berkeley's Graduate Theological Union on the University of California campus, locally nicknamed "Holy Hill." My hope to gain spiritual and intellectual stimulation was based on the high reputation of the school, which included Catholic professors. Nationally, the Hippie movement was flourishing, with literally thousands of youth heading to San Francisco, as the Scott McKenzie song says, *"Be sure to wear some flowers in your hair."*

They were a counter-culture of young people, mostly aged 15 to 25, seeking freedom from the materialistic society consuming their parents. Everything seemed on the brink of change. Men sported long hair in defiance of the clean-cut office look; women refused to shave their legs and underarms, and opted to wear long dresses in an act of resistance to the commercial beauty-queen culture. Both sexes abandoned their watches, a refusal to be enslaved by time.

Breastfeeding in public became commonplace, a rebellion against a perceived Victorian attitude in which sex was unmentionable in mixed company, engaged in only by married couples for the purpose of producing children. The older generation—in the youth culture's perception—believed that giving in to sexual pleasure was a weakness and showed lack of self-discipline; many wives considered marital sex a duty, hardly expressive of intimacy or a sacred act.

This rejection of mainstream culture and its sexual mores, thus seeking to be authentic, led many to fall overboard, irresponsibly engaging in sexual behavior with little consideration of the consequences. To my mind the Hippies needed assistance, in religious language, "saving," not condemnation. In my further study, perhaps I could learn how to be of service to them.

I saw much of value in the Hippies' spirit and behavior. Life was more than having a job. "Life," Sister Joan Chittister says, "is about responding to the great human call to make life more than a series of aimless occupations." The Hippies seemed to hear this call, as well as the hopeful dictum of Leo Buscaglia, author, motivational speaker, and professional "Dr. Love":

> *"Life is continuously forgiving,*
> *amazingly adjustable, always accepting,*
> *and forever encouraging."*

Maybe I could enable young people to see great value in what Jesus taught. Their detachment from worldly goods attracted me, particularly because many of them adopted Saint Francis of Assisi, who lived a life of poverty and held love for the environment, as their patron saint. Francis's love for animals also might have guided their appreciation of all living organisms—in the common mythology, flies were not swatted, but simply swished outdoors.

Hippies seemed to reject institutional religion. Drawn to Eastern spirituality, with its respect for all life and its emphasis on meditation, they sought peace of mind and heart through "Awareness," both outside and within. *"Don't push the river, go with the flow,"* and *"Make love not war,"* were their mantras. Paul Simon's "59th Street Bridge Song" *("Slow down, you're moving too fast")* became the cri de coeur (passionate appeal or protest) of a generation that sought to appreciate the specialness of the moment, the taken-for-granted aspects of everyday life.

We Christians, who claim to be followers of the Word "made flesh," have a negative perception of our own flesh, being often ashamed of it. The Hippies appeared to appreciate their bodies and its functions, showing little or no shame. Perhaps, without knowing it, they were teaching the rest of us that God loves all bodies everywhere. Our bodies connect us to others. It is what all us humans have in common. With the Hippies and the people in Berkeley, I find bodies worth celebrating.

Some, in their efforts to meditate, resorted to hallucinogenic drugs such as marijuana, mescaline, psilocybin, and LSD (lysergic acid diethylamide) as ways to escape the perceived inauthenticity of their elders and to look for answers within. Some were naive and were preyed on to use harmful and addictive amphetamines and opiates by the same objectionable adults they resisted.

The Thinking of Abraham Maslow

During my summer in Berkeley, I took two courses: one in sacred scripture and the other in psychology. The latter introduced me to the thinking of Abraham Maslow, which served as the foundation for a course I taught at Newman the following year. Considered the Father of Humanistic Psychology, Maslow believed that experience is the primary phenomenon in human learning and behavior, an idea that profoundly influenced me in my teaching and preaching later.

> Human beings desire to reach their full potential, Maslow explained, to be mature and self-actualized. Mature human beings do not simply react to situations, but rather proactively seek to accomplish greater things.

Maslow's approach attracted me because of its focus on the positive. Before the course, I'd understood psychology's center of interest to be "fixing what's wrong." I sought to integrate this new positive thinking for me with the teachings of Jesus, who I understood dwelt on the positive, that is, what is necessary to live a meaningful life on earth as in heaven. For me, becoming mature or self-actualized meant becoming the good ground on which the seeds of Jesus' teaching would fall. As I learned to appreciate the power of that teaching in psychological terms, I began to question assumptions that seemed unassailable in my early priesthood, assumptions about who/what holds absolute truth, the nature of good and evil, and the inherent separateness of human beings. In so thinking, *I continued to move toward life on the edge.*

Christ's Resurrection

The sacred scripture course gave me new insights into the resurrection of Jesus. I had been continually searching for new ways to explain or somehow illuminate in homilies the Easter story. I did refuse to introject, after considerable thought, much of what was presented in this Theological Union course. For me and my faith, the scripture is quite clear. As Saint Paul wrote, *"If Christ is not risen, our faith is in vain."* The resurrection of Jesus is key to everything for me. It means believing that this life, as beautiful as it is when we're self-actualized, is not all there is. The risen Christ signifies that Jesus is more than a good, wise man. The point of Christianity is that Jesus is fully human and fully divine—*a paradox and non-dualistic thinking.* As we move farther into the 21st century, I see my faith and practice moving further and further from dualism, enabling me and others to manage paradoxes and apparent contradictions.

In my study at the Theological Union I looked for words to reframe this mystery. The topic and approach intrigued me, and I strove to keep my mind open, to avoid immediate dismissal of the presented material.

The Wonder of Berkeley

At Berkeley I shared an apartment within walking distance of the university's Newman Center. My roommate was a monk from Saint John's Abbey in Minnesota, also attending summer school. We both helped out when needed at the Berkeley Newman center, which the Paulist priests served.

Berkeley, California, was an utter delight. In front of the student union, nearly fifty tables were loaded with literature of political interest, staffed with student activists eager to explain their point of view. Many an hour I enjoyed conversing with these intelligent, committed young people; their concern for the common good was inspiring, although I often questioned their philosophical assumptions.

Joan Baez Gives a Concert

In July, folk singer Joan Baez was scheduled to give an outdoor concert near Carmel. I was familiar with her music thanks to Don Conroy, my friend who played guitar and sang many songs Joan made famous, especially her anti-war songs.

Joan and Ira Sandperl, her mentor, were leading a seminar that same weekend that captured my interest. It was held at the Institute for the Study of Nonviolence that Joan and Ira had founded. I'd asked directions in Carmel, and recognized the Institute as soon as I spotted the simple barnlike structure down a sandy road overlooking Carmel Valley, a gently rolling landscape of vineyards and green hills.

Arriving late, I hurried through a galley kitchen into a large room fitted with rough benches and stools on a bare wooden floor. Some twenty people were seated or sprawled on the floor; each had a notebook, plus the 1966 book, *A Sign for Cain*, by Fredric Wertham. Most participants had read the book and were familiar with Wertham, a Jewish psychiatrist who wrote about violent imagery in mass media and its harmful effects on society. The author focused on 20th century violence, including discussion of alcohol, television, war toys, and advertising. However, I was surprised the discussion made no mention of arms makers.

The book and the dialogue, which Ira facilitated, further demonstrated widespread concerns about protecting children from the psychological harm of viewing violence. Also, part of *A Sign for Cain* addressed the medical professionals involved in the Holocaust. It was all heady stuff and troubling—an intensely stimulating discussion. Being shy in a group of strangers where I have no recognized role, I listened and said nothing.

At three o'clock, Ira invited the group to go outside, explaining we were to spend the next hour in silence. We were not to think about the seminar topics, but rather to "Be quiet" and let the silence speak to us. The others dutifully filed out, suggesting that this was not an uncommon experience for them.

As a priest, I had experienced an enormous amount of silence. In seminary we refrained from talking from 7:30 p.m. until after 8 a.m. breakfast. We were also silent at specific times in prayer or meditation. Each year we spent a week on retreat in total silence at the beginning and end of the school year. I often struggled with the silence. During much of the time, my mind was busy, trying to understand what God was doing in my life, fighting off distractions, consciously talking to God, constantly *doing, doing, doing*. Now, here was Ira saying, "Spend the hour not doing anything; let whatever happens, happen."

I strolled a short distance uphill to a rock and sat, prepared to accept silence. The green and gold Carmel Valley lay at my feet, quiet under the sun but also alive. I could see horses grazing in the near distance, with eucalyptus brush and redwood trees over a ridge. Dubious, I thought, "Go ahead, happen!" Shortly, something did.

The sun was full on my face, a breeze brushed my lips, and I could taste it. It wasn't an out-of-body experience, but rather the opposite: My body was fully aware and attentive. Everything natural around me seemed to take on edges of brightness and an uncanny beauty. A spider, black and gleaming, crawled over a white rock; how pretty it was. I moved my feet, not out of fear, but to give it ample room to continue its exploration, allowing it the freedom that I was coming more and more to appreciate.

It wasn't my habit to notice the prettiness of spiders, but so it was. A pair of indigo swallows soared and dove above me—chasing their winged dinners—weaving even more brilliance into the blue sky.

I appreciated my own freedom as I took in the beauty and the holy presence of this sight, and gratitude filled my heart. But quickly the blessedness of the moment was fractured by the thought, "How could anyone in his right mind kill, mutilate, pollute, or destroy such beauty?" A mental image of the Hiroshima atomic cloud imposed itself on the valley. I must have exclaimed, "No!" as I jumped to my feet, because a girl who had been bending over examining a flower moments before, fifteen feet away, stared questioningly at me.

All of us at the seminar were given a ticket to Joan's concert that evening, one of the few concerts I've ever attended. Joan's singing and the joyful participation of the immense crowd deeply moved me. As her songs carried a cry for peace, the festive behavior of all of us suggested peace was upon us.

After the concert, seminar participants invited me to sleep out with them on a hill not far from the Institute. I kept a sleeping bag in my car trunk, so I gratefully accepted, happy not to have to spend the night alone in a motel room.

Before drifting off to sleep, the young people talked about Joan's inspirational singing, as well as earlier ideas from the seminar. I mostly listened and enjoyed the enthusiasm of these adventurous young people, not to mention the wondrous multitudinous stars.

I woke to the sun streaming through clouds—and found myself utterly alone. All my companions had moved nearly 25 yards away. Trudging toward them, I met gleeful laughter as they explained: Despite pelting my sleeping bag with stones, they had been unable to silence my terrible loud snoring—it seemed to shake the ground. Their only option was to retreat. There were no complaints or condemnation, only acceptance and gratitude that they were able to move away. That was the first I'd ever heard of my sleep behavior—good thing a dear wife didn't need to live with it.

When we returned to the seminar at nine the next morning, Joan Baez made her appearance. Dressed simply and cloaked in her long, beautiful hair, she mesmerized me with her passionate comments. It was inevitable she would draw me into the mutual struggle on the question of the behavior of the Hippies. Joan was convinced that the Hippie movement, with its live-and-let-live philosophy, was detrimental to the peace movement. She wanted so much for those young people who proclaimed, "Make love, not war," to get involved to the point of making a difference.

> **For Joan, it wasn't enough to be against the war; young people and the rest of us needed to act in the spirit of Gandhi's active nonviolence.**

Although I had barely dipped my toe into nonviolent resistance, I wondered whether her position was "absolutist." Because of the Hippies' ideals—that is, their willingness to live simple lives and, in so doing, threaten business growth and success because of their personal austerity—I argued with Joan on behalf of the Hippies, saying: "We need to accept and appreciate their way of life free from competition and striving for success. With technological advancement—machinery now and in the future doing most of the physical labor—it's just a matter of time before there won't be enough jobs for all the people who need to work to make a living." I pleaded, "Let's see the Hippies as a sign of the Parousia, the time when everyone is valued, not for what they do but, for who they are."

Joan, however, would have none of it. After listening intently, eyes glistening, she replied, "Maybe in some longed-for future it will be so, but all a person has to do is open his eyes and look around. You can't help but see the horrible condition the world is in—and, Brother, you can't cop out!"

"Good point, Joan." Later I learned she had made the same argument to folk singer Bob Dylan, to no avail. But she got to me. Her concern was valid. People needed to engage in making the global community a better place, for their own sake.

Returning to Newman in Minnesota

During the drive back to Minnesota in early September, my grateful mind and heart reviewed the benefits of my summer learning adventure in California. I was eager to share these blessings with friends in the Newman community. However, when I arrived I discovered that my friend, Conroy, had left for good.

The hole left by Conroy's departure was huge, far greater than I could have imagined. To replace him, Archbishop Binz (Did he too feel a little guilty?) sent a priest from the College of Saint Thomas, Jack Lee. He was earning a Ph.D. in Communications at the University, so his assignment made sense to me.

Our community, however, was never the same again.

Come Christmas (1967), I had the privilege of presiding at Midnight Mass. The chapel was packed, with people standing in the doorways and jammed into what previously had been the choir loft. My homily was on peace, based on my summer San Francisco experience. When I concluded, the chapel erupted with applause.

I was shocked—it had never happened to me before. In the face of it, I felt humbled.

Minnesota-born Daniel Berrigan: Jesuit Priest, Poet, Teacher, Dramatist, Peacemaker, War Resister, and Truth-teller

Early in 1968, Dan Berrigan made headlines with Dr. Howard Zinn by visiting Hanoi, the capital of North Vietnam, our so-called enemy. In an effort at reconciliation, the North Vietnamese released a captured American pilot to their custody for his return to his family in the U.S. In the process, Berrigan saw the effects of the bombing and napalm on the Vietnamese people. During a later trial, his testimony referred to the experience:

> *Our apologies good friends for the fracture of good order the burning of paper instead of children the angering of the orderlies in the front parlor of the charnel house. We could not so help us God do otherwise. For we are sick at heart; our hearts give us no rest for thinking of the Land of Burning Children and for thinking that other Child of whom the poet Luke speaks...*

Berrigan's actions gave me an idea. Although a stranger to him, I telephoned him like a friend and asked, "How would you like to read your poetry at a program with Joan Baez at the University of Minnesota?"

"I'd be delighted," he said.

Then I called Joan's agent and said, "Would you ask Joan if she would like to do a concert with Jesuit priest Dan Berrigan, just back from Hanoi, reading his poetry at the University of Minnesota?" She liked the idea, and so it came to pass—"An Evening of Folk Songs and Poetry with Joan Baez and Dan Berrigan"—a grand evening for the peaceniks of the Twin Cities.

From Minnesota, Joan and her fiancé David Harris flew to New York, where they were married. (Shortly afterward David went to prison for resisting the draft.)

Dan stayed over in Minnesota, interacting with students in the Newman lounge—an unforgettable time for many of us, especially in light of what happened just two months later on May 17, 1968.

Dan, his brother Phil, a Josephite priest, and my friend George Mische, along with six others (known as the Catonsville Nine), secretly entered the Selective Service office in Catonsville, Maryland, and grabbed 378 draft files (only those classified as 1-A, eligible for military service). They proceeded to burn the files with homemade napalm in the parking lot. Standing warming themselves around the fire, they prayed for the people being killed on both sides of the Vietnam holocaust. They waited and expected to be arrested.

With no attempt to escape, nor any resistance to arrest, the nine Christians nonviolently called the public's attention to the immorality of the war in Vietnam.

On learning of their protest actions, I wrote Dan a note and enclosed a check for $300 to help with their trial expenses. Dan responded by inviting me to the trial, which took place in Baltimore, Maryland, the following October.

Thanks to a friend, I obtained a press card that enabled me to attend every moment of the three-day trial. I vividly remember Dan on the witness stand, testifying, "We only burned some paper to say the burning of your children and grandchildren was abominable, Your Honor."

Astounded, Judge Roszel C. Thomsen replied, "Certainly you don't mean that literally?"

"Of course I mean it literally," Dan fired back. "When we napalm Vietnamese children, we are burning our own children as well." Dan was speaking from a theology of the Body of Christ, in which Christ is the head and we are the members of his body. It was too much for the judge to accept. He rolled his eyes.

The jury met for less than two hours. Supporters congregated on the street and sidewalk outside the courthouse and sang peace songs. The jury came back with a verdict of "Guilty as charged." On hearing the verdict, we all rose to our feet and together began to pray the Lord's Prayer. I couldn't keep back the tears as I choked over the words.

I would never be the same again. I changed from an invisible to a visible war protester living on the edge.

Before the Trial

In our embattled country, shocking events took place. The Reverend Martin Luther King, Jr. was assassinated on April 4, 1968. Robert Kennedy was assassinated on June 6, in that same year. During August 1968 at the Democratic National Convention in Chicago, 23,000 police and National Guardsmen accosted 10,000 demonstrators against the war. The whole nation watched on television as the police mercilessly beat the young protestors. Senator Eugene McCarthy later told me that he was shocked by the blood in and around his hotel. He never got over it.

We were not the America I'd studied in school, the country I wanted to believe in—a nation dedicated to making the world a better place for everyone, consistent with my Christian ideals. My country was nationalistic to the core, with policies designed mainly to promote the national interests of the United States. To this day I wince when I hear a U.S. politician conclude his or her speech with, "God bless America." I pray for the day when politicians and the rest of the country conclude with "God bless every nation, no exceptions."

Conscientious Objection

Students started coming to me to write *conscientious objector letters* to their draft boards. The young men needed letters from priests to corroborate their claim that they had been raised as Catholics not to kill. Of course, this idea was not new, but considering it was a long Emmaus moment for me. I had been journeying with Christ, but until this historical moment and request, I hadn't recognized him in the burning heart within me.

I needed more information to write the letters. I began to study my faith tradition and the politics of war. At the same time I *was* following the news, filled with the struggles of African Americans and Martin Luther King. I was reading his sermons and also using his ideas in my homilies. Before that I was not accustomed to standing up against authority, whether it was church or state. As I learned more and more about the war in writing these letters, my own politics shifted—I disagreed profoundly with the government position.

The defining feature of these times was our country's involvement in Vietnam. It colored every aspect of life and forced us to ask questions most would rather not have asked. Young men faced the risk of being compelled to kill or be killed in the name of a cause they couldn't embrace. It was too simple to view the war as resistance to aggression. Many of us at Newman thought that our country was intervening militarily to prevent the establishment of a Communist government. Religious viewpoints were conflicting too, from those (like Cardinal Spellman) who saw Vietnam as a holy struggle against communism, to those of us who believed the U.S. intervention was an unwarranted disruption of people's lives for political purposes. The Newman Center provided a place where scholars and young people could openly question U.S. policies about the war, in the context of large numbers of draft-eligible young men. Speakers and programs on the issue were numerous, and many relevant historical documents were donated and available at the Newman Library.

As my friend and "counselee" Dale Hammerschmidt neared completion of medical school, he realized that at graduation he would be the youngest physician in Minnesota, and that physicians were drafted by age rather than lottery. So he had to face up to the question of what he could do, believing that this war was immoral: should he resist the draft or apply for conscientious objector (C.O.) status? "Perhaps," he says in a recent letter to me, "the purer stand would be to resist, knowing that becoming a C.O. would displace the problem to someone else." He decided to accept alternate service, proposing that he be assigned to a provincial hospital in Vietnam, treating war casualties. "That was not well received... throughout this process I found the Newman Center to be a place of refuge and nonjudgmental support.... I was particularly thankful for the friendship and support of Harry Bury, who also ended up being author of one of the letters in support of my C.O. status."

Eugene McCarthy Was a Friend

When President Johnson decided not to run in 1967 for the 1968 election, the three major candidates among the Democrats were Hubert Humphrey and Gene McCarthy, both from Minnesota, and Bobby Kennedy. I'd respected Humphrey for his Civil Rights stance, but as Vice President of the United States, he concluded he could not go against the President.

Gene McCarthy was a friend. He and his assistant would visit us priests now and again, around 9–9:30 in the evening at Newman Center. We kept a bottle of Jack Daniels for him there, and he would have a drink, relax, and talk politics until 11 or 12 midnight to our delight and education. Senator McCarthy was a wonderful storyteller. He kept us fascinated with his observations of the political characters in Washington and in the Church. When he decided to run for president, I was eager to vote for him. He was running against the war, on stopping the war if he got elected. Then I watched the bloodshed at the Democratic Convention on TV, and heard the senator's description afterward. It was terrifying.

I became further motivated to oppose the Vietnam War and work significantly for peace.

The Milwaukee Fourteen

Another group of priests and Catholic lay persons, inspired by the Catonsville Nine, set fire to over 10,000 draft files taken from the Selective Service Office in Milwaukee, Wisconsin. These fourteen were arrested and spent a month in prison, unable to raise the $415,000 bail, and were put on trial a year later. One of the participants, a priest, Al Janicke, came from the St. Paul Archdiocese and was a friend of mine. People wanting to show support for these activists, all bound for prison because of their desire for peace, began to wear red armbands, including myself. When anyone asked why, we used it as an opportunity to give our pro-peace explanation and defend the actions of the Fourteen.

Shortly after the arrest of the Milwaukee Fourteen, a deanery meeting of priests took place at the Ascension Hall in North Minneapolis. Archbishop Leo C. Byrne was present among the 150 priests. I dutifully attended the meeting, which concerned Vatican II changes in the liturgy. I wore my black suit, black turtle neck shirt, and the red armband blazing on my left arm, in support of the pacifists in jail.

Not one priest inquired about the significance of the armband. Within a few days, however, I received a scathing letter from the Archbishop asserting that my apparel at the deanery meeting "was another indication of my adolescence." His statement may well have been correct—I've never claimed that I have attained total maturity; I'm still in the process of becoming.

After reflecting on his letter for a day or two, I wrote a response. I asked the Archbishop, "Since I stand with you in opposition to abortion, why don't you stand with me in my opposition to the war in Vietnam?" To his credit he didn't ignore my question, and he was honest with me.

His answering letter stated, "I do not have sufficient information on the war in Vietnam, so I need to trust that the federal government is doing the right thing." I respected his honesty. At the same time, I suspected another variable at play, namely, his fear that if he as a church leader, found information that would cause him to oppose the war publicly, such opposition could lead to the St. Paul Archdiocese losing its tax exemption. If he were alive today, I doubt he would put such trust in the U.S. Government as regards to its stand on abortion and gay marriage.

Participating in a Sensitivity Group

In the early spring of 1969, John Vinton and Lois McGovern, Master's degree students in psychology, had invited some Newman students and me to experience a weekend Sensitivity Group. The session was founded on the vision of Kurt Lewin—a psychologist known as one of the modern pioneers of social, organizational, and applied psychology in the United States. Participants work in small groups of six to twelve over an extended period of time, with the goal of changing human attitudes and behaviors through greater self-awareness—all in an atmosphere of mutual trust and accountability.

> **Participants in the group learned to
> give and receive feedback—*not as criticism*,
> *but as information* designed with a genuine desire
> to enable one another to improve, particularly in the
> area of interpersonal communication.**

The training was completely new to me. I was moved by the effort to be aware of what one is thinking and feeling, and then be willing to share it honestly and openly with friends, associates, even strangers. *I'd never experienced such transparency*. It was intriguing, fun, and a huge step toward intimacy. I relished the opportunity of being open and honest without worry of criticism.

Criticism, I learned, is different from feedback. Criticism can be a personal indictment, a faultfinding mechanism with a degrading tone. Feedback is understood as helpful input. The tone is care and concern, not pointed at a person like a gun, but offered as a helpful tool. Result: The person is more open to a change in behavior. This marked the beginning of my awareness of my personal feelings and those of others. It was indeed enlightening—and it was what I'd been missing in my relationships.

New Structure at Newman

In late summer of 1969, George Garrelts prepared to leave to study Theology at the University of Syracuse under the theologian, Gabriel Vahanian, remembered for his pioneering work in the "God is Dead" movement (not meant literally, but the death of the objectification of God). Archbishop Byrne appointed George Coleman, a popular assistant priest at the Basilica of Saint Mary in Minneapolis, to be the new pastor of the University Church of Saint Frances Cabrini. Jim Kaston was assigned the chaplaincy at the University Hospital and would live with Coleman at Cabrini. John Reardon was ordered to join Lee and me at Newman.

On August 13, 1969, the five of us were summoned to meet with Archbishop Byrne in his office. We all rode over to the bishop's office in my car. The Archbishop laid out his plan, clarifying our responsibilities. He announced I was to be the coordinator (not the director) at Newman. His desire was for all of us to work together as a team, which sounded great to me.

As we traveled to see the Archbishop, I believed our year together would be spiritually fulfilling for the Newman and Cabrini communities. After the meeting, on the way back to Newman Center, I expressed my own enthusiasm for our working together. We needed to depend on each other and have each other's back in the face of what was happening on campus and in the world.

Expecting positive responses after the Archbishop's encouragement, I said simply, "We need to work as an effective team. Could
I have your word that none of us will leave the priesthood for at
least a year?" I thought this was an innocent-enough question since
many priests at that time were leaving the priesthood.

The promise could be a catalyst for discussing how we might
help one another be effective priests. But the ensuing silence
stopped my breath. Not one of the four could give me his word
that he wouldn't leave. I was speechless. From that moment on, my
confidence dwindled that we could live up to our potential, as did
my enthusiasm. I was so intent on making the year a great success,
egotistical on my part, that their "no response" deeply discouraged
me. The uncertainty left me defeated and incredibly lonely, though
without full awareness of my emotional state.

As it turned out, all four of them did leave the priesthood—
not any that year, but because each was preoccupied with leaving,
the Newman apostolate seemed not a high priority. I found myself
hurting for them—the pain involved in such a monumental decision—yet I didn't reach out to them: I lacked the skills. Much to my
regret today, I did nothing.

Mass at the Pentagon

At the trial of the Catonsville Nine, I had met members of the
Catholic Peace Fellowship and students from the Catholic
University of America in Washington, D.C. The Quakers—who
had been reading the names of each U.S. soldier killed in Vietnam
while standing on the steps of the Pentagon—asked the Catholic
Peace Fellowship to do an anti-war, peace ceremony at the close
of the reading. They thought of me. What better ceremony than
to celebrate the Eucharist inside the Pentagon, praying for the
deceased soldiers, and also the peacemakers, seeking to keep
them from dying? Another priest and I were invited to preside
the morning of August 14, 1969, in the Pentagon, a building dedicated to war.

The Catholic Peace Fellowship submitted a request for a permit to celebrate the Mass for Peace in the Pentagon. The reply: "If anyone tries to do so, they will be arrested."

The night before the planned demonstration, an ACLU lawyer warned us that no one should participate except those who were mentally and emotionally ready to be arrested. To that point, I had never been arrested. I didn't consider for a moment what the Archbishop, my parents, or friends would think.

> **It was a question of conscience. I was convinced I needed to act for peace in Vietnam. After writing so many letters, working with young men, and talking and talking some more about peace and war, I decided it was time I put my body where my mouth was.**

Thus, on August 14, the day after the five of us priests had met with Archbishop Byrne, some 30 peacemakers walked into the strangeness of the Pentagon building with its huge wide corridors. It was my first and only visit.

We found a space not far from the ecumenical chapel and placed the canonical (a book for the ceremony of mass) on a portable stand. I had hardly made the sign of the cross to begin the service when a group of policemen confronted us, all men of color, which seemed strange to me at the time. Huge enough to play tackle for the Minnesota Vikings, they were remarkably intimidating.

Polite and professional, however, they informed us we were under arrest and directed us to follow them to waiting police vans. We followed without resistance. I smiled broadly, in imitation of Dan Berrigan when he was arrested. We were transported to a jail in Alexandria, Virginia, which was the cleanest jail I've ever been in.

Women and men were placed in two adjacent cells, out of sight of each other. The cells were 30 x 30 with no furnishings except an uncovered toilet in the far corner. We straightaway continued the mass, praying and singing. At Holy Communion, we passed the body and blood of Jesus from our cell to the women's. Just then, guards came and tried to confiscate the wine, but the women quickly finished communing before the guards could get their hands on it.

Because they hadn't frisked us, the authorities were caught off guard, I suppose because we were peaceful and not unhappy to be invited to their jail. The authorities also assumed we wouldn't be "guests" for long.

The ACLU lawyer arrived at the courthouse before we did. We each appeared before a judge, our names duly noted. All of us pleaded "Not guilty" to the charges of disturbing the peace and trespassing. Our lawyer competently argued for our release on our own recognizance, as we pledged to return for our trial. Less than nine months later, the government dropped the case. The administration didn't want to be seen as against prayer, and our quick arrest had achieved their goal of limited publicity.

I flew from Washington, D.C., back to the Twin Cities that evening. The next day I appeared for mass at Newman—August 15th was a special feast day in the church, the Assumption of the Blessed Virgin Mary. On this holy day of obligation, Catholics are expected to attend mass. The chapel was crowded. The *Minneapolis Tribune* had reported that I'd been arrested and jailed on Friday. So when I walked into the chapel dressed in vestments, about to preside at the Eucharist, people were shocked. They applauded, relieved that I was out of jail and free to be with them for the Eucharist.

Archbishop Byrne was less pleased. He sent me a strong letter about my Pentagon behavior; he cited it as another example of my immaturity. Two days before, he had put his trust in me. In his eyes I had let him down—again. I honestly didn't intend to upset him. In my heart I really was on his side.

> **On the other hand, I perceived my
> behavior as God's will. God was calling me to
> resist the evil of the Vietnam War—taking the initiative
> is part of who I am. I never cease to be amazed at
> what happens when I'm open to take a risk.**

My peace efforts, however—at the Pentagon, being chained at the gate in Saigon, flying into Hanoi to train North Vietnamese, becoming a human shield in Gaza, and even concelebrating the Eucharist with the Holy Father, Pope John Paul II in Rome—*all happened because I was invited*. I responded to these requests as I supposed servants would do. I said, "Yes."

In this instance, not only were Archbishop Byrne disturbed, so were my parents. Relatives called my parents, troubling them with questions, "How come this priest son of yours has been arrested and jailed?" What could my parents say? They didn't understand their priest son *being arrested*. My mother told me about the calls, as if to ask me how she should respond, what to say to such criticism. I didn't know what to tell her. I pictured my mother carrying these criticisms in her heart, as Mary did when Simeon prophesied, "a sword will pierce your soul."

> **I empathized with my mother and was troubled
> that I couldn't do anything about it.**

Nonviolence

More than a year into Nixon's presidency (1969–1974 when he resigned), the war in Vietnam continued unabated. Our many letters to the President and congressmen had no apparent influence on our government's behavior. Protest marches also did not seem effective. Some marches turned violent, which was beyond my comprehension. Many years later I learned that our government planted provocateurs within the protestors to act violently, to alienate the "silent majority." I did not expect my government would do such a thing.

At the time, I had assumed some in the peace movement got carried away in the moment, resorting to violence out of frustration. I heard violent rhetoric from anti-war activists in meetings, who condemned President Johnson and President Nixon. Returning veterans, moreover, reported being spat upon and accused of being "baby killers."

As much as I detested the war, I didn't hate government officials, and I was particularly concerned about our Vietnam veterans and what the war was doing to them. It was because I loved them and I loved my country that I was so vehemently against the war. Even back then, though I couldn't articulate it, I separated individuals from their behavior. I loved Presidents Johnson and Nixon as children of God, but hated their behavior, just as I'd loved President Truman but decried his order to drop two atomic bombs on the Japanese people. As I was growing up, my mother, when I hurt her or others, would ask, "How do you think they feel? How would you like someone to do that to you?" She was teaching me empathy.

To hold a grudge is to hurt myself, I learned; it doesn't make sense to make myself suffer. My faith, moreover, has taught me to love as unconditionally as I can, as God loves unconditionally each one of us without exception. A God-conscious life teaches us how to have love for everyone inclusively and unconditionally. Although I, and the rest of humankind do evil, I perceive our intent is to do good *according to one's own value system*. It's our value systems that need to change and become more Christ-like.

I'm unaware of hating anyone; maybe I disliked a few, so few I can't remember them. Although I received stern letters from Archbishop Byrne questioning my maturity and behavior, for example, I never disliked him. I assumed that if he knew me and my intentions better, he wouldn't be upset.

Frank Kroncke's Invitation

Sometime after Christmas 1969, Kroncke confessed he'd had enough of sitting on the sidelines—our work was hardly sidelines, I thought, but I understood what he meant. He'd joined a group who were intending to take serious action to protest the war. Under the cover of night, they planned to break into several recruiting centers in rural Minnesota and destroy draft files, as did the Catonsville Nine and the Milwaukee Fourteen—in order to raise America and Minnesota's consciousness of the immorality of the war.

Kroncke invited me to join the group, and I seriously considered the invitation. Two concerns, however, disturbed me. First, the nature of the act did not seem to meet the requirements of nonviolence. Unlike Catonsville, the group's intent was to destroy draft records without getting caught; they would be breaking the law without accepting the consequences. Second, the action seemed to be a repeat of Catonsville and Milwaukee, and thus, I surmised, less effective. The movement needed further creativity. If the American public were to be moved to examine the immorality of the war, something more innovative needed to be done. Unfortunately, I had no idea what that might be.

After many prayers, seeking to discern God's will, I knew I needed counsel. Who better to consult than Dan Berrigan? He was at Cornell University in New York teaching while he awaited his sentencing. When I called him, he invited me to visit and stay overnight in his tiny campus apartment.

Our conversation was helpful and inspiring. I outlined my hesitations and my feelings about the war, and my responsibilities at Newman.

He did not tell me what to do. I left, however, determined to act. So many had made enormous sacrifices.

When I returned to Newman, I told Kroncke I was ready to join the protest group. After checking with the others involved, though, he told me, "I'm sorry. But the group is set; members are worried now about adding anybody new." In one sense it was a disappointment, an opportunity lost—to welcome crucifixion, practice what I preached. From another perspective, I could be patient: other opportunities would appear. I accepted their determination, concluding it was the will of God.

I knew that the group planned to hit four different offices. We learned later that among the raiders was an FBI informant. Where the informant was present, no arrests took place. In the other three locations, the FBI were waiting, and Kroncke was captured.

When I heard of Kroncke's arrest, I rushed to Hennepin County jail where he was being held. I was refused admittance despite my assertion I was a priest and his spiritual director. The jail guards, unconvinced, laughed at me. Startled, I'd never experienced this before from civil authorities. A policeman scoffed, "How do we know you're a priest? You don't even look like a priest!" Big mistake—me wearing the turtleneck instead of the clerical collar.

Two days later, the first of several rallies was organized to support the Minnesota Eight, as they came to be called. Two hundred people, including my secretary, Joey, and I marched down Nicollet Avenue to the courthouse. Among a few others, I was asked to address the rally. From the top of the courthouse steps, I defended the actions of the Minnesota Eight. I said, "American violence throughout the world only breeds more violence. If we really want peace, we need to bring our soldiers home. We need to withdraw from Vietnam before more Vietnamese and our soldiers suffer wounds and death. Love is the antidote to violence."

My Second Arrest

Moments after the speeches, a brigade of fast-stepping riot police marched to the front of the courthouse. Then they turned and began to drive the protesters off the street and even the sidewalk. The protesters had nowhere to go. With police batons raised, they shoved people to disperse the crowd. From atop the courthouse steps, I pointed to a spot where it seemed particularly precarious for the young people. Joey and I rushed down the steps just as a policeman pushed a student who he thought was moving too slowly. I cried out, "What are you doing? This is a free country! Citizens have a right to be here on the street!"

Ignoring my shouting, he raised his baton and struck a young person on the shoulder. I grabbed his arm to prevent a second strike. As he pulled free of my hand, the back end of his baton whizzed past my face and struck Joey in the mouth. Blood gushed out. Distraught, I screamed at him, "Do you enjoy hurting people?" He immediately arrested me for "disturbing the peace."

Three policemen ushered me into the courthouse and up to the detention floor. Police there recognized me and taunted, laughing, "You wanted to get into the jail. Well, you finally made it!"

A guard took my fingerprints. One phone call was allowed. I called Newman; no priest was there. I asked the receptionist to call Cabrini and ask the priests at the parish to help me; no priests were available there, either. My secretary found a public telephone and called my dear friend, Bill Carlson, at WCCO Television and described my arrest. He immediately phoned his friend Ron Meshbesher, a renowned criminal lawyer who, despite not knowing me, rushed to the courthouse to defend me.

In the meantime, I was placed in a holding cell with others awaiting arraignment or some other disposition. I found out why it's called "the hole." The room was large enough to accommodate several unfortunates, but windowless, dark, and dingy. I could barely make out the faces of a half dozen inmates who approached me, pressing scraps of paper into my hand. On these were written their names and a relative's phone number; they begged me once I was released, to notify said persons and tell them where they were. I took the papers and promised to make the calls; I saw Christ in each one of the prisoners.

Dazed from everything that was happening, within an hour I was led out of the cell and into a courtroom. When my turn came, I pled not guilty to disturbing the peace. The prosecutor argued that bail be set for my release because otherwise I'd "simply return to the street and continue to arouse the crowd." When I heard this I thought, "That's what the Scribes and Pharisees said about Jesus." My lawyer, who was Jewish, argued, "You let ordinary drunks out on their own recognizance. This man is a man of the cloth; he certainly deserves as much consideration."

The judge wouldn't hear of it. "Six hundred dollars," he proclaimed and hit the desk with his gavel. My wallet contained less than twenty dollars. Suddenly, a complete stranger, a smallish fifty-ish Jewish lady, approached the bench with six hundred dollars in hand. Later she told me that she and poet/writer Thomas Merton were correspondents. I regret I cannot remember her name; I met her only once again, when I returned the bail money.

When my arrest made the local press, once again relatives and acquaintances harassed my mother about my unpriestly behavior. My mother was at a loss as to what to say. If she had defended my actions as a peacemaker, she didn't tell me so.

In January 1971, I returned to Minneapolis from graduate school in Ohio to face trial. My father and friend Jeff Voorhees attended, and I was well represented by criminal lawyer Ronald Meshbesher. I pleaded Not Guilty; and after brief presentations by the prosecution and my lawyer, the judge indeed pronounced me "Not Guilty." *Note:* Unlike my arrest, this result didn't make the papers.

Case Western Reserve University

When John Vinton departed in the fall of 1969 to get his Organizational Behavior (OB) Ph.D. at Case Western Reserve University, I put Case high on my list for consideration of where to go with a fellowship grant I had received from the Danforth Fellowship.

Reading the material describing the subjects studied in Case's OB department, I became even more committed to attend. The curricula/professors taught how to be a change agent at the micro level, influencing individuals and small groups, and at the macro level, to enable organizations and even cultures to change. *Large-scale social change was an objective of mine.*

Captivated as I had been in seeking changes in our hierarchic church and in the U.S. government's war policy—with little apparent effect—I believed Case was the place God wanted me to be.

To be accepted in Case's OB program, I needed to pass an intelligence test, participate in a week-long sensitivity group in Sandusky, Ohio, and be interviewed on campus by certain faculty and students already in the program. I passed the test and attended the T-group/sensitivity training, which again I found fascinating and enlightening. The women and men participating were strangers to one another. Most came from businesses in the Cleveland area. No one's status was revealed—CEO, supervisor, clerk—so that each would learn to trust the others as equals. No one knew I was a priest.

Professor Don Wolf of the Organizational Behavior department at Case was one of two facilitators. We practiced interpersonal skills and behaviors that I could immediately apply in my life, and was moved by the teaching of being non-judgmental, quite unconventional in our society and clearly (to me) in consonance with what Jesus taught.

I had been informed that not only the faculty but also graduate students in the program had input and decision-making power concerning which students were accepted into the Ph.D. program, as well as which faculty were hired to teach. This cooperation between faculty and students—which I did not see at the University of Minnesota, where the students and the administration were often at odds—caused me to conclude that any faculty who could manage the needs of both the administration and the students had a lot to teach me.

After being interviewed by a number of faculty and students, the interviewers met to determine who would be admitted and who would not. One faculty member recommended I not be admitted because I lacked a formal Masters' degree. John Vinton fought for my admittance and won, demonstrating the power of students in the department. It further convinced me that Case was the place where I wanted to study.

Kent State Tragedy – May 4, 1970

While protesting the Vietnam War on campus, four Kent State University students were shot and killed by members of the Ohio National Guard. University students across the United States went on strike, refusing to attend classes. At the University of Minnesota, students not only didn't attend class, many gathered in protest at the ROTC building on campus. The police were called.

At Newman, the student association gathered. During a brainstorming session, we came to an agreement to wear white armbands and stand at the ROTC building between the students and the police. Our intention was to act as nonviolent witnesses, to discourage students and police from attacking each other or endangering bystanders. As human shields, we stood between them, and no violence occurred.

The next night, there was more brainstorming. Because students were not attending class, what could they do? The students themselves came up with the idea of going door-to-door asking citizens what they thought and how they felt about the war. In so doing, students discovered that many people were against the war but felt helpless; they didn't know how they could, as individuals, do anything about it. They saw themselves as impotent."

Again, brainstorming. New idea: Why not invite these average Americans to go to Paris, to meet with the so-called enemy, the Vietnamese. Then we could find out from the Vietnamese how we might help end this horrendous tragedy.

Diana Johnstone, a professor of French at the university, offered to go to France where the Paris Peace Talks were taking place, and ask the Vietnamese how we could be of help. Diana made a quick trip at her own expense and returned to tell us that the Vietnamese would be pleased to receive a delegation from the United States that was comprised of average Americans *who were not well-known anti-war activists.* The Vietnamese leaders were interested in presenting their perspective, which was not being well represented in the American press.

The media had taught us to distrust our own judgment, as Archbishop Byrne admitted to me, for fear of being duped by Communists and people who did not have peace on their agenda. Here was an opportunity to talk with Vietnamese and find out their ideas about peaceful solutions to the war.

The students responded with enthusiasm, "Let's go knock on the same doors as before and announce we've learned what people can do toward ending the war." Excited, the students went onto the "highways and byways" and spoke to the same people: "Here's your chance. Come to Paris and meet with the Vietnamese and get their side of the story."

Most of these people had legitimate reasons why they couldn't go, but thirty people said, "Yes!" One-third could pay all their costs for the flight, hotel, food, and transportation while in Paris. Another third could pay part of the expense. A final third were too poor to contribute anything; among these were two Native Americans whom I especially wanted to be a part of our delegation. I was determined that no one would be left at home because of lack of funds.

A few quick fund-raising events failed to bring in sufficient money. Time was running out and we were $10,000 short. As a last resort, with no idea how I'd pay it back, I borrowed the whole amount from my bank. And off to Paris thirty of us went.

We were a diverse delegation: professors from the University, other educators, business people, community leaders, students, and a few unemployed. Most had done some study about Southeast Asia in preparation for the journey. Marianne Hamilton, a Catholic layperson, mother of eight, conversant in French, was also part of our group and later traveled with me to Vietnam.

Marianne had been a visible leader in the Twin Cities peace movement and was a help to Gene McCarthy's presidential campaign, setting up his speaker engagements across the country. Because she and I were aware that the French had brought about many converts to Catholicism in Vietnam, we suspected we had been misinformed about their status; we hoped to find out more. Marianne wondered out loud: "Could we organize and influence

105

Catholic Americans to have empathy for their brothers and sisters in Vietnam, thus helping lead to an end to the violence?"

The Paris Peace Talks – June 1970

The Paris Peace Talks had gone on for months with little agreement. It seemed for three or four of those months, an argument centered on the shape of the table, which was no small matter—as it indicated the difference between a hierarchical setting and an egalitarian setting. Americans wanted a rectangular table; the Vietnamese wanted a round table so that everyone would be seen as equals.

We spent eight days in Paris. After an initial session on June 27 with a group of scholars to prepare our questions, we met with many, both North and South Vietnamese, and also listened to U.S. State Department representatives.

The day we arrived we heard a misleading statement from Secretary of State William P. Rogers: that the other side had demanded the United States withdraw from Vietnam, and only then would they talk about a peaceful settlement. In my mind, Rogers' statement was meant to make the Vietnamese position sound ridiculous to the American public. Of course every faction wanted a withdrawal, but the peace plans we heard involved much, much more; for example, the improvement of the lives and safety of citizens and soldiers after withdrawal.

On June 29, 1970, we met with a delegation from the Provisional Revolutionary Government of South Vietnam (PRG), as well as representatives of the Saigon government. In all the general sessions we wore headsets in order to receive instant translation.

The following day we held a press conference at the American Cultural Center in Paris and attended an evening reception at the Quaker Center along with thirty members of the Union of Vietnamese in Paris.

The Vietnamese didn't claim with hatred that they would eventually win, but with the patience of certitude. All the Vietnamese groups signaled they wanted liberation and reunification after U.S.

withdrawal, but they would be patient. They politely explained to our delegation that North and South Vietnam were Vietnamese.

Upon returning, all of us were more convinced than ever that the Vietnam War was not only a mistake, but immoral. We were motivated to pass on what we learned from the trip, intent on influencing others to lobby our government to end the war quickly—a typical American attitude. The Vietnamese, far more victimized, were far more patient.

Some of our members set off for Washington where little interest was given to our report. We suggested making peace in Vietnam by bringing the Saigon government, which most of the Vietnamese people perceived as a puppet government, and the PRG together to form a new government, which would then enter into negotiations with the North toward eventual reunification. Our suggestion was dismissed without consideration.

A State Department spokesman said, among other things, "Vietnam has deficient sociology." We were at a loss to understand what that meant. Despite what we perceived as blindness on the part of U.S. policy makers, I trusted they would eventually "get it," that our government could not use its military power indefinitely against the concerted will of our own people.

If we the people were united against the war, we the people could stop it.

John Denver Gives a Concert

Returning from Paris, I faced a $10,000 debt, which weighed heavily on me. If I thought that raising money before the trip was a challenge, post-trip fundraising was near impossible. Nobody I knew was going to donate to a trip that had already happened. Moreover, few were well enough acquainted with the war to understand the value of our recommendations.

107

A Republican friend insisted he could get me in to see President Nixon so I could report directly to him what we'd learned from the Paris peace talks. Dubious, I didn't want him to waste his time trying. His confidence motivated him to bet me one thousand dollars he could pull it off. I didn't have the money to pay him, but I went along, certain that Nixon would not grant me an audience. I won the bet. He paid. So now I had a debt to the bank of only $9,000.

Bill Carlson, my close friend at WCCO TV, and his fiancée Nancy Nelson (a St. Helena parishioner when I was at the parish) invited me to preside at their wedding, June 13, 1970, shortly before our trip to Paris. The ceremony took place at St. Albert the Great church in South Minneapolis; in the homily I managed to talk about peace. Their friend, folk singer John Denver, sang during the service.

When I confided my dilemma to Nancy and Bill, the newlyweds had the idea I might persuade John to do a concert in the Twin Cities to satisfy the debt. They would invite John and his wife Annie, along with me, to dinner at their apartment. I could then, at the right moment, ask John to do a concert for peace on my behalf.

John was just starting out solo as a folk singer, having been previously with the Chad Mitchell Trio, and he was looking for opportunities to solo. He agreed on two conditions—that we secure the new Guthrie Theater in Minneapolis, and "Let's not charge more than you need to pay off the loan." His motivation was twofold: To get me out of debt and to assure a large crowd by charging the lowest price we could. He worried that it might hurt his career if too few people attended.

I encouraged the Newman students to beseech all the request-radio stations to play John Denver's recordings. Bill Carlson, Charlie Boone, Roger Erickson, announcers on WCCO Radio, and others, free of charge, announced the concert as a community service. And the price was right—$3, first-come, first-served.

The day of the concert in late July, I went to St. Mary's Hospital to visit a patient. I, too, was in considerable pain. Jim Breitenbucher, a pre-med student and a friend, noticed my limp when I unexpectedly ran into him in the hospital lobby. He insisted I then and there be examined to find the source of my pain; they discovered a kidney stone, and I ended up in a hospital bed.

I couldn't miss the concert, no matter what. Once the nurse left my room about 7:30 p.m., I dressed quickly, found an emergency exit, and slipped out. Waiting in a car outside was a friend who drove me to the Guthrie Theater, arriving just minutes before I was to introduce John to the audience. My secretary saved a seat for me in the front row.

Playing his guitar without backup, John was everything the people could have asked for. His mellow voice and sparkling, cheerful personality captivated the crowd. The audience begged for more, and he did two encores to an almost full house.

John was delighted. I was elated and immensely grateful. After theater expenses we had just enough to pay off the loan. Again, God had provided a way. Afterward, I snuck back into the hospital and into my room, apparently without being seen. A day later the kidney stone passed, and with it the pain.

On My Way

Less than a month after the concert, an entirely new life opened up to me. With sadness I drove away from Newman, away from a life I loved dearly, which had, in the end, become an unfulfilling, even heartrending, experience.

As my car raced toward Ohio and Case Western Reserve University, my sadness melded with relief. And then came a bit of trepidation. I wondered what God had in store for me now.

CHAPTER 8

Graduate School Beginnings (Fall of 1970)

On Leaving Newman

The drive from Minneapolis to Cleveland, Ohio, took eleven hours. Eager to escape the sorrow of leaving Newman, I sped along in my dark-green 1969 Ford, barely stopping to use the restrooms.

The uninterrupted, solitary drive provided me with ample time to think and feel. It was a chance to meditate, a release from the long months of hard work that were filled with political, community, and personal turmoil. I did feel proud that I'd managed to get everything I owned into the car, including my bicycle.

The simplicity of having practically everything I owned in my car spoke to me of freedom, not mortification or poverty. Again, words come to mind from Kris Kristofferson's song, "Me and Bobby McGee": *"Freedom's just another word for nothing left to lose."* I hardly had to worry about someone stealing my stuff—not much there and not worth much.

Mile after mile, feelings of disappointment flooded my soul. I was disappointed with myself for not being more than adequate as a Newman chaplain. I struggled with a grieving heart, thinking of my weaknesses leading to foolish behaviors. Had I injured people by not being a better priest? Had I given people false impressions when I talked with them, at times perceiving myself inadequate spiritually to meet their needs?

Part of me wished I could have another chance at Newman. Another part of me said I was running away. My failures, particularly in the past year, troubled my conscience. I thought I'd failed at living a life that would attract others to become nuns, priests, and brothers. I didn't build an effective Newman team. I didn't influence significant others to follow the nonviolent Jesus. I failed to make peace with my archbishop. Some dear people I hurt.

To my mind, I'd failed to be the priest I intended to be— a bitter disappointment. The thought that God had another plan for me entered my mind, but wasn't salient or foremost.

As the miles drifted by, I had a conversation with myself. If Archbishop Byrne had asked me to stay on, I told myself, if he had said those three simple words, "I need you" or "Christ needs you," I would have given up my fellowship and remained at Newman. I'd have had renewed energy and spiritual fervor, determined to be a better team player. I wasn't blaming the Archbishop; it was simply an observation.

If I had left with the Archbishop's blessing, I might have felt more at peace. Instead, feeling rejected and in exile, my unawareness of my resentment got the better of me. The unwelcome emotion amplified as I thought about the Archbishop driving out to the cabin where his former secretary was vacationing and asking him, "Will you do me the favor of being the director of Newman Center?" Bill Hunt graciously accepted. I grew calmer as I remembered what I did to ease the transition for Hunt before I took off for graduate school by bringing him and the staff together on retreat to plan the coming year's activities. I so wanted to ensure the long-term pastoral and sacramental missions of the Newman Center, particularly the emphasis on seeking peace with justice. I believed strongly that a commitment to social justice in the hearts of many is linked inextricably to faith.

Passing slowly through the Chicago traffic and picking up speed across Indiana, I began to feel more confident than disappointed. I looked forward to graduate school—another mountain to climb, a new opportunity to grow, and develop maybe even a mission. The way ahead seemed both clear and uncertain.

As I entered Cleveland with an element of optimism, I thought about my reasons to avoid living with priests in a rectory or at a university Newman Center. For me to do so would include being heavily involved with the needs of people and students. I recognized my difficulty saying "No" when faced with a person in need.

Consequently, I arrived at the determination *not* to connect with the bishop of Cleveland or any of the priests. Being incognito seemed the best approach.

I didn't find a Catholic community of lay people, either. I attended St. Anne and Our Lady of Peace churches near my apartment. Both displayed a pre-Vatican II spirit, people hurrying in and out of church without greeting strangers. Participation was a passive and joyless affair and lacked the enthusiasm I was accustomed to at Newman. I was disheartened and missed Minnesota so much that it was an effort even to attend mass, and it became a duty, not a joy.

Homebody

John Vinton invited me to stay with him and his wife until I found a place of my own. He had urged me to apply to Case Western Reserve University's Organizational Behavior program, and successfully argued for my acceptance. But I was eager to be on my own. In less than a week I settled into a small modern apartment about a mile and a half from the University.

I bought the least expensive furniture I could find, together with dishes, utensils, pots and pans, ready to do my own cooking and cleaning for the first time ever. A late bloomer, it was time I became responsible for myself. Armed with some of my mother's recipes and a fancy for experiment, I looked forward to the challenge and freedom of keeping house.

Never having lived by myself before, I discovered it to be both engaging and peaceful, a freeing experience. Nobody to tell me what to do, but no one to lend a helping hand either—an invitation to grow, which I readily accepted. I learned a valuable lesson: To be interdependent, one first must be independent.

After a time, independence grew old. Once I learned the basics of taking care of myself, cooking and cleaning lost the appeal of novelty. However, my situation motivated me to put up with it, since *there were no alternatives*.

Having recently recovered from a kidney stone and at the time nursing a stomach ulcer, I gratefully accepted the slower pace of school, to which I was unaccustomed. I found it an utter delight to attend classes in the daytime, and then be responsible for nothing in the evening but reading and studying, without the constant interruption of a screaming telephone. I wish everyone could have this opportunity. How about giving everyone who can't find a job a chance to study, or write poetry, or play a musical instrument? For me, the healing and peaceful fall of 1970 was like being on retreat.

Challenges

One standout exception was a near altercation at a professional football game. "Broadway Joe Namath," quarterback for the New York Jets, came to town to play the Cleveland Browns. John Vinton chanced upon two tickets and invited me, for a change of pace. I was enthusiastic. Then, though without preplanning, but because of my anger at my country's war policy against the Vietnamese people, I didn't stand for the National Anthem. I considered my action an expression of our first amendment right to "freedom of speech…peaceable assembly, and petition of the government for a redress of grievances." Such symbolic protest was not uncommon in the Vietnam years, but was uncommon in a sports venue. Not understanding my intentions, five muscular male Browns fans accosted me and threatened to beat me within an inch of my life. In their eyes I was being unpatriotic. They assumed I hated our country. Surprised, I crouched deeper in my chair. Thankfully, just then the game began on a positive note, distracting my attackers. Near the end of the game, I managed to slip away and lose myself in the departing crowd. Whew!

I had a similar experience earlier in Colorado. After visiting my sister at her Carmelite monastery, I was driving back to Minnesota when I stopped at a small-town coffee shop. In an effort to be friendly, I joined a conversation between several truck drivers. In making a point, I mentioned as a favorable example the priest James E. Groppi, who led people of color in a march through Milwaukee in a protest for social justice. It was angry poor whites that pelted them with rocks. How could these poor whites feel good about themselves if they couldn't see others as "less than"? The truckers responded with such anger, I was lucky to get out of the place unharmed. Outside, others saw things quite differently from my friends and me, and furthermore, did not take kindly to opposing viewpoints.

The experiences taught me that at Newman and in graduate school, I lived in an intellectual ghetto. If I were to influence others to think and feel differently, I needed to consider the context.

In the spring I had another rude awakening. One bright morning, running late for class, I thought I'd better drive to school. In the garage below my apartment, I searched and searched for my car, pacing the concrete aisles to no avail—somebody had actually stolen my car. I called the police. Without even coming out to talk to me, and with no apparent empathy or compassion, the policeman said over the phone: "Forget about getting your car back. It's practically hopeless. My guess is it's on its way west. Cars like yours are converted into dune buggies for desert fun." He told me to report the theft to my insurance company for whatever compensation I could get.

It wasn't much. Enough money, however, to add stupidity to injury by buying a used British MG of *very* poor quality, notwithstanding it was a sharp-looking green convertible. Parts for foreign cars in those days were hard to come by. Many a day I spent time and money in the repair shop, until I got rid of it a year later. Learning experiences, though valuable, can be expensive.

New Community

As I expected, my classmates were 23 to 32 years old, considerably younger than I was. Like me, all confessed they were "on their way to somewhere else," Cleveland being a necessary stopover. I too expected, on finishing, to return to the Archdiocese of St. Paul. In the end, I was the only one who remained in Cleveland after graduation.

Five women and seven men made up our 1970 class. Eight of the twelve finished, earning a Ph.D. Once the faculty accepted a student into the program, they were committed to doing all they could to enable that student to be successful and finish. The faculty worked at "building a learning community," their stated mission and practiced value, if not entirely successful.

Gestalt Institute of Cleveland

A number of our department's graduate students also attended the Gestalt Institute of Cleveland, a three-year program meeting once a week, except in summer. It complemented our Systems Thinking course at Case, because Gestalt theory holds that the mind understands external stimuli as a *whole* before perceiving their parts. We were taught that to understand another person or an event, we need to consider the entire situation (the whole picture), and then the components that create the particular form at a given time.

Following the teaching of psychiatrist and psychotherapist Fritz Perls, the Institute placed heavy emphasis on raising self-awareness and influencing the interconnection between the individual and his or her surroundings.

One of the results of this psychological training *was learning how to cry*. I learned it's okay, that is, okay for big boys to cry. In fact, it's an actual sign of maturity. Tears of gladness, tears of sadness—it doesn't matter.

Our culture, however, didn't accept the idea back then, just as today our society doesn't grasp that it takes a more courageous person to love one's enemies than to confront or defeat them.

I needed to cry, but being of German descent, I didn't know how, nor was I apt to give myself permission. Gestalt psychology taught me to be aware of and accept my feelings as blessings. I then appropriately enabled myself to cry.

I also came to appreciate the benefits of laughter. So enveloped in seriousness, my body and soul needed an escape. I needed to not be serious all the time. I learned to take to heart the advice of Pierre du Pont (founder and CEO of DuPont Industries, and a magnate of Organizational Development) when he told his staff: "You have broken the Fifth Rule. You have taken yourself too seriously. What are the other rules? There are no other rules."

I grew up never seeing a portrait of Jesus laughing. Later, traveling in Asia, I came upon statues of smiling Buddhas. Why so much emphasis on the suffering Jesus, I wondered, and no mention of times Jesus must have laughed. The Christian religion urges both the young and old to be serious. Yet sacred scripture encourages us to rejoice in Christ our savior.

My Gestalt experience reminded me of the spirit of the Hippies, not to push the river, go with the flow, enjoy the ride, and laugh as you go. Live in the present. We can accept life as a miracle and a mystery. I believe that Jesus, notwithstanding his final circumstances, did this. He certainly knew how to accept life as it comes.

The prodigal son in Jesus' story didn't appear to be a happy fellow, even when he was out and about, being prodigal in spending all his inheritance; nor was his dutiful older brother happy. On the other hand, the old man, their father, knew how to rejoice, have a good time, and laugh from the belly. In my current interpretation of Jesus' story, the father is God. Jesus came to earth to tell us what God is like. But I didn't get it for a long time that God is a God of laughter, and it isn't just okay, it's manly, to laugh through my tears.

The Gestalt Institute reinforced:

- My understanding of the error of trying to find harmony, peace of mind, and happiness on one's own.

- Separation from others cannot bring genuine happiness.

- Happiness comes through the fulfillment of love, which is not concentrated on self, but rather on community, with whom one shares this love.

CHAPTER 9

My First Trip to Vietnam (1971)

Research—Summer 1971

In early summer 1971, Professor Frank Friedlander gave me another chance to learn methods of academic research. Serendipitously, at the same time, I heard about a conference to be held in Paris in June: "International Assembly of Christians in Solidarity with the Vietnamese, Laotian, and Cambodian People."

There would be opportunities to meet with Vietnamese from across the political spectrum. I intended to meet as many Vietnamese people as I could, and then travel to Vietnam to continue my research. My question would be: "What do you think and how do you feel, as a Vietnamese, about the presence of American soldiers in your country?" I wanted to know if the U.S. military was considered an asset or a liability.

Frank approved of my research question and methodology. Two classmates, Jeff Voorhees and Carolyn Lukensmeyer Hirsch, offered to join me in this adventure, which pleased me no end.

Our plan was to fly to Paris to attend the conference, then to India to visit Mother Teresa of Calcutta, and on to Vietnam. I had never visited Mother Teresa's community. While visiting the U.S., she had visited me many times, and now I'd have the chance to see her in her home community. And Jeff and Carolyn were more than eager to meet her.

People asked how I financed these trips. In the end, I used money from the Danforth Fellowship to pay for the trip. Future trips were financed through the generosity of Peter and Mary (of the Peter, Paul and Mary trio), who gave concerts in Minneapolis to raise funds for my peace work.

Reporter Tom Fox Approaches Me

An hour before takeoff at the New York City airport, a stranger approached me and *surreptitiously* put a small piece of paper in my hand with the name and address of a Vietnamese person living in Saigon. Tom Fox was a reporter for the *National Catholic Reporter* newspaper, later to become its editor, then publisher. How he knew of me and my mission is still a mystery.

I had heard of Tom, however, and knew he had been evicted from Vietnam for filing dispatches judged to be unfavorable to the South Vietnamese and American war effort. When he introduced himself, I readily grasped the paper. He disappeared as quickly as he had come. I slipped the note into my wallet. In the moment, I had no idea how significant it would be to our trip.

Paris Mission

Paris in June is always a sensual treat—sweet-scented flowers everywhere and the aroma of French cuisine. At that time, though, I was too focused on our mission to appreciate the amenities. Jeff and I attended meetings with various groups, spoke with many individuals, and visited with friends from the year before. When I strongly pressed the Vietnamese representatives, I received assurances that, once Vietnam was reunited, no punishments would be administered to the people in the south. All would be forgiven.

Relief and Disappointment

I wanted to believe the assurances from these representatives from North Vietnam. As it happened, they were not present or in control when the northern forces rolled into Saigon in 1975 and occupied the south. The military brass knew how to strategically fight a war; however, they were clueless when it came to winning the peace. True to their military socialization, the North Vietnamese couldn't trust strangers, even fellow Vietnamese, and proceeded to condemn and punish anyone in the south who was in a position of power for colluding with the enemy. As a consequence they also punished or ignored many ordinary citizens. They did not appreciate their southern brothers and sisters in the National Liberation Front (NLF) and the Catholic Third Force, who worked at life's peril for unification. Fear and ignorance led the North Vietnamese to ignore their counsel.

Many of my friends in the south who had invited me to help them reunify the country, were ignored or threatened when offering differing ideas. Tran Ngoc Bau, my dear friend and confidant, who later escaped to Switzerland, was among those who were treated harshly and whose life was in danger.

Doan Van Toai, a student leader in the resistance to the Thieu regime, was sent to an "education camp." (See his book *The Vietnamese Gulag*, Simon and Schuster, 1985.) The result was horrific suffering and concomitant resentment of the Communists among the people in the south. To this day, many in the south refuse to refer to Saigon by its new name, Ho Chi Minh City (HCMC).

As I reflect almost fifty years later on the Communists' behavior, it is difficult to control my sorrow at the folly of the military leaders. Instead of coming in as liberators, they marched in as conquerors and treated the people accordingly. Instead of thanking and rewarding those in the south who joined them in freeing their country from a puppet regime set up by the Americans, they reacted out of fear, and trusted no one but their own contingent.

Their fear prevented them from leaving the people be—those people who had worked with the Americans, many simply to put food in their families' mouths. The North's behavior led to a whole generation of suffering and prejudice that set back development, not only in the south, but also in the north. It is reminiscent of the persistent antagonism that, to this day, breeds hatred and hostility among southerners in our own country, estrangement a century after the Civil War. Today, the Middle East suffers similar discord and worse conflicts, as we Americans made the same mistake in Iraq.

North Vietnamese Priests

The big surprise for me at the Paris conference was the presence of two Catholic priests from Hanoi. Because our meeting was in solidarity with the Christians of Indochina, their presence from North Vietnam made sense. Most of us, exposed only to the Western press, had the impression that Christian churches in North Vietnam were nonexistent. We were led to believe that the Communists had closed all the churches, and that believers in Christ were persecuted. To describe the enemy as practically devils, allowed bombing them into oblivion to be seen as less reprehensible.

The two priests were elderly and frail. Speaking through an interpreter, I learned one was the pastor of St. Dominic Church in Hanoi. Whether they were being careful or were under close surveillance, I had difficulty engaging them in conversation about religious freedom or the condition of the church in North Vietnam.

In the evening after our encounter with the two priests, Jeff and I went for a quiet stroll along a Parisian avenue to discuss what we had learned that day. The air was fresh but damp and cool, and a fine mist polished the stone and marble buildings. So deep were we in conversation as we slowly walked Avenue Kleber, around the Centre De Conferences Internationales and the Place de la Concorde, we barely noticed the famous structures and sculpture. We trusted the elegant, flat-hatted gendarmes to shepherd us through the traffic.

As we wandered, we pondered how we might use our introduction to the North Vietnamese priests to advantage in peacemaking. Jeff came up with an out-of-the-box suggestion: "Let's telegraph the Pope, telling him about the priests, and offer to bring them down to Rome to visit with him."

I agreed enthusiastically and added, "I could hide a camera in my cassock, and as the Pope greets and embraces the two priests, I could snap a picture. We could release it to the western press. The entire western world would see there is a viable Catholic community in North Vietnam instead of a bunch of 'godless Communists.'"

Our plan so excited me that I could hardly sleep that night. First thing the next morning I asked the Vietnamese priests if they would be willing to go to Rome to visit the pope. Surprised, they promised to let me know. Just before noon, they told me they could go. Quickly I telegraphed Pope Paul VI with our idea, and waited. The next day I received a telegram from the Vatican saying the Holy Father was too busy to see us, but that a Paulist American priest, Tom Stransky, would be happy to receive our delegation at the Vatican on Saturday morning on the vigil of Pentecost. I was disappointed but not surprised because the idea had been a long shot. On hearing the news, the two North Vietnamese priests declined to come to Rome with us.

Rome...but Not a Holiday

I was eager to go to Rome, and so was Jeff, as was an American Franciscan priest, who with six of his lay companions had also come for the conference. They had planned to go from Rome north to Assisi to visit the birthplace of St. Francis, and they saw the Vatican as an important stopover opportunity to speak to church officials about the war.

We arrived at the Vatican Saturday morning. It was the Vigil of the Feast of Pentecost. The American priest at the Vatican greeted his fellow Americans with friendliness. We shared our information from the conference, but our dialogue soon turned into a debate. I complained to him, "Had John XXIII still been pope, he wouldn't have been 'too busy' to see priests from North Vietnam, given the tragedy going on in that country." I suggested he would have been eager to learn about the conditions of the church in North Vietnam—and the thinking of at least some U.S. Catholics about the war.

As I would have done in his position, this priest defended John's successor Paul VI, arguing that, "Paul is a good man, simply different in personality."

I wasn't having it. I protested, "If we came with a donation of a million dollars, check in hand, I bet the Holy Father would find time in his busy schedule to see us." Of course, I couldn't know that, and was only expressing my frustration. Our host didn't refute my accusation, simply dismissed it. In the end, I'm sad to confess, I left the meeting in a huff.

Protest in Rome

In my mind I'd already planned a protest action, expecting a fruitless ending to our Vatican visit—a self-fulfilling prophecy. Later in the afternoon, having borrowed vestments and resources for a home Mass from a local Italian parish, I took a taxi to the steps of St. Peter's Basilica in Rome. As I climbed inside, decked out in alb, stole, and chasuble, the driver didn't blink an eye, as though priests in Rome traveled all the time in attire to do Catholic mass.

Jeff was waiting for me when I arrived, along with the Franciscan and his group, and members of the Italian press whom I'd alerted. We ascended the multiple steps to a space that enabled us to set up a small table with bread and wine. As I gazed from St. Peter's Square, glittering in the afternoon sun, to the majestic statues of the twelve apostles above, the thought came to me, "This is exactly what I was ordained to do."

The Franciscan priest assisted, but being out of costume, didn't vocally concelebrate. I began the mass as the rest of us sang peace songs: "Where Have All the Flowers Gone?" "All We Are Asking

Is Give Peace a Chance," and "Oh Freedom." Elderly ladies climbing the steps to pray inside the Basilica paused to celebrate with us. My three-minute homily asked that we pray for peace. Just as I finished giving Holy Communion to nearly fifty participants, the Swiss Guard, dressed in street clothes, interrupted the ceremony.

Unable to give the final blessing, I gave my celebret (a card issued by my archdiocese that identifies me as a priest) to the officer to prove I was a legitimate priest. He then marched us off to a room inside the basilica. Because the Vatican hasn't had a prison since 1890, the officer (we later learned from a reporter) called the Italian police in an effort to convince them to incarcerate us. Thankfully, the Italian police refused on the grounds that "breaking of church law" was outside their jurisdiction, and because we were in the Vatican state, not in Italy. Because of the Feast of Pentecost, had we been jailed we might well have languished in a cell for a week before getting a court appearance.

Frustrated and exasperated, the officer looked at me sternly and spoke with authority in English, "Leave Rome immediately and never come back."

Rumor has it that Saint Peter, twenty centuries earlier, received the same orders. The thought pleased me. We were on our way, anyway—"to somewhere else"—and I had no intention of returning to Rome. God's providence held otherwise.

In the future...not only would I return in October with letters for bishops at the synod from the Vietnamese church, but in 2004 I'd be concelebrating mass again on those same steps, with Pope John Paul II at Mother Teresa's beatification.

Stopover in Israel

Late Sunday afternoon, Jeff and I met Carolyn at the Rome airport. The next day at Carolyn's suggestion, we changed our reservation to fly to Israel before heading to India. Changing reservations in those days, thankfully, unlike the present, amounted to a simple phone call and no added cost. We changed reservations often throughout our trip whenever it served our purpose, no questions asked.

In Israel, we visited one of the graduates of our Organizational Behavior program, Saul Eisen, who was teaching at the University of Tel Aviv. He shared his OB experience with Israeli students, who also found participation in decision-making strange. Once the concept was understood, however, students took to it. They got it: the way to run an organization is with everyone's input.

Years later, Pope Francis demonstrated such effective leadership by tapping eight cardinals from around the world to advise him on governance and reform. It amazes me that in the 21st century many leaders of organizations still follow the dictatorial behavior of command and control.

Our visit to Israel lasted only three days, so I intentionally saved my visits to the holy places for another time. We did visit the old city in Jerusalem. I was troubled to note in the summer of 1971 that the Israelis treated the Palestinians as second-class citizens. Walking through the old city, I paused to sit and drink tea at an Arab shop. I asked the owner a question: what was daily life like for him? He complained that not being Jewish, he was forced to show identity papers nearly every day. In addition, they didn't have one-man, one-vote power. Because he was a citizen of the country, I asked the man why this was so. The man sighed with an expression of hopelessness. He said, "Palestinian families have five or six children, and the Jews have only two at most. The fear is that, in time, the Palestinians would outnumber the Jews, and it would no longer be a Jewish state, but an Arab state." I walked away wondering how the Palestine/Israeli situation would end. As I write in 2018, almost fifty years later, I'm still wondering.

I wish I had been wise enough at the time to state, "If the Israelis had created a situation wherein most Palestinians could get rich, the Jews would not need to worry because the Palestinians also would begin having two or fewer children."

The three of us flew to New Delhi and on to Calcutta (now Kolkata). Because of bad weather, our flight was postponed a day, and the airline put us up in, what for us was a luxurious New Delhi hotel, at their expense.

Lost in Calcutta

Night had fallen by the time we landed in Calcutta. As we walked down the steps and onto the tarmac at about 10 p.m., it felt as though we were descending into a furnace. The heat, even at that late hour, combined with our fatigue, very nearly did us in.

Once inside the terminal, I called Mother Teresa's convent. She knew we were coming, but neither she nor I had known exactly when. Mother answered, a nice surprise. Because it was so late, she advised us to get a hotel room, and she would pick us up the next morning.

By the time we rescued our luggage, the airport appeared descrted—no one behind an information desk eager to assist us. We expected to find a taxi to take us to a hotel. We found one man who was unable to converse with us in English, so Carolyn mimed sleep, and I drew outlines in the air of a large building. My frustration grew. Exhausted, I detested not being able to communicate. Finally, the man motioned us to follow him and he led us to a taxi. Relieved, we climbed inside, only to face the same challenge. But the driver nodded and put the car in gear as though he finally knew what we wanted.

The darkness and his slow driving served to increase the anxiety of the three of us. The farther he drove, the darker it got. With no streetlights, we could see only by the dim lights of buildings on either side of the road. Suddenly we came upon a building ablaze with lights. I made the mistake of assuming it was a hotel and yelled at the driver to stop. He understood that word, or its intensity. He pulled over, and we jumped out eager to escape. Just as quickly—though after we paid him—he disappeared into the night. We were distressed to discover it wasn't a hotel at all but a closed office building. My heart sank. How could I make such a mistake?

We set off into the pitch darkness. Lugging our suitcases and without a flashlight, we literally stumbled over sleeping bodies on what appeared to be a sidewalk. Eventually, Jeff said, "This is futile. You two stay here with the suitcases—it doesn't make sense to walk around like this—let me go off and see what I can find." His suggestion made sense to Carolyn and me so we agreed.

In the dark, with nothing moving, waiting seemed endless. I began to worry that Jeff wouldn't find us again, though I said nothing to Carolyn. But he did return, saying. "I found a place. It's not much, but it has a bed."

"Anything," I said in relief, wondering how he did it and how he found us again in the darkness. We grabbed our luggage and carefully picked our way among the sleeping bodies, speaking in whispers so as not to disturb the sleepers, and to keep track of one another. We had less than a block to go.

Our accommodation was a single room with a large bed and a working ceiling fan. One naked light bulb furnished pale light. Thankful, I noticed a much-needed latrine. The three of us immediately arrived at the conclusion that the bed was big enough for all of us. Even though I'd never slept with a woman, under the circumstances I didn't give it a second thought—we desperately needed sleep. And the price was right, three dollars a night.

Moments later, as I lay in bed, with Carolyn in the middle between Jeff and me, I thanked God I wasn't alone. I couldn't imagine being here all by myself. The gentle whine of the overhead fan and Carolyn's soft breathing introduced another thought: "Of course, I know I'm never alone, God is always with me, but still, God and I would have had a hard time tonight without Jeff and Carolyn. Thanks, God."

Following Mother Teresa

In the morning, I once more phoned Mother Teresa. She and a driver arrived quickly in a jeep. In her soft white sari with the blue stripes, her small slender body belied the spiritual giant she was. She greeted us joyfully but in a businesslike manner, as if to say, "It's about time you got here, there's work to be done."

As the driver inched his way through the traffic, passing count-less beggars, Mother chatted away, explaining to Carolyn and Jeff the call she and her sisters had been summoned to answer: "To care for the hungry, the naked, the homeless, the crippled, the blind, the lepers—all those people who feel unwanted, unloved, uncared for throughout society, people who have become a burden to society and are shunned by everyone."

Her order, the Missionaries of Charity, was endeavoring to fol-low Jesus's lead in tending to physical challenges and then spiritual needs of the poor. Mother Teresa told us, "Today somebody is suf-fering. Today somebody is hungry. Our work is for today. Yesterday has gone, tomorrow has not yet come, and we only have today to make Jesus known, loved, served, fed, clothed, sheltered."

As soon as we arrived at the motherhouse, Mother Teresa wasted no time taking us to "the house of the dying." In the glaring hot sun, the sisters daily drove a makeshift fleet of rickshaws and navigated the crowded streets, returning with ever more people in acute states of distress and neglect, some of them just hours from death. At the time of our visit, the people's needs were appalling. Millions of refugees from the war over the separation of Bangladesh from Pakistan, as well as uncontrolled immigration, had created a crushing socioeconomic burden for India. The sisters also searched garbage cans for newborn babies, unwanted because their mothers were financially and/or emotionally unable to care for them. Our hearts broke. I wanted this to be just a terrible dream from which we'd awake and find nothing but happy families.

The moment we opened the door to enter the low cavernous building, the stench almost knocked us over. At first I held my breath. It took all my strength not to turn and go back outside in order to breathe. Though the windows were open, the heat caused the smell to hover like a malign presence. With no breeze and only a few floor fans, relief was impossible. Of course I couldn't just leave. I determined to "suck it up" as I watched Mother Teresa rush to attend a dying patient lying on a floor mat, lifting his head to give him water.

Mother once told an interviewer that she saw Jesus Christ in the faces of the poor, the outcast, the maimed and the dying. She described them as Christ in "distressing disguise," and said she believed they all deserved what she called "the delicate love of God." In 1977 she said, "I think it is really important that we all realize (the poor) are our brothers and sisters, and we owe them love and care and concern…they give us much more than we give them."… "They're such strong people, living day-to-day with no food. And they never curse or never complain. We don't have to give them pity or sympathy. We have so much to learn from them."

Mother Teresa lived and served with a generosity that continues to challenge me. It was evident that Mother Teresa walked her talk, as did the other nuns. Their behavior calls forth the best in me. In my eyes she stands tall because she was able to organize a good-sized team of people devoted to the same purpose. I so wished to be able to do that as well.

The large room held some seventy dying people, each lying on a floor mat. The sisters moved among them and ministered to their needs. I watched Mother Teresa move from person to person, get down on her knees and apply a cool wet cloth on the forehead of each as she spoke comforting words into their ear. She did everything she could to relieve each one's anguish. The other sisters did the same as they administered medicine. People were dying here, yet in their last moments they were receiving love and respect, not facing death alone.

The three of us followed Mother's example. Kneeling at the side of a dying person, I changed the cloth on his or her forehead and look into glazed eyes. Unable to communicate in their language, I blessed each one and prayed in English. During this time, I no longer smelled the terrible odor. Somehow my nostrils got used to it, and Jeff and Carolyn reported the same experience.

At one point, Jeff later told me, Mother Teresa spoke with a woman who was near death. Mother Teresa turned to Jeff and said she had asked the woman why she was clinging to life, and the woman replied that she wanted to see her son. Mother put Jeff's hand in the woman's and asked him to be her son for that moment.

The dying woman said some words Jeff could not understand, and he nodded and smiled at her. When she had finished speaking, Mother told her now that she had got her wish, she could close her eyes and go to her maker.

After some time, Mother approached us and motioned that it was time to leave. She next led us to the building that housed the babies. That large room was much brighter and had no odor. Nine large mattresses were scattered about the floor with at least eight one- and two-year-old babies playing on each one. The three of us were drawn like magnets, each to one of the beds to sit down with the babies. Immediately they began to crawl all over us. We hugged and played and comforted them. Some of the children seemed non-responsive at first, and the nuns encouraged us in our play. I looked up and saw the nuns and Mother watching us, all smiles. Here language was of no account. These babies needed touching and hugs.

We spent most of the day holding and playing with these tiny abandoned children of God, moving from mattress to mattress, and shooing flies away from their faces. Mother went off to do other work. I've often wondered what happened to these children. The sisters ran a grade school to teach them when they got older. Today Mother's legacy continues via the many outreaches of Mother Teresa Children's Foundation, through which lives have been changed. Their programs have helped and continue to help children all over the world, who would never otherwise go to school to receive an education.

Mother invited us to return the next day and asked me to preside at the community Mass, which I was honored to do. No mention was made of our sleeping situation. Celebrating the Eucharist for these sisters I so admired was a humbling experience. I can't remember my homily—their presence and work were the most telling homily.

Bangladesh Refugee Camp

After Mass and breakfast, Mother Teresa announced we were going out to a refugee camp. No argument from us; we were eager to go wherever Mother wanted. Jeff remembers that before we left, a young priest had come into the room out of breath and flustered, trying to deliver his urgent message. Mother gave him a glass of water with lemon and told him to drink it and compose himself. He finally told her that cholera had broken out, and his pastor had sent him to her to get vaccine. She scribbled a note on a piece of paper, put it in an envelope, and gave it to him with instructions where to go to be given vaccine. As he jumped up to depart, she stopped him and made him sit back down and have another drink. When she was sure she had his attention, she told him that when he got back to his pastor with the vaccine, he was to remind him that if he ever got his hands on any money, *he owed her some.*

The same driver and open-air jeep delivered us to a camp not far from the city. On the way, Mother prepared us for what we were about to see. At the moment, a civil war raged between the east and west in Pakistan, separated in the north by India. After the partition of British India in 1947, a new nation of Pakistan was born, although divided into two distinct geographic and cultural areas, East and West Pakistan. The western area held the greater political and economic power. Decades of exploitation of the people in East Pakistan led to popular uprisings and brutal crackdowns. Eventually the East declared its independence and named itself Bangladesh.

The civil war drove millions of desperately poor refugees from East Pakistan into East India. Mother Teresa's neighborhood, similarly destitute, could not handle the influx. The refugee camps were desperate in their need for help from the global community. The sisters were overwhelmed distributing food, clothing, and medicine and also administering to orphans and to women who had been raped by soldiers.

The poet Maya Angelou's words flooded my mind, "Evil [is] what millions of ourselves do to millions of ourselves."

At the camp, Mother's sisters moved among the people with gentleness and strength. The people were ravaged and hungry. The sisters gave them aid, medical care when possible, and eased their suffering. Everywhere you looked were makeshift pup tents. Those

132

who could stand looked to us as if we had come to deliver them from a horrible dream.

One couple asked Mother to come and examine their sick baby. She went over to the child and checked his vitals while speaking to the parents in their language. Returning to us Mother confided, "The child has cholera, and it's very contagious." Cholera is carried by flies—flies swarmed the feces that was mounded everywhere.

As we walked slowly back to the jeep, Mother told us, "When the monsoons come in a few months, all this will be under at least a foot of water."

"What will these people do?" I asked. It was far beyond my imagination.

And, the first time I'd heard Mother come even close to complaining, she said, "Only those who manage to sleep in trees will survive."

I surveyed the scene. Not enough trees in evidence for even the healthy to climb. Abhorrent, true—the old, weak, and very young would die.

As we climbed back into the jeep, Mother asked us, "After lunch, would you go to the U.S. Consulate and seek help from the Americans for these refugees?" Of course we would. We'd do anything to help these people. I was grateful Mother had thought of this, but at the same time I worried. Success would take a miracle. Because we were anti-Vietnam War activists, I suggested, we were the last persons the American government would heed.

Mother Teresa's driver took us to the U.S. Consulate at 1:30 that afternoon. We asked to speak with the Economic Adjudicator. Although we had no appointment, we didn't need to wait long.

We began by saying Mother Teresa had sent us, hoping her name would carry weight. We described the devastating conditions at the camp, and Mother's dire prediction that the camp would be under a foot of water in a few months. We tried to convey the refugees' desperation. It was not news; the officer said he was aware of the situation. He politely promised to send our request for aid on to Washington.

It seemed highly unlikely our request would bear fruit, that the U.S. would send relief. The bloody war—the Pakistani army fighting with mostly American firearms and led by U.S.-trained officers—had not brought about a change in policy. The carnage and filthy conditions among the refugees, when they became public, horrified people across the global community. Nixon was rumored to favor Pakistan over India because India remained neutral toward the Vietnam War, and because of Nixon's special relationship with the Pakistani head of state.

As we expected, nothing came of our request.

In Thailand, Disbelief

From India, we flew to Bangkok, Thailand. Through the intercession of Carolyn's friend, we were invited to a delicious lunch with the U.S. Ambassador Leonard S. Unger outside on the Embassy grounds. We were served lunch in a gazebo that had lizards crawling on the posts and rafters, and a monkey on a tether between some trees. The Ambassador treated us with genuine kindness. We related our experiences in India and the refugee camp, in hopes the ambassador would reinforce our request for U.S. aid. He showed concern but remained noncommittal. As far as we know, he did nothing. The ambassador did, however, arrange, at our request, for us to meet with the Embassy's Economic Adjudicator the following morning.

At the meeting, Carolyn questioned the Embassy officer about U.S. plans for the economic development of Thailand. We were stunned by his response: "Because the Thais are notorious for not working or planning for the future, our intention is to run electric lines into all the small villages in northeast Thailand, the poorest area, and then give each village chief a television set. In their culture people come and go in each other's homes; eternally invited. The villagers will gather in the chief's home; when they see all the ads on television for products they can buy, they will be motivated to work hard and plan how to get these consumer goods." He explained that if they had a bumper crop of rice this year, they wouldn't plant next year and that the goal with the televisions was to "teach them to want things so they will work harder and plan more."

The three of us were shocked, stunned into silence because these remarks were so preposterous, it should have been funny. But of course it wasn't funny. How I wish I'd said, "Why not invest instead in education and health care, which would contribute to physical wellbeing and social principles of ethical conduct? In an atmosphere of ideas, good will, and tolerance, progress can be made in building a Thailand that's healthy for all its people." I hadn't sufficient information to do so, thus we simply looked at one another in disbelief.

CHAPTER 10

An Invitation to Return to Saigon

Strangers in Saigon – First Visit, October 1971

Monday morning, we landed at the Saigon airport. Fighter jets lined the runway, hidden inside individual camouflaged hangars. With U.S. passports, we moved quickly through airport security and Customs. I suppose South Vietnamese officials assumed we were coming to aid in the war effort; why else would Americans come to war-torn Vietnam?

Once we were outside, taxi drivers vied for our attention. We were at a loss as to where to go—strangers in a mighty strange land. "Downtown" was the best we could suggest.

In the twenty-minute drive through heavy traffic of trucks, motorbikes and bicycles, we noticed at every intersection ominous tall shelters surrounded by sandbags. Perched on top sat Vietnamese soldiers behind machine guns eyeing the traffic, as if an attack was imminent. This was an ugly and surprising sight.

We were dropped off near the Continental Hotel, which we later learned was the hotel where Graham Green wrote his novel, *The Quiet American*, during the early stages of the Vietnam War. Ragamuffin street kids, in their efforts to survive, sold the book to tourists in Saigon for years. I've purchased at least three copies and read it several times.

The Continental was too rich for our pocketbooks, so we walked west toward the Cathedral of Notre Dame. After two blocks we came to an ancient dilapidated hotel. We stepped inside where we found very young and very pretty Vietnamese girls lounging on seedy furniture in a carpet-less lobby.

Our satisfactory experience in Calcutta encouraged us to take a ten-dollar single room on the fifth floor, this time with two beds, one for Carolyn and the other for Jeff and me. In the elevator, we had to hoist ourselves by a rope pulley to get to our room. We laughed at the thought that the elevator was as perilous as the streets below. The room was clean, though, and the cold-water shower worked. I would have preferred a warm shower, but in that extreme heat it wasn't a major issue.

Once situated, we started off in search of the person whose address Tom Fox had slipped to me at the New York airport. We asked for directions and found out it was within walking distance of our hotel. At the door of a small house built in the 1920s, I took a deep breath and lightly knocked. After a few moments a narrow slit in the door was slid open, and a pair of eyes appeared. It reminded me of speakeasy entrances in films about prohibition—when one saw the eyes in the opening, one whispered, "Joe sent me."

A man's voice said something brief in Vietnamese. I quickly said that Mr. Tom Fox had given us this address and that we hoped to talk with willing Vietnamese persons. He may have suspected we were reporters like Tom. I slid a card through the opening with the name of our hotel and room number. The voice promised to contact us.

On the way back to the hotel, Carolyn suggested we get directions to a marketplace. Once there, Carolyn went directly to a table selling cloth. She found the material she wanted and received directions to the home of a seamstress nearby. She went immediately, with Jeff and me tagging along, and was promptly measured and told to return in five days for her áo dài, the traditional attire for Vietnamese women. The costume is a tight-fitting silk tunic, with a padded coat worn over pantaloons—very beautiful and very modest. Carolyn and the seamstress managed the exchange with neither knowing the other's language.

The next day we received a message to return to the address that Tom Fox gave me, with instructions to come in the afternoon. We arrived to find the home filled with over a dozen Vietnamese men—some professors; some priests; a social worker, Ngo Cong Duc; a member of the legislative assembly; and owner and publisher of *Tin Sang*, a Saigon daily newspaper, of which there were more than a dozen. The Vietnamese appeared to want to share their thoughts to whoever was willing to listen.

The group also had many questions about what we wanted to do. They designated Tran Ngoc Bau as our guide and connection to them because he worked for Lutheran Christian Services and was fluent in English.

We told them we would like to meet students and any other people they thought would be important to our efforts: reporters, other professors, and clergy—Vietnamese people who could speak English. I wanted to learn, for my research, what the common people thought about the presence of American soldiers in their country. Because I was unable to speak Vietnamese, I couldn't just walk up to people on the street, so I needed referrals and a translator such as Bau. We also told them we wanted to be of assistance to them in whatever way we could, *not only taking, but giving as well*.

As it happened, it *didn't* happen. We were able to visit with only a few "average citizens." Even with a Vietnamese translator, I sensed that people were guarded in what they revealed to Americans, afraid to express their honest feelings. Consequently, my research sample was skewed heavily toward the intelligentsia, the people who spoke English. With Tran Ngoc Bau and sometimes a different escort, we visited with students, Buddhist monks, priests, and even the Archbishop of Saigon, Nguyen Van Binh.

I liked the archbishop immediately; the twinkle in his eye was mixed with sadness and compassion. No doubt he walked a fine line between priest and laity, and between those who favored the American presence and those who did not. Publicly he was careful not to show his hand. To us, he spoke positively of both groups, those who favored Americans and those who didn't. He did not say anything negative. He understood our sentiments and treated us with utmost kindness and respect.

Ngo Cong Duc and *Tin Sang*

Ngo Cong Duc invited us to visit his newspaper, *Tin Sang*. Whether because of genetics or diet or both, most Vietnamese tend to be small in stature, but not our host. Not only did he stand tall, his solid muscular body seemed ready to take charge, reinforced by a strong voice.

When we arrived at the newspaper plant, outside were stacks of newspapers piled high over our heads that had not passed the censors. The South Vietnamese inspectors would check the daily paper, and if they found anything objectionable, they would not let the paper be delivered, so the papers were piled in eight-foot-high stacks in the alley outside the plant. On entering Duc's office, I spied a loaded pistol on his desk within easy reach of his right hand. He explained that the government viewed certain articles as "unpatriotic." We assumed the only reason the paper was allowed to publish at all was to give the appearance of a free press, and because Duc was an assemblyman.

I finally got up the courage to ask about the loaded gun on his desk. Duc responded in all seriousness saying, "There are a lot of violent people out there." Each time soldiers came to censor another issue of the newspaper, Duc was prepared, lest they seek to murder him in the process. Saigon was a city in trouble, and we didn't know what, if anything, we could do to help. It was a desire to assist that motivated our courage, similar to swimming out into the deep to save a drowning person.

Visit to Quảng Ngãi

Thursday morning Carolyn and I visited the U.S. Air Force headquarters, asking if we could fly to Da Nang and then back down to

Quảng Ngãi to visit the prosthetic hospital, which the American Friends Service Committee (AFSC) operated. We'd been advised that military transport planes flew back and forth between Saigon and Da Nang daily, and the chance of catching one was good. Sure enough, the officer in charge didn't question our motives. He may have assumed we were working for the U.S. military. Because of my briefcase, we didn't appear to be tourists or renegades. "Report back at 1:30 p.m.," the officer said as he verified the availability of seats for us. I was tempted to salute and proudly respond, "Yes sir!"

Jeff needed to make his Saturday noon flight to be back in the United States by Monday to teach at Cleveland State University. Carolyn and I were scheduled to fly back to Saigon Saturday morning from Da Nang, but we couldn't count on getting back before Jeff's plane was due to depart. Jeff spent the time in Saigon with students and Buddhists monks.

Thankfully, the flight to Da Nang was uneventful. To avoid ground fire, our route took us over the ocean, about a mile from the coast. However, as we landed in Da Nang, the airport was under rocket attack, so our flight to Quảng Ngãi was delayed for several hours as we hunkered down.

Fortunately we weren't bombarded for long. Servicemen and others present took the attack in stride, which assuaged fear on our part.

Eventually, the all-clear siren sounded. In dark night, we hurried aboard the plane and made the short flight over enemy territory *to* Quảng Ngãi. The kind Quakers, surprised to see fellow Americans, welcomed us and gave us each a room and food. During the night, Carolyn and I were kept awake by a raging battle that appeared to draw ever nearer.

Friday morning, we toured the hospital and observed the work of these religious Americans. They made prosthetics—artificial limbs, not only for injured soldiers but for any and all who came to them, especially children, most of whom had been injured from stepping on landmines when at play. The staff iterated the challenges they faced because of insufficient prostheses supplies.

My Lai Village Tragedy

In the afternoon, at our request, a Quaker staff member took us a short distance to the village of My Lai where an American military atrocity had been committed. Three years previously, March 16, 1968, a platoon of U.S. troops on a search-and-destroy mission, led by Lieutenant William L. Calley, brutally killed many unarmed civilians.

According to testimony that had come to light less than three months before our arrival in Vietnam, the U.S. soldiers dragged dozens of people, including young children and babies, into a ditch and executed them with automatic weapons. The massacre ended only when Warrant Officer Hugh Thompson landed his helicopter between the soldiers and the fleeing villagers and threatened to open fire if the massacre continued.

When checking various sources on the Internet in 2018, the number of deaths ranged from 347 to over 500. This included old men, children and women, many of whom were also raped. As one report stated, "The brutality of the My Lai killings and the official cover-up fueled anti-war sentiments and further divided the United States over the Vietnam War."

Carolyn and I walked slowly and silently through the village. What could we say? I pictured what had taken place then. We examined the ditch where the innocents were massacred. My heart was heavy with sorrow.

People we encountered in the area shied away from us. They had seen only a few Americans since the slaughter took place. I had bought chewing gum and candy on the way there from people selling from their huts at the roadside. In the village I attempted to give the treats to women and children. When they allowed me to venture close enough, they would reach out, take, and then quickly run off, not trusting Western strangers.

Even these almost-50 years later, I can still say that my visit there was somber and saddening.

Setting the Stage

Saturday morning Carolyn and I flew back to Saigon on another U.S. military plane. Joyfully we bumped into Jeff a few moments before his plane left for the U.S., and after a quick sharing, he was gone.

That evening Carolyn and I felt honored to be invited to dinner at Duc's home. In the afternoon she'd picked up her áo dài from the seamstress. She looked strikingly beautiful; the gold silk set off her light brown hair—and she won the hearts of the women and men with her effort to dress as a proper Vietnamese woman. It was politically wise as well, curbing somewhat the anti-American feelings beginning to run rampant among the people the U.S. sought to help in the south of Vietnam.

The Vietnamese priests were clothed in white shirts and black pants, unlike the long flowing saffron-colored robes Buddhists monks wore. When on official church business, priests wore black suits with a white collar in public, similar to U.S. priests. For casual wear, Vietnamese men dress in long pants, usually a dark color, and a short-sleeved shirt. On official occasions, the convention is for men to wear dark suits with long-sleeved shirts and ties.

I never observed men or women wearing shorts in public. Modesty is a high value in their culture. Families were scandalized when their daughters, in an effort to attract American soldiers, began to dress like American women.

At dinner, I couldn't help but be struck by the patriarchy in evidence—the Vietnamese women prepared the delicious dinner and ate in the kitchen, including the hostess, Duc's wife. All the men and Carolyn, the exception among the women, ate together in the dining room.

Speeches followed dinner, a custom still today—the longer, the better. That night, topics centered on people's suffering and frustration as the war dragged on. Many expressed gratitude about the three of us coming to Vietnam. Soon it was my time to respond.

I didn't know what to say. Carolyn would have represented us far better, but was not asked. I made an effort and said that the three of us were humbled by their generous acceptance of us as Americans, given what the U.S. was doing to their country, and that we deeply felt their affection. Because the audience was largely priests and professors, many of whom we'd met the previous Monday, I ventured to say: "When I was in the seminary before ordination, it was pointed out many times how blessed I was because, as a priest, I was entering into a marvelous brotherhood. Unfortunately, my experience has been that few priests want to be my brother; most want to be my superior." Loud laughter erupted. They understood completely. I then told them that Carolyn, Jeff, and I experienced a genuine brotherhood with them. I likened them to family. Smiles and applause followed.

Ten Priests and a Bishop, Please

One of the priests then spoke up: "We need you to do us a favor."

I wanted to say, "Anything," but bit my tongue.

He continued: "We would like you to find ten priests and a bishop and come back here in October and do a demonstration against the presidential election. General Nguyen Van Thieu is running for election, but it is a fake election. It is an election in appearance only to convince the American people that democracy exists in South Vietnam, unlike in the North." He was alluding to the propaganda that North Vietnamese were evil Communists, while the people in the south were democratic people seeking freedom from oppression.

Another priest added, "The election is scheduled for October 3, and there's no way Thieu can possibly lose."

Yet another priest said, "Thieu was a friend of President Nixon even before he was elected President of the United States. President Nixon developed a 'back channel' to persuade Thieu not to cooperate with President Johnson because South Vietnam would get a better deal once Nixon was elected. Nixon communicated this information through the Chinese supporter Anna Chennault (born Chen Xiangmei), whose husband led the Flying Tigers and who was close to South Vietnamese officials. Following Nixon's advice, Thieu refused to join the 1968 peace talks."

> Note: Internet sources explained that The First American Volunteer Group (AVG) of the Chinese Air Force in 1941–1942, nicknamed the Flying Tigers, was composed of pilots from the United States Army Air Corps (USAAC), Navy (USN), and Marine Corps (USMC), recruited under presidential authority and commanded by Claire Lee Chennault.

How accurate this information was I didn't know. Clearly, it was true for the men in the room. And everyone knew that "promising peace with honor," Nixon won the 1968 election against Hubert Humphrey.

A History Lesson

Maybe my confused face caused Bau to conclude that Carolyn and I needed a history lesson. Bau said, "When the French were defeated in 1954, approximately 100,000 mostly affluent Vietnamese Catholics left the north and came south because they were taught to fear the Communists. Since they had cooperated with the French and adopted Catholicism, they concluded the Communists would punish them, and take their land and possessions. These Vietnamese Catholics have become the largest and most active constituency supporting the Thieu regime. With the Americans entering the war, they were convinced the Communists, like the Japanese in the World War II, would be defeated, and they then could return to the north and reclaim their homes and property."

We were there to learn from the Vietnamese, to obtain their perspective on what had been happening in their country.

I got the picture. Religion and politics, together with excessive wealth, are a volatile mix. It wasn't my place, though, to comment. Wanting to understand better, I asked, "Isn't the wider Vietnamese Church promoting peace?"

The priest Lau spoke up. "The Church is one of the greatest obstacles to peace in the south. Politically, South Vietnamese Catholics are a well-organized group. Even though they are only ten percent of the population. Because of the French influence, they occupy more than half of the positions of command in the government, 50 percent of the army officers, 40 percent of the deputies in the National Assembly, and 65 percent of the senators. They are fiercely anti-Communist—their catechetical instruction taught them that communism and hell are the same. They believe Communists are children of the devil and must be exorcised."

I was struck by Lau's strong language.

The Catholic Third Force

These Catholics with whom we were eating represented a minority group of Catholics, who were, nevertheless, growing more vocal and influential. They were called the Third Force, Catholics who had come to the conclusion that the war was fruitless. When the Americans first came to their country, Bau confessed that they were optimistic like their brothers and sisters who had come down from the north that the war would end soon and peace would prevail.

As the war dragged on, however, they observed more and more innocent women, children, and old men being killed. U.S. bombers dropped herbicides (Agent Orange) and other chemicals that were contaminating the countryside. Not least, the alien American culture had become more attractive to the youth. The Third Force came to the conclusion *that the medicine was much worse than the sickness.* They believed their country would be far better off if the U.S. soldiers would just leave—so convinced were they that they could attain a peaceful settlement with their Vietnamese brothers and sisters in the north.

This conclusion had not been easy, yet once determined, it became an obsession of the Third Force. They just wanted the Americans and their bombs, and their Thieu puppet government, to be gone.

The Catholic Third Force, although critical of the South Vietnamese government, would not join the National Liberation Front and take up arms. They were nonviolent, in consonance with the principles of Jesus, Gandhi, and Martin Luther King. That was the main reason I identified with them and found it worth the risk to accept their invitation to return and conduct a demonstration.

But what kind of demonstration? "Well," Bau declared, "like we already said, we'd like you to find a bishop and ten priests, yourself included, who would protest with us against the upcoming fake election."

"Why ten priests and a bishop?" I wondered aloud.

"Because the strongest constituency supporting the South Vietnamese government are these 100,000 conservative Catholics who fled from the north," he explained. "If you can find ten priests and a bishop to protest the war, it could have a profound effect on their consciences. Maybe, just maybe, they will begin to question the war and join us to seek a nonviolent peace. Your action would say, 'Jesus died on the cross for Communists too, not just for Christians.'"

I would be back in class in October. It was already late June, so I worried: How could I find ten priests and a bishop by October? I didn't know any clergy in Cleveland, and perceived that I was somewhat estranged from the priests in St. Paul. Also, I couldn't forget my shortage of money. Danforth Foundation had granted me another $5,500 fellowship, but for only one more year, and I had no money coming from the Church. I had paid my way on this trip, and would have to do the same in October. Nonetheless, *I couldn't say no to my friends in this desperate situation.*

I said, "How are we going to do this? How will we stay in touch?" I suspected my government had me under surveillance, especially the last year at the Newman Center. (Mechanical difficulties with

147

our phones led to my belief they were being tapped. Maybe in Cleveland, too, for all I knew.) What if the government intercepted and read my mail, or the South Vietnamese government read theirs?

Someone suggested a code name. "How about calling the demonstration: A Mass for Cardinal Spellman?" This suggestion brought on more laughter. These Catholics were obviously aware that the Cardinal of New York had made strong statements supporting the war.

While visiting U.S. troops in Vietnam in 1965, Spellman famously quoted a U.S. Revolutionary War hero in declaring, "My country, may it always be right, but right or wrong, my country." The Cardinal's quote betrayed an attitude that mirrored the arrogance and ignorance of America. "My country, right or wrong" is nationalism at its worst. Cardinal Spellman was also known to have described the Vietnam War as "a war for civilization" and "Christ's war against the Vietcong and the people of North Vietnam." ("Vietcong" was the word for the soldiers of the National Liberation Front, southerners fighting the civil war against the South Vietnamese government and their U.S. counterparts.)

Pentagon Papers

On our return flight to the U.S., Carolyn and I were greatly encouraged to learn of Daniel Ellsberg's release of the Pentagon Papers to *The New York Times* newspaper, which published excerpts on June 13. The Pentagon Papers were a history of the United States' political/military involvement in Vietnam from 1945 to 1967.

They revealed that the U.S. had expanded the war with the bombing of Cambodia and Laos and coastal raids on North Vietnam by U.S. Marines, none of which had been reported by the media in the United States. Ellsberg said he leaked the papers to end what he perceived to be "a wrongful war." Learning of Ellsberg's action, I was encouraged. Maybe it would be easier now, I thought, to find a bishop and ten priests to participate in the demonstration.

The Hunt Is On

How shall I do it? I wondered. I couldn't put an ad in the newspaper or even a Catholic publication stating, "Wanted, ten priests and a bishop to do a Demonstration for Peace in Vietnam in October."

I wrote Bishop Thomas Gumbleton, a young auxiliary bishop in Detroit who had publicly questioned the morality and wisdom of the Vietnam War. He responded kindly, but said he wouldn't be joining us because, after careful consultation with his advisors, he concluded that the action didn't seem prudent or effective at this time.

Next, I wrote to the bishop of Pueblo, Colorado, Charles Buswell, who had marched against the Vietnam War and was known to volunteer in soup kitchens. He had a reputation as a "gentle soul who led a simple life and always advocated for the poor and immigrants."

I was amazed at the honesty of his reply. In addition to saying he would not be going, he told me why: "I'm afraid to go." In his note he enclosed a check for $100, "to help with" my expenses.

During a visit with my sister at her monastery in Littleton, Colorado, she suggested I ask Denver's auxiliary bishop George R. Evans, thinking he might be interested. However, when I visited with him, although he listened as if in agreement, he said "No," without giving a reason.

Throughout the summer, mostly in Minneapolis, working with peace colleagues, I kept searching for ten priests. I didn't know whom to ask. I perceived that none of my former classmates who were in the priesthood shared my concerns about the war. In retrospect, I wish I had contacted university Newman chaplains who, at that time, were dealing with draft-age, anti-war young men and might have been open to the Vietnam demonstration. It escapes me why I did not think of that.

I quietly asked over a dozen priests. None said yes.

A priest from the Winona diocese in Minnesota, John Dee, used to appear from time to time in my office at Newman Center. I never understood why, but he would drop in occasionally, and he was the only priest that did so. He played guitar and put on programs to teach about Jesus both inside and outside the liturgy. On the occasion of one of his visits, I chanced to ask him to join the demonstration for peace in Vietnam. To my grateful surprise he answered without hesitation, "Yes." He turned out to be a good match.

I received an invitation to attend an August organizational meeting of Clergy and Laity Concerned About Vietnam (CALCAV) in Ann Arbor at the University of Michigan. I gladly attended, welcoming the chance to find more priests. I found only one, Bob Willis, a Jesuit priest from California. His experience was similar to mine: he was studying for a Ph.D. in psychology; he was a student of Carl Rogers, renowned for his knowledge of Counseling Psychology.

I spoke directly to Bob, whom I'd come to admire from his contributions in the meetings. "Will you go with me to Vietnam to do a demonstration for peace?"

"I don't know. What's it about?

I explained simply, "The Young Christian Worker movement is planning a demonstration in Saigon against the war, at the time of the Vietnamese presidential election in October. They're convinced that the Catholic people of Saigon need to see that American clergy are actively against this war."

"Are others going?"

"I contacted three bishops, but all three declined although they applaud the effort. I asked a number of priests who publicly oppose the war, but so far I have only one other, John Dee from Minnesota."

"When do you need to know?" Willis asked.

I looked at my watch. It was 11:30 p.m. "How about in half an hour?"

"I'll meet you back here at midnight."

He came and agreed to go.

Leonard Hirsch, a senior student at Case, asked if he could come along and take pictures. He was Carolyn's husband, and so had knowledge of what I hoped would be a secret trip. I happily agreed. Len was one of the "stars" of the Gestalt Institute of

Cleveland—politically astute. Physically he reminded me of a New York street fighter. A no-nonsense guy, his large muscular body and strong voice sent the message that he could take care of himself.

Nearly September and I had the commitment of only three others. Disappointed, I sent a letter to Tran Ngoc Bau in Saigon asking if it would be possible to postpone the "Mass for Cardinal Spellman" until Christmas. By then, I explained, maybe I could find more priests and a bishop. To be honest, I was hoping they would agree so I wouldn't need to miss any classes.

Approximately two weeks later, a note arrived with the simple words, "With or without a bishop, the Mass for Cardinal Spellman must go on. Please come." The moment of significance in their eyes was the presidential election. The note convinced me that we were desperately needed. I notified the others to plan to leave September 27, and we each would take different planes in case we were followed by the FBI.

I wrote a letter to the professors and each of the 45 students in the Organizational Behavior community explaining why Hirsch and I would be missing classes for a few weeks. I made copies on the department copier and arranged for Jeff to pass them out once we arrived in Vietnam. "Soon after you receive this letter," I wrote, "you'll know the purpose of our absence."

On Our Own

Once we'd arrived and reconnected, Tran Ngoc Bau updated us on what had been happening in his country since my visit the previous June.

Two events stood out in terms of our mission:

One, the Catholic Third Force had formed an alliance with the radical An Quan Pagoda Buddhists. These Buddhists distrusted all Americans and would have nothing to do with the likes of us. Therefore, in fear of jeopardizing this newly formed and strategic alliance, Bau told us he and the priests would not be joining us in the demonstration. Moreover, it seemed to the Third Force leadership that our action would be much more effective if it were an all-American mission. We were on our own, but they would provide whatever materials we needed.

Second, the Catholic Third Force group asked that our protest target be the United States Embassy, and that we chain ourselves to the auto entrance gate. Surprised at this turn of events, we nonetheless agreed. We had come to serve. Jesus' prayer in the Garden of Olives came to mind: "Not my will, but Thine be done."

The protest date was set for Saturday morning, October 2, at approximately nine o'clock in the morning the day before the presidential election Sunday, October 3.

On Friday morning Bau invited us to the home of the Apostolic Delegate with thirteen Vietnamese priests; with the exception of Hirsch, all of us would be decked out in our flowing black cassocks. I hadn't worn a cassock since before going to Newman Center in 1965, so I borrowed one from Father Minh, who was close to my size. I still have it, a coveted remembrance and relic of the fateful week in Vietnam.

The Apostolic Delegate is the Pope's representative to a particular country, such that the prelate is in regular contact with Rome. After knocking on the door of the bishop's residence and asking to see him, a staff member told us that he had no time to see us. Undeterred, we sat down on the porch and waited. It took more than an hour for the Vatican official to find the time and emerge.

The French bishop wasn't argumentative. He listened to our complaint about the war and about the Church's silence. Willis was particularly eloquent in describing the Church's behavior as shameful in the face of killing innocents. The bishop's response, given in French, was denial, as he sought to make excuses for the Vatican's silence and the Church worldwide. We walked away determined to do even more. In the evening, the An Quan Pagoda Buddhists called a peace conference at their pagoda. The police, in turn, placed barbed wire fences around a square block of the Pagoda to prevent anyone from attending the meeting. Bau invited us to join other demonstrators at one of the barricades. The objective was to, at a given signal, together lift the barbed wire out of the way and make for the Pagoda, daring the police to shoot us all.

Suddenly, behind us, Vietnamese youths tipped over an American truck and set it on fire. So adept were they it looked like they had done it many times before. The police vacated their stations and headed for the truck to pursue the young boys. That was our signal. All of us pushed the barbed wire rolling fence aside and made for the pagoda. The police recognized our trick, turned instantly, and began firing teargas canisters at us—we kept running toward the pagoda. A canister swept past my right ear, nearly striking my head. I felt its wind. Landing twelve feet in front of me, it exploded. Tears blinded me. I moved quickly to my left and found a crease in a stone building, which shielded my body. I covered my eyes with a handkerchief and prayed. I stayed there for at least half an hour until the shooting subsided and the smoke from the canisters slowly lifted. The street was deserted. Carefully I made my way back to the hotel, thanking God I was still alive. Later I learned that the teargas had also blinded Willis, and a small Vietnamese boy led him by the hand to safety.

The next morning after our breakfast of noodles, Ngo Cong Duc showed up with a printed handout message in Vietnamese and English, which was to explain our actions with the chain and locks that would bind us to the Embassy fence. Duc then traveled with us to the Embassy and wished us luck as we climbed out of the taxi. We began our brisk walk to the Embassy gate.

CHAPTER 11

Hanoi: Another Invitation (September 1972)

Coming Home

Weary in body, I returned to Cleveland, Ohio. The following week our class was expected to take a qualifying exam. The Organizational Behavior Department at Case Western Reserve University had recently hired a new chairperson. In an effort to be more rigorous, the faculty agreed to give an exam for the first time in the ten-year program. If we managed to pass, we would be eligible to write two qualifying papers, leading to permission to write a dissertation. Our test called for us to answer seven out of ten questions concerning behavioral theories and practices in organizations. We were given ten days to complete the exam.

Still reeling from my Vietnam experience, I called my friend Willis in California, begging for help. From his studies with Carl Rogers, he sent me some ideas taken from counseling psychology that I found usable for my answers. I didn't consider drawing from that material as cheating, but rather as research. Three of us, me included, failed. Arthur, the only student of color in our class, and Jeffrey Voorhees, who had been to Vietnam with me earlier that summer, also failed. It was particularly disappointing for us because, after working on the exam for ten days, we felt committed to our answers. It was not simply that our answers weren't satisfactory; we heard feedback that in failing, we personally were "not good enough, did not measure up."

I was particularly disappointed in my performance, because I had previously expressed concern to one of my favorite professors, Don Wolf, that I hesitated to sit for the exam, having just returned from Asia and Europe. He urged me to go ahead, saying, "Write what you know, and teach the faculty." Needless to say, my efforts left much to be desired.

Thankfully, a second chance was given in the spring. What I learned from the first experience was that I should not try to teach the evaluators, but write what I perceived they wanted and expected to read. Both Jeff Voorhees and I passed. Sadly, third person did not, and was disqualified.

Shortly after my return from Vietnam, the dean called me to his office. I suspected he was upset with my political activism, but couldn't admit it. He expressed his displeasure with me for having used department resources (copier and paper) to print my reason for missing classes and going to Vietnam. I offered to pay for the costs. With humor, I shared the experience with my student colleagues, which was the usual way I managed the authority's efforts to discipline me.

Under the guidance of my professor, a team of graduate students was introducing the concept of autonomous work teams to the ALCOA's office staff. ALCOA had engaged the university to aid in their organizational development. I was privileged to be a part of this intervention, and valued the experience. A number of ALCOA workers, however, said they would not cooperate with our department's intervention if I continued on the team. Having read in the newspaper about the chaining incident at the U.S. embassy, they regarded me as an enemy of our country. Suresh Srivastva, the head of our department, stepped in. He warned top management that he would withdraw all our consultants if I were not allowed to participate; he then facilitated a meeting in which I met with my accusers. I spoke of my love of my country, which motivated me to seek to make it better by using my first amendment right to free speech. In the end, I was allowed to continue.

Another Invitation to Return to Vietnam

The following September of 1972, not quite a year after the chaining experience in Saigon, Catholics in Hanoi invited me and Marianne Hamilton (now deceased), a peace activist from Minneapolis and one of the founders of Women Against Military Madness (WAMM), to come to Hanoi. This invitation was a response to my request the previous October to visit the North after our protest in Saigon.

Our hosts wanted us to train North Vietnamese delegates who were attending a peace conference in Quebec, Canada, and show them how to relate to the Western press. Marianne and I were prominent organizers of this International Conference of Christians in Solidarity with the Vietnamese, Laotian and Cambodian People to be held in Quebec, Canada. We hoped that the presence of North Vietnamese on the continent would influence the U.S. electorate to vote for Senator George McGovern, rather than give President Richard Nixon a second term.

Marianne and I were to be a part of a larger delegation of peace activists. Our mission was to bring three prisoners of war back to the United States. Three U.S. pilots had been shot down in an area controlled by the Pathet Lao, and were to be released as a gesture of reconciliation and, it was hoped, to influence the U.S. electorate to vote for McGovern, who had promised, if elected, to end the Vietnam War. The Vietnamese preferred to release these pilots— not to an official government body but to several peace workers, along with Marianne and me. Two family members of the pilots also accompanied the delegation. Another father had been undecided whether to join the group. The Pentagon called him continually, urging him to have nothing to do with the expedition. Ultimately, he followed the Pentagon's advice and decided not to go.

Cora Weiss, a well-known peace advocate, and director of the Committee of Liaison with Families of Prisoners Detained in Vietnam, assembled our group. Along with others including David Dellinger, one of the "Chicago Seven " protestors, and Professor

Richard Falk, Cora had been organizing mail exchanges between families and prisoners. Marianne Hamilton had been with our group during the 1970 Paris Peace talks. She speaks French, an asset in Vietnam, and she knew some of the Vietnamese diplomats from Paris and other peace conferences.

Rev. William Sloane Coffin, the original person characterized for Gary Trudeau's Rev. Scott Sloan in the *Doonesbury* comic strip, was already an icon for spiritual progressives. His mission to free the pilots was controversial, publicized in North Vietnam as a peace initiative, and in the U.S. as Communist propaganda.

After the war, in 1977 Coffin wrote a book, *Once to Every Man*, about his involvement with peace activism during Vietnam War. These powerful words are from his book:

> "We needed to do something. More than ever, I was afraid that if we Americans failed to respond to these admittedly painful and stubborn problems, our apathy would brutalize us. Social justice would remain an abstraction, while the pursuit of security, comfort and luxuries took us over."

None of us were naïve, I believe, in undertaking this journey, or expecting to be lauded for returning three captured pilots. What I knew about North/South Vietnam politics I learned, not from U.S. newspapers, but from earlier trips and from talking with the Vietnamese. My experiences with Catholics in Saigon led me to trust them. My witness to the Vietnamese people's suffering convinced me that we needed to do this trip. If we were used as propaganda, so be it; our trip was in the service of peace. My mother, however, worried, obviously concerned for my safety. I was not sensitive enough to appreciate her concern. My conscience, anyway, took precedence.

Two notable U.S. journalists were part of the trip: Peter Arnett, a stellar war correspondent famously responsible for recording the oft-quoted phrase, "We had to destroy the village in order to save it," and John Hart of CBS News. Hanoi had cleared Hart for the occasion, but he was not allowed to bring his sound system or cameramen. Two Japanese were to provide the cameras, and would meet him in Hanoi.

I had a secondary objective on this trip: to research the freedom of the Church in North Vietnam, hoping to demonstrate that the Communists were not preventing believers from practicing their faith, as U.S. propaganda asserted and U.S. Christians assumed.

On September 16, we began our trip to Hanoi to bring the prisoners home. We arrived first in Bangkok, Thailand. Marianne and I had left in such a hurry we didn't get the required cholera shots. Waiting a day for an Air Thai plane to Vientiane, Laos, we were able to get our shots.

In Vientiane, where I had spent a week the year before, the whole delegation came together. Marianne and I visited my friend Mr. Tran at the North Vietnamese Embassy, and received our visas. He was pleased to learn that I'd finally be able to visit the north of his country. The next day Aeroflot, a Russian transport plane, flew us into the city of Hanoi.

The two family members, Minnie and Olga, wife and mother of two of the pilots, were dressed to the nines, looking beautiful for the final leg of our trip, trying to be composed. We couldn't imagine their emotion, being so close to seeing their loved ones, agonizing over what their men must have suffered, having been shot down and imprisoned.

Most of our group was up and down in the aisles like tourists, taking pictures of Minnie and Olga, as well as the view through the plane's windows. Marianne leaned over and whispered, "They must be dying inside, everyone asking how they feel, people taking pictures of them all the time." I nodded in agreement, as I wondered whether the POWs would be at the airport.

We passed over the Plain of Jars, a wasteland made by American bombs, then the hills and trees of Sam Lorah province. The Jars constitute a mysterious collection of ancient stone cylinders, some of them weighing over a ton, believed to have been fashioned by nomadic tribes more than two thousand years ago. Hundreds are scattered across the war-scarred countryside of northern Laos, where the U.S. bombarded the area with more bombs than it dumped during World War II on Germany and Japan combined. Hard for me to imagine and understand. Ironic to be an American under American bombs, I was thinking, knowing the attacks would not be called off just because of us.

As the plane descended through the clouds, we began to make out the patterned roofs of a small village and lush green carpets cut by winding ribbons of water and square patches of rice paddies. The sight of the lovely land brought tears to Marianne's eyes. Its beauty helped distract us from fear of the danger and devastation awaiting us.

Arrival in Hanoi

Heavy clouds dominated the last leg of our flight, and the weather was rough, as was our rather abrupt landing in Hanoi. The sudden stop on the short, single runway jolted everyone. Once on the ground, our delegation was met by Chief Justice Pham Bach with a host of smiling young men and women carrying a bouquet of flowers for each of us.

Before the official greeting could commence, sirens and a bomb alert that sounded like our civil defense signal, interrupted the proceedings. The North's anti-aircraft missiles usually were silenced during civilian flights, so bombers often followed closely behind. As quickly and efficiently as our hosts could gather us, we were hustled into bunkers. Minnie was in tears, but Marianne was upset and angry, so I held her tightly. Angrily I said to Marianne, "You'd expect that our government would be careful not to bomb a mission of mercy designed to free our pilots!" The Chief Justice comforted us, breaking the tension, "You meet some of the best people in bomb shelters."

The young people who met us were from the Committee for Solidarity with the American People (Viet My). Most of them were women because the men were off fighting. Mr. Trong Quat was their leader. Once we were out of the bomb shelter, Mr. Ngyen served as our guide and interpreter. He hurried Marianne and me into a car to take us to the city. I hadn't realized until that point that our group had been separated into two distinct commissions. The Coffin group contained the relatives who would meet the pilots, and our religious group would train the North Vietnamese for the Quebec conference, and meet with Catholic leaders.

Captured American Pilots

In the airport, Mr. Quat asked if the pilots would accompany the delegation to visit hospitals and bombsites. "Hard as that will be on them," Coffin answered, "they will." "In that case," Mr. Quat said somberly, "They could be released very quickly." Minnie and Olga reluctantly agreed with this suggestion. A squad of Russian autos came to pick them up, with a separate jeep for John Hart and his equipment.

Most of us noticed that our Vietnamese leader appeared worried. He really had no idea when the pilots would be released. Another verification that in every organization communication is poor. We Americans were expected to learn things on our own. Coffin assured Quat that our group had a special feeling for the Vietnamese—*that we were friends because we had deliberately refused to be enemies.*

Coffin later told me the Committee for Solidarity took their group to a military compound. Minnie and Olga were led off to a private space to first reunite with son and husband. Coffin's group and many members from the world press waited for them to emerge.

Before the pilots were brought in, an officer made clear to the crowd that the pilots were being released to "The Solidarity Committee for the American people," not to representatives of the U.S. military. The three pilots—Major Edward Elias, Lt. Norris Charles and Lt. Mark Gartley—faced unimaginable conflict. They were grateful for their release, but to whom could they express gratitude? They were not collaborators, and did not want to be misinterpreted in any way. They felt guilt leaving their fellow prisoners behind, and perhaps helping their captors at the same time.

Again, from Rev. Coffin's book, I am paraphrasing what he wrote:

> With the North Vietnamese returning the three pilots, it was what was needed to get the war back where it belonged—on the front page of all American newspapers. The "Bring our boys home" banners had great appeal to Americans—and the President started to bring our boys home.

The Catholic Committee in Hanoi

Our Hanoi lodging was the Hotel Reunification. Many things were called "Reunification," highlighting the genuine desire of the Vietnamese leadership and people to be one nation. On our arrival, the Committee of North Vietnamese Catholics was waiting to greet Marianne and me. To our joy, Mr. Pham Van Kham, whom we both had met previously in Paris, was there, as well as three priests, all known to one or the other of us from Paris or another conference. It was heartening to see familiar faces.

We had hardly greeted one another when an air-raid siren again interrupted the welcome. We hurried down to the hotel basement bomb shelter. As we settled onto the hard wood benches, I wondered if our trip here was going to be spent under cover in uncomfortable places like this. I looked at Marianne, who seemed on the verge of tears. I nudged her with my elbow and winked as I said, "You'll get used to it," hoping to get her to relax. There was nothing we could do. We were in God's hands. In a few minutes the whole group began sharing stories, with humor that put everyone at ease. In less than half an hour, sirens sounded once again, wailing that it was safe to leave the shelter behind.

Our hotel rooms were large enough for several people, not like in Saigon or Vientiane, though the huge tropical fan on the ceiling was reminiscent of those rooms, and it was equally hot, with no air conditioning. A large coffee table was set for tea, along with a thermos of hot water and two bottles of warm beer. Guests who didn't trust the water, I speculated, might trust the beer.

It was time to relax and settle in, but as soon as I was ready for bed, another alert sounded, so I hurried down to the shelter. During the long wait, I fell asleep on the hard bench. After a time, Marianne later told me that she tried to return to her room, but hotel staff forbade her until the all-clear siren sounded. Throughout our stay in Vietnam, descending into and emerging from bomb shelters was a common occurrence.

Many Vietnamese people were involved behind the scenes to make things go well for us. They seemed overanxious to protect us from harm, and eager to procure what they thought we needed. My interpreter Tri was always cheerful and spoke excellent English.

Marianne's interpreter was less adept in English, but could not do enough to serve Marianne. At the earliest opportunity, the interpreter took Marianne to a fabric shop where a tailor made her a comfortable and culturally attractive áo dài. Marianne was delighted with the pajama-like suit, well cut but loose and lightweight for the climate.

**Our kindness towards each other showed
that we were not enemies, but friends.**

We'd been given a list of possible activities besides the training, and were invited to propose our own. The Catholic Committee wanted us to survey the damage both in Hanoi and in the provinces. Our own wishes were that we meet families, and could travel to the province of Vinh. The latter was not possible because of the danger and inability to travel the bombed-out roads.

The next evening, we had dinner with some of the Catholic Committee friends, including Mr. Pham, whom we knew better than the others. He claimed that the Catholic Church in the North fared better than in the South because there are still more priests and more times of worship. He said, "Hanoi is a good city. There are no robberies, no beggars, and the attitude among the people is positive despite the war. They support each other."

Pham went on to say, "The National United Front encourages Catholics to join in defending their country. Bishops still have problems with this because Bishop D. John Dooley and the Council of Bishops made a resolution in 1951 that forbade Vietnamese Christians to participate in activities with Communists. Clerics, for the most part, are hesitant to speak out, but the people no longer follow the hierarchy, and they're asking an end to the resolution. Such an order does not reflect the morality of Jesus, only the interest of French colonialists." (The French were defeated in 1954.)

Freedom of the Church

On Sunday morning, Marianne and I attended mass at the Hanoi Cathedral, within walking distance of our hotel. We'd heard that Catholics came to church at early dawn because air attacks were less likely then. The cathedral was filled, men sitting and kneeling on the left and women on the right, about equal in number, so Marianne and I separated.

The only Latin hymn during the mass began the service, the choir singing "Asperges Me" (Wash me from my sins, Oh Lord). The remainder of the prayers and songs were in Vietnamese, and the ritual was pre-Vatican II; during the mass the priest was facing the altar, not the people. Some hymns were familiar to my ears, being Latin and English hymns from my youth translated into Vietnamese, such as "Panis Angelicus," "Queen of Angels," and "Ave Maria." The people's piety and reverence captivated me. They followed their missals carefully, voices loud and clear, heads bowed, eyes lowered during the communion, except for a few teenagers who did distract me. I prayed and thought about my Carmelite sister, who would have been comfortable worshipping with these Vietnamese Catholics.

After mass, we slowly made our way back to the hotel, observing as much as we could. Although it was still early, the streets were filled with hundreds of people on bicycles, much activity, circles of people squatting on the sidewalks, talking. I wondered how this bicycle culture could fight so gallantly against their technologically capable foes.

We passed Wuat Lake with the lovely Tran Quoc pagoda, the oldest pagoda in Vietnam, now located on an island in the middle of the lake. As we walked down a tree-lined boulevard that students had planted, we noted the French architecture of its graceful buildings. Elegant, well-kept former homes currently housed government offices. On a commercial street, we noted the spirited, lively activity down a long row of small boutiques: leather, fabrics, shoemakers, and bakeries. Obviously, Sunday was not a day of rest in this culture. Life abounded on this street. A few months later, much of this was demolished in the 1972 Christmas bombing.

On Sunday afternoon, we spent some time in the hotel conference room going over the current situation and coaching representatives to the Quebec peace conference on how to describe their lives without animosity, in what they perceive is a civil war. My hope was that I could facilitate a process whereby they could witness to U.S. citizens that the Vietnamese are mothers and fathers who love their kids, go to work every day, pray and sing—like human beings everywhere. Their message at the conference would be that they mean no harm to the citizens in the United States, and that they believe the American people as well do not wish Vietnamese people any harm. The U.S. government is mistaken—that because the Vietnamese have a Communistic government, it doesn't make their people evildoers. My task was to enable these Vietnamese representatives to communicate this message in a way that Americans could hear it, change their minds, and vote to end the war against Vietnam in the November election. (As it turned out, the meeting in Quebec was successful but received little press in the United

States. The American people hardly knew the Vietnamese were on the continent.)

Our meetings always had an endless supply of tea and bottled water. These beverages were augmented with tiny candies and small, round seasonal cakes. Since it was near the autumn festival, the cakes were rich. One cake was glazed like a Christmas fruit-cake, and another was almost all sugar and nuts. A small wedge was sufficient sugar for me. Wherever we visited, no matter how poor, a ceremony of serving these delicacies took place before the talks. Meetings were in Vietnamese with Tri interpreting, and occasionally, they would break down into small talk and chatter.

Members of the Catholic Committee could all speak French. Sometimes Marianne was too anxious to wait for translation, and would press a point directly in French. My two years of French under Father Ralph Broker at the minor seminary was hardly adequate to keep up with the conversation. I wished I'd been a better student. But Madame Cam, a lawyer and Catholic representative in the National Assembly, spoke English well. Both of us became fond of her, and although she appeared shy, she responded eloquently and was straightforward. She was pleased to say that 125 women were in their National Assembly, which is similar to our United States Congress. She asked Marianne, "How many women are in your Congress?" When Marianne said, "You can count them on your fingers," Mme. Cam beamed with pride and said, "You must work on that, we need more women."

Five of the government ministers were women, and they played an important role in North Vietnamese affairs. Vietnamese women in general contributed greatly and suffered much as the war dragged on. The lawyer's three children had been left with her mother in Saigon in 1955, thinking they'd be reunited in a year. The U.S. had thwarted the 1956 election for unification, and she hadn't seen her children since. She reported, "Please understand, reunification with the South is one of our deepest yearnings." As she spoke, I imagined President Abraham Lincoln saying much the same thing during our horrendous civil war a century earlier.

We asked many questions about the freedom of the Catholic Church in the North, and kept being reassured. Mme. Cam seemed bewildered by our questions, and would counter, "But we are all Vietnamese!"

Her words reminded me of the Reverend Martin Luther King praying that one day little black boys and girls would walk hand in hand with little white boys and girls—all Americans.

The committee then spoke about the Catholic population, 1,200,000 souls in twelve dioceses. Thirteen bishops were appointed by Rome; all were native Vietnamese. Five hundred churches had already been destroyed in the war. During President Johnson's years, the bishop in Vinh was killed during the bombing. I wondered how I might get this information to Catholics in the United States, many of whom are led to believe few Catholics remain in this Communist country, and that they are not free to worship God.

When we met for dinner, Marianne was wearing her handmade gift. The traditional áo dài was made in one day, and everyone oohed and aahed over its craftsmanship. "Now I feel like I fit in," she laughed, "I feel like dancing!" She twirled around the floor. The hotel kitchen staff came out and applauded. Marianne bowed and curtsied, to everyone's delight. Unfortunately, Marianne passed away in the summer of 2017. Not before, however, founding Women Against Military Madness (WAMM), an active anti-war organization.

Traveling by Night

On Monday, we staggered downstairs at 4:00 a.m. to set off for the provinces. Because of the continued bombings that I assumed were designed to break the spirits of the Vietnamese people, we traveled by night in an army jeep to Nam Ha and Ninh Binh provinces. Our open jeep was camouflaged on top with branches. As we climbed aboard, we noticed a stack of steel helmets perched on the back seat. We were urged to keep the headgear in our laps, just in case.

At an outpost at Hanoi's city limits, Tri got out to present our papers. Marianne followed, camera in hand. Another jeep crammed with French journalists approached the outpost from the other direction, and Marianne snapped a photo. A mistake. Immediately two guards confronted and sharply questioned her. Poor Tri instantly raced over to intervene and explain. Questions and answers tumbled on each other in two and three languages as the French joined in. Why? Why not? Guards want to know. "Posterity." What? "The little house and the jeep." "No." "Sorry, didn't know. My first roll, they can have it," Marianne stammered.

"No, No," Tri assured and consoled Marianne. "I'll take care of it, but don't snap any more until we are clear of the city." The guards were obviously edgy, and I understood why. We were coming and going, but they lived there. A bomb could end their lives at any time. They couldn't be too careful.

It was a learning experience to find out, politically and practically, what could and could not be photographed (no bombed bridges, dikes, or military). We could take pictures of loaded trucks, bomb damage, and perhaps the wounded if they consented. Also, it was only courteous to ask villagers' permission before taking their pictures. I was surprised at how shy they became when asked. The countryside itself, or a water buffalo often with a boy riding atop, were okay to photograph. Marianne established a habit of asking, "Can I take?" The down sweep of the hand meant, don't take. Sometimes, Tri would snap a photo if we were busy— we found Tri to be a most diligent individual and very kind. Later, he would joke with us, "I'm a member of the proletariat, I don't understand you capitalists."

Although Tri was not a Christian, we depended heavily on him for interpreting our encounters with Christians in the North. During a private conversation, Marianne asked what he thought life was about. Without hesitation or embarrassment, he said, "I think life is about helping each other and sharing with each other." The two of us fell silent as we thought about our nation's bombs falling upon a people who apparently cared deeply about human rights. After a few days of interpreting religious talk, we dubbed him "Bishop Tri." By the time he'd interpreted my homily on the last day, we called him "Cardinal Tri."

Our trip to the provinces was haunting—it took four hours to go ninety kilometers (almost 56 miles). The road was a mass of stones from filled-in bomb craters. Our driver, an expert at vehicular improvisation, skirted innumerable unfilled holes, and threw the clutch to grind through others. Wedged between Mr. Tri and me, Marianne stayed in place by hanging on to a metal bar in front of us. We gripped the doors firmly, and I prayed they would not spring open. Only the autumn moon lit our passage.

We met Soviet trucks along the way, and I often saw ammunition stashed under various trees. The rice fields and glistening leaves provided us a camouflage cover. All along the roadsides, people unloaded rice sacks, carrying them past broken trucks, and loading them again into another vehicle. All were busy, and I could imagine Americans doing the same thing to protect our country if attacked—thinking that we would act no different than the Vietnamese if we feared an invasion.

Everywhere we looked, we saw busy people or social gatherings. While the two of us were pained and confused seeing the ravaged land, the people simply went about their business. The small groups gathered by each house reminded me of my youth as neighbors sat on their front porches discussing politics and watching their children at play. Here they were having breakfast or tea amidst much talking and laughing. "People here keep up activities, cope well," Mr. Tri pointed out. "The American purpose is to bomb dikes and roads, but we have determination. Our life is still blooming even among the craters. You have seen it." Yes, Marianne and I saw a bomb hit a road in the distance, and shortly afterward, eighty to a hundred old men and women emerged from the forest with shovels in hand, working to fill in the crater quickly to enable passage to continue.

With the approaching morning sunlight, its passengers weary, our jeep turned off the road onto what seemed a small path through dense brush. As we came to a clearing, within a minute or two, children surrounded and skipped after us. A small pagoda that had been turned into a guesthouse dominated the scene. This was Nam Ha. With its rustic surroundings and houses settled under trees, the hamlet couldn't be seen until we were practically upon it. Farther off, I could see water buffalo standing like statues in green fields of rice alongside dikes. Several women with baskets balanced on their hips and heads crossed footbridges.

We were led inside the pagoda to find breakfast waiting. After we'd washed and rested through the heat of the day, Mr. Viet Tung, a pleasant-looking, serious, soft-spoken man, shared with us more background information. Proud of his province, he wanted to make it live for us. Pausing to think while our translator spoke, he resumed where he'd paused, seamlessly, sadly, looking straight at us, asking us to understand. Nam Ha was, for the most part, a Catholic village. People raised rice in an area of 500 kilometers (300 miles) of dikes with water from the Red River and the Da River. "Because our village is forty kilometers from the sea," Tung said, "planes come often."

"We defeated the Mongols three times in the thirteenth century; our drums called people to fight against feudalism. Now, after the French, we must defend ourselves against American military. *When will it end?*" Tung asked.

After a long pause, Tung continued. "In our people's struggle, Christians played a vital role. The priest, Lan Quang Hoc, who led people against the French in 1900, wore wooden shoes like our peasants. Many famous priests supported the people's struggles. As Christians who follow Jesus, we have tried to live in peace. But we wanted to be free of the French—and simply be Vietnamese, as God created us. We envisioned Vietnam being one country. But no, a Western treaty divided our land. Consequently, the fighting continued, and we were caught up in it whether we wanted to or not."

He told Marianne and me that under President Nixon's administration, from April 15 to September there were over 2,000 sorties, and 530 attacks that dropped 3,000 tons of bombs. I don't know how he knew the numbers, but I didn't question his figures. At his invitation, we followed him out to the square. He showed us an exhibit of charred rice, and melted glass and steel that was caused by small fragmentation bombs. I bent to examine an exploded guava bomb fragment, and on it, I noticed the name Honeywell. Sadly, I confessed, "Marianne and I live in Minneapolis where these instruments of death are manufactured." He simply nodded.

"In April and May we were shelled every night from the U.S. 7th fleet, the Air Force and Navy combined," he explained. "In Nam Dinh, sometimes there were as many as 30 sorties. In the whole province, there was no place that was not attacked."

We were to see it for ourselves. In the city of Nam Dinh, the provincial capital and the North's second largest city after Hanoi (120,000 souls), destruction was everywhere. We toured by jeep and on foot, down streets of dwellings charred and broken, almost a ghost town. Our steps slowed as we looked in horror. From time to time, people came to doorways to watch us. Children ran up to us, and then stood back and stared. Marianne walked up to one doorway where several women stood and extended her hands and asked: "Ma mere, mon amie, que puis-je dire?" (My mother, friend, what can I say to you?) An older woman took her hand, smiled and stepped aside, bowed in a gesture to bid us enter. Hospitality was given even here, despite the suffering our fellow Americans caused. However, our guide said "No," as we had much to do. Marianne thanked the ladies, for offering more than they knew. I reluctantly walked away from them because I had wanted to enter and see how the Vietnamese lived.

At the hospital, we picked our way through ruins, and looked out of broken windows across the courtyard. "This was the pediatric ward," said Tung, with its broken corridors and gaping roof.

Seventy percent of the town was in ruins, including the hospital. "Don't you mark hospitals with red crosses on roofs?" Marianne asked naively. "Not anymore," our guide answered. (Afterward, hospitals were camouflaged.) "We must keep vigilant. We disperse persons so we can limit casualties, but we can't protect our houses, or schools, or the places where we must live our lives."

Near the coast, we were again horrorstruck, this time at the devastation of Phat Diem, which had been a religious complex with an ornate cathedral, displaying a blend of Gothic and Chinese architecture. There had been numerous chapels, a school, a Carmelite monastery, and housing facilities. In its countryside setting, it reminded me of the monastic community at St. John's Abbey in Collegeville, Minnesota. I was told Phat Diem is to Vietnamese Catholics what St. Peter's in Rome is to European Catholics. The only residence left intact was that of the bishop, Bui-Chu-Tao, whom we met there. We could plainly see his grief when he invited us to inspect the damage, but he quietly declined to accompany us because it was too painful. I suspect he was suffering from PTSD.

Just a month before our visit, bombers came twice on July 24 and August 15. On August 15, worshipers were celebrating the feast of the Assumption of Mary. The cathedral environs contained no gun emplacements, factories, or storage tanks, nothing that could be construed as a military target. Simply, a beautiful symbol of the people's faith in God was destroyed. There we also met Mother Ngo, whose Carmelite monastery had been bombed to bits. Dazed and bewildered, she said that she didn't know where the Sisters were, or what to do next. She asked where she should go, but I could offer no advice or even encouragement. So many grief-stricken people that day were talking about family members who had been killed or injured I simply could find no words of consolation. "God's will" on the lips of an American, even a priest, would have been cruel and hypocritical. I wanted to go beyond sympathy and have empathy.

In a tiny hamlet nearby, everything seemed at peace. I sang "Grandfather's Whiskers," a camp song with gestures for the children, who giggled and hid behind each other. We strolled down some Eden-like paths—at the end of one were toilets, holes fronted by a bamboo screen from knees to neck, with an idyllic view that dispelled discomfort and embarrassment. But the mud! My God, the mud! The constant drizzle caused us to sink almost ankle deep when we strayed from the path. Marianne finally pinned her pajama legs up to her knees, which made the kids giggle.

In this quiet place, we spent part of the night. Our guesthouse had two large rooms lined with bunk beds swathed in mosquito netting. Between the rooms was a smaller washroom containing double basins filled with water, and a long trench below. When we'd finished with the basins, we poured the water over our bare feet in the trench, which was a great pleasure in the heat. We retired early, exhausted and depressed after all we'd seen.

Two hours later, a loud crash woke me, and left my heart pounding. I waited, expecting someone to come and take us to the shelter, but no one came. Soon heavy rains came with thunder and lightning. Despite my relief, I couldn't sleep any more. I kept thinking of the nights of terror people in this land were living through, long nights and long days.

In the early morning, we set off before light dawned. Throughout the journey, the people we met were very patriotic, even though religious. For example, we were taken to an anti-aircraft gun where three Catholic young people were the sole operators of the powerful instrument of death. Proudly, they showed us the citation they'd recently received from the government for downing two enemy aircraft. I asked the girl, "What makes you happy?" She responded through our interpreter, "I'm the gayest when I'm shooting down an American plane." Sadness immediately gripped me—I'd so wanted her to have said, "When I'm in school learning things." But school was not on anyone's mind.

Echoing many of our conversations, the province chief of Nam Ha had told us, "To do our duty for our country, to protect our people, we think is the will of God. We are proud to be Vietnamese and

Christian. Vietnam is one country, and we can't rest until the nation, North and South, is free of the invader and its puppet Thieu."

It seemed many North Vietnamese Catholics had to make an earnest, disciplined effort to prove their patriotism. More and more youth were joining the army to avenge the deaths of their family and friends. We had to conclude that the bombing, far from destroying their morale, was erasing personal and religious differences, and unifying them in their common struggle for survival. Would this unity remain when war was no more? Could Catholics, Communists, and Buddhists build community? We could only hope so.

My impressions of the North Vietnamese—Catholics, Buddhists, and secular Communists—were that they had much in common with our traditionalists and fundamentalists in the United States. Evident was a strong ethic of emphasis on hard work and self-discipline, and rejection of gambling, drinking, and dancing. Prostitutes and beggars that I'd seen in Saigon during my former trip were absent in the North. Everyone seemed to have a task, even children, working with their parents in the rice paddies, or clearing away debris.

We came to a ferry crossing at the Red River, where a girl of around nineteen guarded the road and directed traffic from midnight to 8:00 a.m., the times when most travelers passed over. I asked her how she liked her job. "It's my duty," she answered gracefully; "I'm proud to serve my country." During our brief conversation, while we waited for permission to proceed, she told me through the interpreter of her boyfriend fighting with the army in the south. She hadn't heard from him for over three years. In response to my next stupid question, she nodded sadly that she missed him.

Then she blew her whistle. With a jerk, our jeep leaped forward; after 75 yards, we crowded onto a flat boat to make the precarious crossing. Out in the middle of the river, I was thankful not to see American bombers because *we were an easy target*. As we hustled off the boat on the other side, an air-raid warning signal pierced our ears. Our young female guide tried to usher me into the muddy bomb shelter. I resisted, fumbling with my camera, intent upon taking a picture of the attacking American planes. She insisted, tears filling her eyes. She would not go into the shelter without me. Her tears shook me and I gave in, following her flashlight into the dark tunnel as the planes droned overhead. I thought afterward, she probably saved me from deafness, because the bombing was close.

The Decoys

Back in Hanoi, the newly released POW pilots were also traveling with their families and Coffin's group while we were in Nam Ha. Once freed, they'd had suits made—and their diet changed. The bombing lessened because Nixon had curtailed the sorties in the vicinity of Hanoi until the freed pilots were out of the country. The men looked well, we were told, though subdued and taciturn, obviously beaten down by their ordeal. They were happy to talk with Americans, but we had a general agreement not to press them to answer questions. Out of concern for them, I refrained from taking their picture.

Meanwhile, we understood that our International Control Commission (ICC) plane, carrying observers from India, Poland, and Canada, established under terms of the Geneva Accords, had been forced down two days previously, and the CBS film of our trip was confiscated. Coffin's group sent a telegram to President Nixon stating the conditions of release again; the main point was that it was to be a civilian escort. The politics of the pilots' release was becoming complicated, as we later learned from U.S. newspapers: Secretary of Defense Melvin Laird had threatened court martials should the pilots make any "disloyal" claims. Welcome home.

Over the next days, the pilots did indeed follow some of the same itinerary we did, and as William Coffin reports (*Once to Every Man: a Memoir*, Athenaeum, New York, 1977), the sight of child amputees brought tears to their eyes. Still, their anguish over the buddies they left behind was dominant in their hearts. Gartley, one of the freed pilots, admitted quietly that things looked different on the ground.

The pilots had ample time to think during their imprisonment. They were allowed to listen to vetted radio programs, and didn't find Radio Hanoi at all impressive. Earlier pro-peace visitors had left articles on the Pentagon Papers, George McTurnan Kahin's 1969 history of the war, *The United States in Vietnam*, co-authored with fellow Cornell professor John W. Lewis. Prisoners open to other points of view read the documents, which had some influence regarding how they thought about the war. Others deep in their own ideological frame of mind refused to read the materials.

Our plan was for Coffin and his group to take the pilots through Russia into West Berlin while Marianne and I became decoys, flying into Vientiane, Laos, the route we'd taken into the country. A squadron of U.S. military and more world press were waiting when Marianne and I descended from the Russian passenger jet. When the pilots did not follow us, U.S. officials became exceedingly disturbed. They showed their disgust, walking away from us without so much as a comment when we informed them the pilots had not accompanied us. I felt dismissed. They asked no questions about the pilots' health or frame of mind.

News traveled quickly even in those days, however, and U.S. officials guessed at the pilots' Berlin arrival. Our hopes that the pilots could have a free-and-open press conference were dashed as moments after exiting the plane, they were grabbed quickly by U.S. officials and whisked away before they were able to say anything. Nothing was heard from them until well after the U.S. presidential election. I have never seen them again, although I would like to. I wonder how they now view their experience and the Vietnam War.

On Wednesday, September 20, Marianne and I were invited to tour the War Crimes Investigation Commission in Hanoi, located in an office museum exhibiting military material. In an exhibit of unexploded bombs, the antipersonnel bombs were the most hideous. The trade names of American companies were stamped on the weapons. Deeply mortifying to Marianne and me was to read various statements written on the bombs such as, "Vietnamese fuck you." I wondered if those Americans who wrote such insulting words attended Christian churches and claimed to believe in Jesus, who pleaded with us to love our enemies.

After lunch we were taken to visit Mr. Khanh, editor of the Hanoi newspaper, *People's Daily*. Once more, a bomb alert interrupted our conversation. By now, Marianne and I, along with the Vietnamese people, were veterans at this disruption, and we scurried across a small courtyard to descend to a concrete room, where conversation resumed. "Death falling on people is tragic, but the demolition of spiritual life is more tragic," Mr. Khanh continued calmly in broken English. "We're doing what Jesus Christ would have done, struggling for freedom, willing to suffer for a century against French, Japanese, Eisenhower's war, Kennedy's war, and now against those using Vietnamese to fight Vietnamese"—he seemed to stare at me—"as your forefathers did with the Indians in your country. Nixon spends a billion dollars to increase the Saigon forces, and the money attracts people who have lived hard lives. It means you Americans buy people's souls."

It wasn't a time for us to quibble with Mr. Khanh's theology, history, or politics, even if I saw his theology differently. Marianne and I simply listened, nodding, communicating that we understood his pain. He needed empathy and compassion, and he received it from both of us.

Someone came down to tell us we could leave the shelter, and we emerged into sunlight, but for me the darkness of our discussion lingered, reinforced by the pain, suffering, and destruction we'd witnessed since our arrival.

Later that afternoon, a news conference with the international press in our hotel drew 200 people. I was amazed at the size of our "audience," and at the depth of the questions. Marianne gave a short account of our impressions and expressed our gratitude. Then, speaking from the heart with no script, I felt inspired as I related how our experience on this trip to North Vietnam had affected us. Mr. Tri interpreted as I spoke with passion, giving our understanding of the political situation. The press was also interested in our views of the situation of the Vietnamese church, as well as about the upcoming international assembly in Quebec.

When the two of us came down for dinner, Tri was waiting to eat with us. He seemed to be looking at us in disbelief, and just said "Excellent, excellent." He meant the news conference. He was proud of us, and voiced how pleased he was to have been interpreting. He claimed it was the largest news conference the Vietnamese-American Friendship Committee (Viet-my) had ever gathered.

Meeting with the Cardinal Archbishop of Hanoi

After dinner we met with other committee members to go over the next day's events. During the discussion our hosts asked if there was anything else they could do for us. This was my chance. And it was not planned, so on impulse, I asked, "Would you be so kind as to arrange a meeting for us with the Cardinal of Hanoi?"

"Well, you know," Mr. Pham confided, "the government doesn't have a very good relationship with the Cardinal—I don't think he will see you." I understood him to mean, we have no influence with the Cardinal, so he will not satisfy a request from us.

Feeling hopeful, I encouraged him, "Try. Maybe the Cardinal would be willing to see a Catholic priest from America." My intent was to make a connection that could be a step forward in mending the rift between the institutional church and the Communist government.

The day after making the request, the Catholic Committee was astounded and excited beyond words when the Cardinal Archbishop of Hanoi, Trinh-Nhu-Khua, agreed to meet with Marianne and me on Friday morning. "This is the first time he has ever received an American priest," Pham exclaimed with obvious pleasure. But then he cautioned us with all seriousness, "Do not ask him any questions. This is a huge first step, and we must move slowly while at the same time persistently, without alienating him." What I interpreted from his polite words was "We perceive this visit as potentially great progress, don't screw it up." We agreed, reluctantly, not to be our typically American impatient selves.

The next morning, when Marianne and I walked in, the Cardinal was sitting beside and to the left of his Vicar General, his trusted advisor. I liked the Cardinal immediately. With his portly figure and smiling eyes, he reminded me of Pope John XXIII. He was a roly-poly fellow, very pleasant looking. The Vicar General more resembled most Vietnamese, slender with gentle eyes.

No introductions were made, the assumption being that we knew whom we were meeting. Mr. Tri was not present because both our hosts spoke English, although the Vicar General never spoke directly to us, nor did Marianne speak other than to ask a question of the Cardinal. I was assumed to be the leader of our delegation, and we followed the Vietnamese protocol—in meetings, statements and questions are addressed only to the leader of the respective parties. Yet, the atmosphere was delightfully cordial. Beer and cakes were presented and pleasantries shared. Tea was served in little cups with typical Vietnamese biscuits, like crackers.

I remember asking the Cardinal, "What are the major challenges facing the Catholic Church here?" The Cardinal replied that only eighteen priests served approximately 180,000 Catholics in the archdiocese. Moreover, the seminary was closed and young men were expected to fight in the war. He explained the troubles he had with the government, namely, that he was not free to teach all the things needed to be taught about the Catholic Faith. Catechism and religious education materials were sometimes confiscated. In addition, he had many financial challenges owing to the war, with serious damage to church properties from the bombs. "The greatest obstacle to regular worship, of course, is the American bombs," the Cardinal reiterated.

He went on to say that, as we could readily understand, his most serious problem was the lack of priests. On the other hand, he proudly emphasized the strong faith of the people, especially in the countryside, saying, "Some walk literally miles to attend Mass on Sunday."

I replied with understanding and empathy. At the same time, I noticed that, unlike many of the priests and lay Catholics we'd encountered, the Cardinal didn't express his support and understanding of the government's challenges, and we didn't press him.

Finally, I took the initiative, *because he asked me,* "Is there anything I can do for you, Father?" I should have expected it, but I didn't. Again, I said what came to my mind, and I answered, "Oh, your Eminence, I would so like to say Mass in Hanoi." I hadn't come to Hanoi with that intention, but when he asked me what I would like, it was clear to me: celebrating the Eucharist was the priestly thing to do. What could be a better sign of peace, a way of making peace?

The Cardinal appeared a trifle flabbergasted. I don't know what he expected me to say. Looking troubled, he murmured to his Vicar General in Vietnamese. They carried on a brief conversation, then the Cardinal replied, "You know we're not up on Vatican II, and we don't concelebrate masses here."

I said, "That's okay, your Eminence, I can say Mass by myself." They put their heads together and spoke again, he and the Vicar General. Then he asked, "Where would you want to say it?" The only church I knew of, and where Marianne and I had attended Mass the Sunday before, was the Cathedral. So, I said confidently, "The Cathedral would be fine."

"When?"

"Tomorrow morning, because we are leaving tomorrow afternoon." After conversing once more with the Vicar General, the Cardinal consented. Our departure was filled with happy smiles. I couldn't wait to get back to inform the Catholic Committee. After overcoming their disbelief, they were even more excited and thrilled than I was because they saw it as a breakthrough.

Celebrating the Eucharist in Hanoi

Later on Friday, we received word from the Cardinal's office of a change in plans. I was welcome to say Mass in any church in Hanoi *except the Cathedral.* I had no idea what that was about. I was at a loss to come up with another church. Then I remembered a priest I'd met in Paris, when my friend Jeff Voorhees and I attended the Paris peace talks. He was pastor of a church named Saint Dominic. I said quickly, "How about St. Dominic Church?" Permission was granted, and on Saturday morning at 6:00 a.m., I would preside at Mass in Hanoi.

John Hart, the CBS newsman, appeared more elated than I was. He prepared to videotape the whole Mass, and arrived way before 6:00 a.m., so his Japanese film crew could get all set up.

Marianne and I arrived at Saint Dominic Church also before 6:00 a.m. I recalled that the Communists would watch for American bombers and, if danger arose, warn their Catholic neighbors attending Mass. Evidently there was no ill feeling between loyalists and practicing Roman Catholics. The strife was simply between the government leaders and the church hierarchy.

Thus, when I caught a glimpse of the crowd outside the church, I immediately concluded the secular neighbors were watching out for their friends inside the church. Maybe so, but not entirely. As Marianne and I stepped into the church proper, we found the place packed. True, it was a small building compared with the Cathedral, holding less than 500 people, but every seat was taken and people sat shoulder to shoulder in the pews. I couldn't help but notice people peering in through the windows. The church didn't have stained glass or air conditioning, so the windows were low and wide open, making it easy for the people to put their heads in and achieve at least a one-sided view.

We started up the center aisle and the thought hit me, "Oh my goodness, I can't say Mass in Vietnamese, I don't know the language. It doesn't make sense to say Mass in English because nobody will understand what I'm saying or doing. I need to say Mass in Latin." Now this was 1972. In the U.S. we'd stopped saying Mass in Latin in 1964, and I had not used Latin in seven years.

When we approached the front pews, I had another surprise. The freed pilots, with Minnie and Olga, were in the very front pew, with Coffin's group directly behind them. Marianne squeezed in next to Cora Weiss.

Walking into the sacristy, I was grateful to find a priest who was maybe in his thirties, who seemed to me like a young boy, partly because his head came up only to my shoulders. I asked if he had a Latin missal. Smiling, he cheerfully obliged me. His English was poor, but we used hand signals to communicate.

When he offered to serve the Mass, my gratitude increased. As I began the Mass, with the Vietnamese priest kneeling beside me on my right, our backs to the people, I couldn't remember all the Latin prayers I used to know by heart. No problem! My priest server coached me through them, both of us saying the prayers softly enough so, at best, it sounded like mumbling to the people. Once I climbed the steps to the altar, all the words were in the missal. Feeling more confident, I prayed them loudly and with vigor as we did in the old days in the U.S.

My server read the Sacred Scripture in Vietnamese. Unfortunately, I failed to prepare a homily, not expecting a crowd, and surprised by the presence of the pilots and the other Americans in the front two rows. Not to give a sermon, though, would have been seriously inappropriate. I swallowed hard—gazing at Olga, then Minnie, and finally the pilots. My talk was short and unremarkable but I spoke from my heart. My message was simply, "All human beings, Vietnamese, Americans, and every other nationality, color, and creed are children of our one Father. Our dear God, consequently, calls us to live in peace with each other." It probably didn't matter that I lacked eloquence. I believe the spirit of God was active in the church, despite me.

Years later at a peace meeting, I chanced to meet again the Reverend William Sloan Coffin. Relaxing after dinner over coffee he said, "You know you Catholic priests are lousy preachers!" My mind quickly went back to my sermon that day in Hanoi with Coffin present. He himself was a remarkable preacher. I remember visiting the Riverside Presbyterian Church in New York where he was pastor, and finding printed copies of his previous sermons in the vestibule. His staff published his words each week because of the many requests. But before I had a chance to agree with him, he added with apparent envy, "But you Catholics have the Mass."

Celebrating the Eucharist with the Vietnamese faithful was an intense experience for me. As we prayed together, I experienced solidarity, unity, even intimacy with those beautiful people that my dear country was bombing unmercifully. I whispered "Corpus Christi" and placed Holy Communion on each Vietnamese tongue. I was and am convinced that Jesus Christ could and would break down the prejudices that kept our two nations and peoples apart. These were devout human beings who wanted nothing more than what most people desire, namely, freedom, autonomy, sufficiency, and safety for themselves and their families. That can't be too much.

When the Mass was over, Mr. Tri asked me, "Do you want to know what the people are saying about this?" I answered, "Oh, yes, please tell me." I so wanted the spiritual happening to be effective and meaningful for all present. "They're saying," Tri offered with pleasure, "we know he is a real priest because he said Mass in Latin."

When the people got the word from the Communist government that an American priest was coming to say Mass, they were skeptical. They did not completely trust their government. They wanted to check it out for themselves. My Latin convinced them I was genuine. I had never before considered the Latin mass such an excellent means of communication.

Enlightenment

What conclusions did I reach about the American presence, and about religious freedom in North Vietnam? It was clear to our delegation that both the Vietnamese leaders and people made a distinction between the U.S. government's intentions and those of the American people. If Vietnam were the only major issue on the ballot in the 1972 election, the Vietnamese were confident that people in the United States would vote for Senator McGovern because he promised, if elected, to end the war. My many visits to Vietnam after the war confirmed this attitude. The people appear to love Americans, and are honored when we come as tourists to their country.

With regard to freedom of religion, two things came to my mind at the time: First, freedom is not absolute. It is not a question of either/or, but rather one of degree. Second, I believe Christian development goes through three stages of spiritual growth.

People in the *first stage* place emphasis on discipline and practice: prayer, administration of the sacraments, catechetical instructions. I think it's important that people pray, but more than saying prayers is the necessity of living a Christian life.

In the *second stage*, Christians involve themselves in the corporeal worldly works of mercy: feeding the hungry, clothing the naked, taking care of the sick, and the like. Although this behavior does not address the sources of a society's ills, and can be paternalistic, a hungry person cannot wait to eat until the system is changed. These works need to be done, but such works are not enough.

The theology of liberation well describes for me the *third stage*. This is the revolutionary stage bent on changing an unjust system. At this level, energy is devoted to freeing humans to determine their own destinies. Here the religious person exists at the edge of society and is vulnerable to rejection by the state or other power structures, which have their own agendas.

The state might tolerate the role of religion in the first two stages of faith. This was the case, I believed, both in North Vietnam and in the United States. The government is pleased when believers are urged to say their prayers and perform the worldly works of mercy. When the poor are ministered to, they are not as likely to revolt.

Archbishop Dom Helder Camara expressed the idea clearly: *"When I give food to the poor they call me a saint. When I ask why they are poor, they call me a Communist."*

When faith calls for confronting injustices, however, it is a different matter altogether. Resistance becomes an act of conscience, and few governments have allowed such freedom. My own experience in the United States during Vietnam pointed to our government's reluctance to permit serious challenge. My arrest for attempting to celebrate Mass in the Pentagon to pray for peace (discussed in a earlier chapter) was a reminder that Americans' freedom to radically critique our government is limited. Only small proposals for change are tolerated, I concluded.

Likewise, in North Vietnam, I observed Catholic Christians are free to worship, free to teach religion to their fellow Christians, and free to care for the poor and those in need. They are not free to criticize the government. I was convinced, however, that bombing the North Vietnamese into oblivion is not the way to liberate my Vietnamese friends. Dead, they cannot lead a meaningful life. They cannot act on their consciences and confront their government, nor can they pray, or care for their children or the unfortunate. If left alone to determine their own destiny through their human and religious faith, the Vietnamese people may well liberate themselves. They do not need American soldiers to do it for them.

Returning Home

After arriving in Vientiane, Laos, I took the first plane I could back to the United States traveling via Paris. Just before taking off for Hanoi the week before, an API photographer who was not allowed to come with us into North Vietnam, had given me his camera, asking me to take photos for him and deliver them to their office in Paris. I wanted to stop in Paris to deliver the camera and photos to the API office, in hopes they would find them valuable enough to help financially support my journey. I was traveling on borrowed money. Unfortunately, since I had no photos of the pilots, only of the Vietnamese people and the devastation, they were not interested. They did take back the camera.

In the meantime, Cora Weiss's husband had arranged for me to be on the *Today Show* in New York. I flew directly from Paris to New York and checked into a hotel. I was scheduled to be at the station at 7:00 the next morning. It was an opportunity, I thought, to share another perspective of what was going on in North Vietnam, in hopes of enlightening the American electorate.

At 5:00 a.m. I was awakened by a call from the station telling me not to bother to show up. My TV interview was cancelled. No explanation was given for the cancellation so I simply went back to my school. I was disappointed at the missed opportunity.

I believe no portion of my Mass that was filmed by John Hart was allowed to be shown on CBS, since none of my friends commented later that they saw it. Years later, I contacted CBS in an effort to obtain the videotape, and was informed they did not have it in their files. What happened to the videotape is still a mystery. As with many attempts at delivering the peace message, government pressures may have prevailed against these tapes becoming public.

Nonetheless, upon my return, I joyfully set to work in preparing for the International Conference in Quebec and to welcome my new Vietnamese friends to our continent. I continued to hope and pray that our meeting, with their presence, would move the hearts of the American public.

Pope Paul VI pleaded just seven years earlier at the United Nations:

> "If you want to be brothers (and sisters), let the weapons fall from your hands. You cannot love with weapons in your hands… It suffices to remember that the blood of millions of men and women, numberless and unheard of sufferings, useless slaughter and frightful ruin… unite you with an oath which must change the future history of the world: No more war, war never again! Peace, it is peace which must guide the destinies of peoples and of all humankind."

CHAPTER 12

A Catalyst for My Personal Development (1972)

PhD Candidate

In the spring of 1972, I passed the comprehensive exam that I had failed the previous fall. Further requirements before becoming a PhD candidate involved writing a research paper and a theoretical paper demonstrating my ability to meet the challenges of completing a dissertation.

I used the research I had done in Vietnam as the foundation for my research paper. For the theoretical paper, I depended on personal experience and recent research on the priesthood, entitling it: "Notes on Intimacy and Relativeness: An Autobiographical Sketch." The process became a catalyst to significant personal growth. In retrospect, I realize that writing it was preparation for this story forty years later.

I became aware of having been stalled, for many years, at psychologist Eric Erickson's "identity level" of my emotional growth—retaining an adolescent's shyness, unable to share my thoughts and feelings. Archbishop Byrne was on target when he accused me of being an adolescent, but for the wrong reasons. While writing the paper, I came to realize that graduate school, Gestalt training, and changes in personal relationships, had contributed to my personal growth as a person and a priest.

My research into what was happening to priests in America in the 1960s made me aware of a new sense of self that had evolved over time through efforts both awkward and painful. The research revealed how immature that my priest colleagues and I were emotionally, and even spiritually. Forty years old and highly trained in the priestly profession, I was nonetheless still an adolescent emotionally. Beginning at Newman, and on through my studies in Cleveland, I became highly motivated to grow, even if it meant shifting away from traditional institutional values toward personal ideals and convictions.

Maturity at 40?

My faith tells me that in the theological sense, in the sense of being reborn in baptism, we are children of God. Should we not, therefore, act like children before God? I think no. That is childishness. In Saint Paul's letter to the church at Corinth, Greece, he said, "When I was a child, I spoke as a child, I understood as a child, I thought as a child, but when I became a man, I put away childish things."

It is one thing to be a 14-year-old adolescent; it is quite another to be a forty-year-old adolescent, like I was at this point in my life. I needed to be open to God in the fullest degree of my existence, creature to creator, son to Father. I became aware that I had a lot of growing up to do.

As a priest I was invested with authority and position in relation to the laity in the pews. I came to recognize that I failed to distinguish between myself and the priestly role I played—celebrating the Eucharist, preaching, hearing confessions, presiding at weddings, and other priestly work—and identified only with those qualities I needed to perform that role. I was unaware that I personified my priestly power and position in relating to family and friends—for example, my mother referred to me as "Father" to the end of her life.

In failing to distinguish myself from the role I played, I lost myself; I wasn't my authentic self, and was still immature. Although my priestly power was given only for the performance

188

of my ministry, I identified with these powers and placed a mask between others and me, between God and me.

Not only did the mask intervene between the world and me, it also caused me to repress that which I found unpleasant in myself. Consequently, I lacked a free, open relationship with God.

Friendship and Maturity

I also discovered that a person without a friend is impoverished. I needed to relate to at least one adult human being. Some of my colleagues found this relationship in the human person of Jesus. But for many of us, myself included, the need was to have an open, honest relationship with a mature adult through whom we could grow up. Unfortunately, this was not so clear to me then, and it became a slow awakening.

Over time, maturity develops through a dialogic encounter in which two people share their selves openly and honestly. We are created for a personal encounter either in marriage or outside of it. A sign of Jesus' humanness is that he was pleased to have close friends among His disciples, as well as Mary, Martha and brother Lazarus, and Mary Magdalene.

> **As I was coming to love and accept myself, despite my weaknesses and mistakes, I was becoming more ready for the love of a friend.**

Graduate school and the Gestalt Institute enabled me to become more aware of myself and to love myself. I didn't need to be a cleric to be loved and accepted. My colleagues at Case became my friends, and for the first time in my life, I could assume I was acceptable and was loved no matter what unacceptable things I had done. I didn't need to conform to another person's or an institution's value system to be accepted. I evolved toward a greater confidence and warmth in close relationships with others, including women, with whom I had previously been aloof and bashful.

Previously, I never shared myself with another. I had been good at sharing ideas, but not *self*. I devoted myself to work. This excessive attention to work made me feel secure. It wasn't "messy," as Pope Francis urged People of God to be when he visited Brazil during the summer of 2013: "What is it that I expect as a consequence of World Youth Day? I want a mess... I want trouble in the dioceses! ...I want to see the Church get closer to the people. I want to get rid of clericalism, the mundane, this closing ourselves off within ourselves, in our parishes, schools or structures. Because these need to get out!"

At no point in our priestly training were we encouraged to engage in conversations regarding our own personal feelings or vulnerabilities.

I was using work-duty as a shield against love and intimacy. Avoiding intimate relationships—which require sharing oneself—was a way for me to avoid uncertainty and be in control. I needed to call the shots, because I was a product of church structure. We were taught to follow the law, not personal needs. I agree with the Jesuit priest writer Peter McVerry who said: "...the message of the gospel is a message of radical solidarity and a message of radical inclusiveness where we *share* one another's burdens, where we reach out to everybody...to make them feel valued and respected. Yet because of the *structures of the church,* that message is lost, and not only is it lost but it is seen as totally irrelevant."

Aspects of Friendship

In one of the Case T-groups/sensitivity training, we discussed various aspects of friendship. One person described friendship as the "union and discussions" he had with colleagues at work. He experienced a wonderful sharing of ideas, and this formed the basis and substance of their friendship. That description reminded me of the delightful relationships I had with Garrelts and Conroy at the Newman Center.

Another person in the group said an example of friendship is to work together in a common cause. This statement reminded me of the men and women who worked with me in my peace efforts during the Vietnam War, such as Marianne Hamilton, who went with me to Vietnam, and Arlene Gibbs who helped me raise money for the cause. She was instrumental in bringing peace activist Mary Travis, and on another occasion, Peter Yarrow (both of "Peter, Paul, and Mary") for a concert.

Yet another T-Group member defined friendship as communication and sharing of self with another. This definition surprised us. When she was asked what she meant by communication of self, a discussion ensued, and the group came to realize that radical, deep friendship means sharing with others our most personal thoughts and feelings—no secrets—and discovering ourselves through the process. In retrospect, I *wasn't surprised* that it was a woman who brought this up.

I was leery of opening myself to another person. Maybe the other person wouldn't like the real me. The outcome would be unpredictable, out of my precious control. But I needed to try.

> **So during those years I ventured forth.**
> **And I'm still at it, at 88 years young. It wasn't like**
> **opening a door wide all at once—more like venetian**
> **blinds slowly opening as my trust developed.**

I realized that the difficulties I experienced at St. Francis Cabrini, St. Helena, and the Newman Center were self-inflicted. I wanted acceptance, but I sought it through contrary means—I spent my

191

hours with needy parishioners believing that, because they needed me, I was fulfilling my own needs. I wasn't communing with them. I meant well but it was not relationships of equality, it was more top-down.

We are meant to live in community, communing with each other. Even when in mental prayer, we aren't alone; we're communing with God. My mistake was I assumed communing with God was all I needed. I thought that constantly being with others, giving away all of myself to them, would bring me comfort. I remained on the outside looking in.

The realization was a long time coming that I was more than a priest, and didn't need to identify myself through that role alone. My psychological growth continues and explains how I've been able to aggressively meet the forces of authority as my own person.

I concluded God wanted me to be respected simply as an individual human being—because God created me. The same goes for everyone else...we are all equal.

PhD Dissertation

It's commonly said that people study psychology to better understand themselves. The challenges facing me and other priests in the middle of the 20th century moved me to study the priestly role. My maturation in graduate school and at the Gestalt Institute provided the background for my PhD dissertation.

I hypothesized that one aspect of psychological development is the ability to avoid passive obedience and to think and act in accordance with one's conscience. I wanted to investigate this hypothesis via a sample of American diocesan priests. I wished to understand why so few Catholic Christians and particularly their leaders were willing to confront the immorality of the Vietnam War and other injustices in our midst—racism, poverty, sexism, and prison oppressions.

Professor Donald Wolfe agreed to chair my dissertation committee, ably assisted by three others. With permission from the respective bishops, I sent a long questionnaire to parishes with two or more diocesan priests in five dioceses in the United States. Thankfully, 278 of my fellow priests, including 94 pastor-associate pairs, took the time to respond.

My literature reviews for the dissertation included a number of studies done in the early 1970s that showed a significant number of priests, similar to American males in general, were psychologically (that is, mentally, emotionally, and behaviorally) underdeveloped. This finding was surprising and unsettling to many in the church, given priests' careful selection and lengthy training with the expectation that they become leaders in the institutional church. The findings were not so surprising to me because of my recent studies and personal experiences. I'd learned that healthy development is relational, that maturity involves being both independent and interdependent.

These studies of priests concluded:

A. Underdeveloped priests showed a lack of integration of emotional and intellectual growth. Rather than confronting this lack of growth, the priests became adept at smoothing over the deficiency through intellectualization and a skilled use of other defense systems. Their understanding of themselves thus did not match how others perceived them.

B. Underdeveloped priests were uneasy with intimacy, that is, responsible closeness with other persons. Sexuality was not integrated in their lives, such that many priests functioned at a pre-adolescent level of psychological growth. (No wonder pedophilia was revealed as an issue soon after these studies.) Experiencing difficulty and discomfort with adult relationships, a substantial part of a priest's life, deprived them of a deep source of personal and work satisfaction. They sought satisfaction in such hobbies as golf or skiing.

C. Among the underdeveloped priests was evidence of passivity, exaggerated docility, and a tendency to identify themselves through the role of the priesthood rather than through their own personalities. They tended to mistrust themselves, feel unworthy, and often held back from using their full capabilities. They tended to have ambivalent attitudes toward authority, on the one hand wanting its protection and direction, while on the other resenting it and using it in ways to project their own problems onto others. They expressed poorly realized religious faith, and this deficiency, together with personal immaturity, had a strong influence on their not living up to their religious ideals; for example, lack of trusting in God, so that they would complain about the actions/misbehaviors of others.

Characteristics of Mature Priests

These findings confirmed what I had discovered about myself in my struggles with both personal identity and intimacy. The studies further described characteristics that genuinely *mature* priests manifested: Mature, developed priests focused on social ties that connected them with the rest of the universe. They acted toward creating a better future for themselves and others; fostered intimate relationships that enabled them to be more themselves; cultivated a spiritual life that included union with God and union with all others, and maintained a group of friends who expressed a positive outlook on life. Their intent was to work at something that brought out their best gifts, their deepest commitment—and not to fixate on their incompetencies. Behaviorally, they contributed with greater cooperation and creativity, out of freedom rather than duty. Each was a work in progress, not a finished product.

My own arrested development had been fostered by an organizational climate and training in which obedience, passivity, and defensiveness were the norm. Simple awareness of my immaturity was the first step in the direction of personal growth. To grow I needed to overcome my passivity—take initiative, think for myself, and stop "going along" to "get along."

> The reason that fellow priests didn't recognize or support my work was suddenly clear—passive obedience to the laws of the church and government immobilized them.

Also, I concluded that I needed to exercise greater freedom in my own life and the work I was doing. Challenging my government's policies toward Vietnam was singular personal growth. Such incapacity was the reason so few priests were involved in the civil rights movement with The Reverend Martin Luther King, or the struggle for justice of the grape-pickers with Cesar Chavez immigration injustice, or the injustices of poverty or prison conditions throughout the global community.

Double Bind

A double bind is a psychological predicament in which a person receives from a single source conflicting messages that allow no appropriate response to be made. This dilemma is another reason that so many priests didn't/don't participate in the struggle for social justice—they were/are faced with contradictory demands— what the parent, manager, or bishop says is contradictory to what the person senses as the other person's unexpressed wish or command. This double bind interferes with the individual's ability to find him/herself, and develop in a stable and constructive fashion.

195

The Church itself is the agent of a double bind for the parish priest and university chaplain.

Church teaching calls for the People of God to be involved with *human* dimensions, of equal value to sacred dimensions. This teaching was my basis for becoming a priest.

> For me, social action was clearly an avenue to the realization of *agape*, the divine love that needs to penetrate humans and social and religious structures, bringing us to God.

Various publications have provided data that I am paraphrasing below:

The Vatican is clearly involved in politics. It has a permanent presence in at least 40 international organizations including the United Nations, the European Council, the Arab League, and the Organization of American States. The Vatican radio broadcasts in 47 languages. I am told Pope Francis has 40 million Twitter followers, increasing of a rate of 25 percent every year.

The Vatican has diplomatic relations with about 193 countries in our world. Vatican diplomats, who are largely bishops and priests (no women), are heavily involved in peace negotiations in countries such as Venezuela. Political actions of the Popes appear to serve as a template for peaceful church actions everywhere. What makes the Popes' interventions significant is that they are not confined to internal communications within the church but are shouted from the rooftop.

Hence Pope John Paul II was an important political figure in the fall of dictatorships, most especially in Poland and Soviet Union. I am told that Mikhail Gorbachev praised Pope John Paul as "the world's most left-wing leader," drawing on his opposition to poverty and injustice. Gorbachev indicated that the end of the Communist control would have been impossible without the Pope's action.

Pope Francis speaks out against war, nuclear weapons, poverty, discrimination, and corruption. I so appreciate his statement in paragraph three of *Amoris Laetitia*, "that not all discussions of doctrinal, moral, or pastoral issues need to be settled by interventions of the magisterium." Pope Francis signals trust in decentralization with decisions to be made at the pastoral level. He wants priests to serve the people—not use them.

Yet parish priests and campus chaplains are experiencing a double bind when they enter the political realm or even speak out specifically on political issues other than abortion. Bishops and pastors tend to come down hard on priests who address social issues that might anger affluent church members causing a likely decrease in parish support. Opposing the "Herods of today," as Pope Francis described political leaders who impose their power and increase their wealth, can lead to criticism from above.

To fulfill our vocation in all its fullness, however, priests need to be practically involved in pursuing political virtue, good civil habits, and performing works of justice and love. Protest marches and prayers are needed. Living our lives outside the sanctuary, as though we believe what we preach, is what will be truly evangelical and attract the young.

To see the world with empathy through the eyes of the poor is what Pope Francis is urging us to do and then act. Unfortunately many of us priests were not trained for such activity.

During my interim years of training (1945–1955), a second-level message came down from my instructors. This message emphasized a *sacred-role* orientation, with little regard to the *human* element. The teaching stressed the value of obedience and downplayed initiative, creativity, and personal/human encounters. Therefore, the training had a marked de-emphasis on pastoral activities that would reflect the human dimension in action, namely, developing interpersonal skills, for example, the ability to be both empathetic and compassionate, to be aware of and be open and honest about what one is thinking and feeling.

After ordination and until graduate school (1955–1970), this expectation continued. Both my pastors and the laity expected me to concentrate on sacred activities: baptize, hear confessions, say mass and give communion, anoint the sick, and preside at marriages and funerals. In addition, I should give an interesting sermon and of course, pray. I believed I was equipped with the knowledge and tools to fulfill only my sacred role—be a "good priest."

My dissertation research revealed that priests who had accepted their role as "dispenser of rituals" confessed to being happy as priests. Those priests whose activities, or intended activities, were pastorally oriented, or were balanced, however, were significantly less happy and satisfied. They perceived their priestly vocation to be out in the streets, as stated above—doing community organizing, helping the poor, and seeking social justice—therefore, they found themselves experiencing a double bind. The universal church in its theology, we assumed, was calling us to be involved equally in the sacred and the human, the changing of the world, while our bishops, pastors, and laity expected us to limit ourselves to the sacred and castigated us for making justice, as Jesus did, the center of our lives.

My dissertation helped me understand why the fifteen years of my priesthood before graduate school (1955–1970) were not the fulfilling experience I expected. I had envisioned that in becoming a priest I'd be an instrument of change—personal, spiritual, social, economic, and political.

**I believed, and still do, that everything
needs to change such that the global community
becomes the Kingdom that Jesus came to establish,
and priests are intended to be leaders in this process.
It is what I signed up for.**

I had encountered a double bind. I had internalized an inclusive theological orientation that was the stated intent of the church. At the same time, I experienced a job description and lifestyle that, as the church hierarchy insisted, was antithetical to an integrated orientation. The consequences for me were threefold: psychological underdevelopment, no associate/pastor interpersonal relationships, and marked dissatisfaction and frustration in my priestly role—all of which I'd been previously unaware. In the absence of introspection, I assumed I was happy (I didn't expect much), and I assumed I was doing the best I could.

Preparing my dissertation, particularly the analysis of survey results, increased my awareness and understanding. I knew I didn't want to return to the dysfunctional environment of a parish priest. I needed social justice work and a life in which I could continue to grow. It didn't seem too much to ask and seek.

CHAPTER 13

Various Positions I Applied for... and Those I Held

Archdiocese of Saint Paul

In 1974, I graduated with a Ph.D. in Organizational Behavior and Administration. I was eager to be an instrument in the training of future priests, to enable them to grow psychologically and to have the human skills to be effective pastors, not simply administrants of the sacraments.

Shortly afterward I returned to the Archdiocese of Saint Paul and made an appointment with the seminary rector, Monsignor William Baumgartner, who had been my philosophy professor 25 years before. He was a thoughtful and committed priest, and I assumed I would not only receive a fair hearing, but I had high hopes I would be welcomed with open arms to join the seminary faculty.

Having looked over my transcripts, and before I got a chance to describe my dissertation findings with the implications for priestly training, Monsignor stated, "I'm sorry, but the seminary curriculum doesn't contain what you are prepared to teach." His demeanor implied that he didn't believe it *should* be part of the curriculum. The finality of his tone kept me from pointing out the benefits of my newly acquired knowledge. Afterward, I wished I had disagreed and explained that what I was able to bring to the seminary was exactly what future priests needed to know to be effective pastors. But I didn't.

However, on a brighter note, Monsignor suggested I apply to teach in the Archdiocese's College of Saint Thomas, "because their curriculum includes the subjects you're prepared to teach." I walked away happy with the thought that I could bring my knowledge and pedagogy to the students of Saint Thomas College.

I visited with the new Archbishop John Roach, and stated unequivocally that I didn't do all the work needed to obtain a doctorate in order to do parish work. He was sympathetic to my motives and determination. Neither could I return to the University of Minnesota Newman Center where Bill Hunt, the director of Newman, and his team of associates were doing a commendable job. I requested, therefore, an appointment to the faculty of Saint Thomas College.

Archbishop Roach responded, "In the old days, the archbishop could simply assign a priest to the college, but no more. President Monsignor Terry Murphy, and the faculty now determine who joins their faculty ranks." I perceived this change as progress; for the archbishop to simply appoint me or anybody else with no input wasn't in the spirit of Vatican II. Archbishop Roach did offer to write a letter of recommendation for me, and I was sincerely grateful. I presumed the recommendation would do the trick, and I thought the college would be happy to have me. Over the years I have cultivated the habit of thinking positively about most everything—a habit that generates happiness.

Three members of the Saint Thomas business faculty interviewed me; I had no meeting with President Monsignor Murphy. Coming away from the interview, I was convinced I had favorably impressed my interviewers, who had especially liked my intention of researching and publishing a book. However, I made at least one mistake.

I said that in addition to teaching I intended to do organizational consulting, because I could then bring the consultant experiences and current business practices into the classroom. The practice would provide current examples or case studies of how agents of behavioral change work. Students would learn from my successes and failures. Over time, I could bring students with me to the consultations, so that they would receive hands-on experience in enabling organizations to change for the better.

This mistake led to a letter of rejection from Saint Thomas. The reason given for rejection: my intention to consult with companies in addition to teaching. "Unlike large universities," the letter explained, "Saint Thomas prides itself on being student-centered with teaching being the priority," with the expectation that the professor be devoted solely to teaching. The letter suggested I might be better suited to teach at a university where the emphasis was on research. "Good luck," was their final comment.

Although somewhat disappointed, I surmised there was another unspoken factor in the rejection. At that time, anti-war activists were receiving much publicity for picketing Honeywell Corporation in Minneapolis. A mere eight miles from the college, Honeywell was one of Saint Thomas's major benefactors. It was easy for me to rationalize that the main reason for my rejection was my peace-making history because the college's president was well aware of these activities.

He was reasonably concerned that I might join the Honeywell brigade of demonstrators—and I agree. I would have participated in the protest and made statements to the press. How would the president of Saint Thomas explain to Honeywell decision-makers the protesting behavior of one of the college's professors?

One's loyalty to an institution weighs heavily on other values, seemingly leaving no place to go.

So my hope of working in my archdiocese didn't come to fruition. With Archbishop Roach's support, I applied to the National Catholic Welfare Conference, a lobby in Washington. Had I been accepted I would have been able to contribute to two far-reaching letters to Catholic Americans, one on peace and the other on economics. I also applied twice to Catholic Relief Services (CRS). Rejected by both with no reason given, I found solace in Thomas Merton's words: "We must make the choices that enable us to fulfill the deepest capacities of our real selves." I could only think that God had another mission for me, and that I would pursue my dream according to God's leading.

Psychotherapy: Beech Brook

Because I was in debt from my education and needed money with which to live, I returned to Cleveland and began to search for a teaching position. None appeared. I eventually accepted a position as a psychotherapist at Beech Brook, a 120-year-old treatment center for emotionally disturbed children and their families. The pay was a whopping $12,000 a year, and would help in repaying a $10,000 student loan that I secured after the two-year Danforth grant ran out.

> **As it turned out, similar to the United States government, I remained permanently in debt, even in my old age, because working for peace can be a costly affair.**

Working as a psychotherapist at Beech Brook had its successful moments, but not often. The work was challenging, a good way to use mediation and psychological skills I'd been taught, and I did find great joy when I was able to assist a family in moving ahead.

The milieu reminded me of a similar sense of ineffectiveness I'd experienced in my parish priesthood days, when the culture's racism had greater impact on parishioners' behavior than my Sunday homilies. If I could change the *environment,* I came to assume that I could be more effective long-term in positively influencing family life.

After I'd been at Beech Brook for three years, in 1977 an earlier graduate of our Organizational Behavior Program at Case invited me to join his consulting firm. I jumped at the chance. I saw it as an opportunity to participate in an environment consonant with my abilities and education. This company consulted to both profit and social-profit organizations. The company had developed a successful track record in implementing positive change among transit companies, thus much of our business came from such companies.

The training focused on the human side of enterprise: leadership, conflict management, team building, self-knowledge, and workforce motivation—all the kinds of training I had hoped to facilitate for future priests at the seminary. In the late seventies, I found it a valuable learning experience and was grateful to develop new skills, such as visualization.

Teaching and Learning at Baldwin Wallace

In June of 1980, a professor invited me to join the Baldwin Wallace College (BW) faculty and become both an assistant professor and associate director of the Master in Business Administration Program (MBA). I was honored and relieved to accept.

I'd never taught full-time before, but it has been a remarkable learning experience for me over three decades, and I have enjoyed the students immensely. I taught both undergraduates and graduates in the Business Division, courses in management and organizational behavior—team building, and the like.

We began to take students abroad on study tours, and I was fortunate enough to travel with the marketing professor taking students to the Holy Land in 1982. As part of our trip, we visited Egypt, both Cairo and Luxor. We had an opportunity to visit many holy places. I observed and struggled to understand the conflict between the Palestinians and the Israelis, but back then, from my brief perspective as a visitor and my own history with another beleaguered population, it was a sorrowful but incomplete picture. More intense involvement was in my future. Having co-led a study tour with this professor, I began to guide tours on my own and we traveled, during the next 20 years, to such places as Costa Rica, Japan, China, and later Vietnam.

Conversant in Costa Rica

In 1989, I was promoted to full professor. The previous year I had been granted a sabbatical to study Spanish in Costa Rica, and during the seven months from June until after Christmas, I enjoyed, for the first time, living abroad. I was blessed and felt delighted to live among poor families. From my host family, I learned to speak their conversational Spanish, while attending language school for six hours a day. Being able to order what I wanted at the market increased my confidence. Just purchasing a bus ticket to another Central American country was a treat, and my journey included carrying on small talk with fellow passengers in their language.

I discovered learning a language is a practical way to study another culture.

Unlike my experience in the States, everywhere I traveled in town, at the beach or in the rainforest, I was met with welcoming smiles. I prayed that someday fellow Americans could greet strangers, including immigrants and people of color, with such welcoming kindness.

Interest rates in Costa Rica were at 20 percent, making it nearly impossible for the average citizen to borrow money to build a house. Unemployment, consequently, was commonplace. I learned that people needed to be able to borrow money at a reasonable rate to buy their own homes and to start businesses, so that employment could increase.

A major blessing, in my opinion, was the absence of an army. Costa Rica constitutionally abolished its army in 1949. The people were proud of this, and wouldn't consider solving the unemployment challenge by creating a standing army, which is what I had experienced in Egypt.

Experiencing Liberation Theology in Nicaragua

A major motivation for my learning Spanish was to help me understand and perhaps influence what was happening politically in Central America. As I became more comfortable with the language, I traveled to Nicaragua and Guatemala.

In Nicaragua, before the Sandinistas were fighting the Contras (who were being supported by the United States) over half the country was illiterate. After the Sandinista victory, the new government encouraged university students to go out into the countryside and teach the people to read and write. The Sandinista Front for National Liberation's (FSLN) literacy campaign is often seen as their greatest success. Over 100,000 Nicaraguans participated as literacy teachers. Within six months, half a million people had been taught rudimentary reading, bringing the national illiteracy rate down from over 50 percent to just under 12 percent. One of the stated aims of the literacy campaign was to create a literate electorate able to make informed choices. UNESCO recognized the success of the literacy campaign with the award of a Nadezhda Krupskaya International Prize.

I made an effort to connect with Witness For Peace, an organization of Americans engaged in helping the Sandinista government by informing the people of the United Sates about what was actually happening in Nicaragua—very different from reports of the U.S. mainstream press. For whatever reason, I didn't receive a warm welcome, perhaps because they suspected I was a CIA operative.

I did, however, interact with the Quakers—a peace church comprised of mostly Canadians and people from the U.S.—and a Catholic parish in Nicaragua City. The Quakers introduced me to a liturgy of silence, after which some attendees shared their personal meditations. The service was prayerful, thoughtful, and had amazing participation. I was impressed and gained an understanding of the importance of silence in Catholic liturgical practice.

I witnessed Liberation Theology in operation at the local Catholic parish during a Sunday night mass. The priest led a dialogue homily with full and active participation, and hearing how the people applied the scripture to their current situation moved me immensely. I was able to follow almost everything with my newly acquired Spanish. The women in particular were not only articulate, but spoke with intensity. The liturgy was a grace-filled springboard for the faithful to go out and make a positive difference in their communities, according to Gospel values. The experience gave me so much hope for Nicaragua. I've noticed that few refugees and migrants have sought to enter the United States from Nicaragua. Perhaps, if we would compete less with neighboring countries and cooperate more with them, fewer people would seek to sneak into our country.

Surprises in Guatemala

In Guatemala I sought to visit Gregory Schaeffer, a priest from Minnesota whom I'd coached in football at the minor seminary when he was a freshman. He had a vibrant parish, San Lucas near Lake Atitlan, and these parishioners were growing spiritually and financially under his leadership. Much to my disappointment, he was in Minnesota at the time of my visit. His associate most graciously received me, and let me sleep in the pastor's bed. His room was simple, sparse of decoration, but had a comfortable king-sized bed. His associate took me with him into the countryside where we concelebrated mass in Spanish among the poor peasants. The little chapels in the mountains were open to people and animals alike— no one noticed when a pet dog attended the ceremony.

In this parish, the church went to the people instead of the people coming to church. It was evident how integrated were the sacred and the pastoral in the lives of the people. They were inseparable, a reflection of the findings of my PhD research fifteen years previously, wherein priests blending Catholic action with administering the sacraments were not only mature but also effective.

As I rode the bus between my friend's parish and Atitlan, a caravan of soldiers halted our passage in the middle of the highway. A captain mounted the bus steps near the driver and loudly ordered all the men to exit through the front entrance. Clutching my U.S. passport, I obediently followed the others to the front. Descending, I showed the captain my passport, fully expecting him to respect it. He hardly glanced at it and motioned for me to stand with the others at the front of the bus. Again, I obeyed without objection. While not overly confident, I don't remember being afraid. My body stood straight among the smaller Guatemalans, tense, ready for any eventuality.

The soldiers checked the bus to make sure no male was hidden among the women. Finally, with a wave of the captain's hand, the males standing in front of the bus were directed to re-board. I then noticed that my companions were middle-aged or older. Looking out the bus's rear window, I saw that those left standing behind the bus were young men, even boys, being lined up and led away—simply snatched from their mothers, conscripted to fuel their government's war against the peasants fighting for freedom and equality.

I had another surprise while traveling in the mountains. I came upon Israeli soldiers training the Guatemalan government's troops. Later, in Thailand, I was to stumble onto U.S. troops training government soldiers long after the Vietnam War had ended.

I learned that, in selling arms to developing countries, part of the deal was to teach the buyers how to use the sophisticated (although outdated) equipment.

Professor-in-Residence: Hong Kong

Free from administrative responsibilities in the 1991–1992 academic year, I was able to be on sabbatical, and so I accepted an invitation to be a visiting professor-in-residence at Hong Kong Baptist University.

The opportunity came through the intercession of a professor Bob Graham who had taught at Baldwin Wallace and later accepted a professorship at Hong Kong Baptist University. I was blessed to have a friend in this professor—he and his family made my stay in Hong Kong a joyful learning experience.

At first, because I was unfamiliar with the culture, teaching Chinese students was quite a challenge. Chinese culture is family-oriented and group-centered. For instance, in college classes in the U.S., when students are asked a question, many hands go up, offering to take a stab at a correct response. In China, on the contrary, not a single hand appeared when I asked an open question. At first, I thought they might be shy in the presence of an American professor. I tried then to call a student by name: "Ms. Chang, do you believe you can motivate the workers you supervise?" Ms. Chang sat quietly, her eyes closed. Quickly, students all around her began speaking to her in Chinese. I had no idea what they were saying. Eventually, I learned they were giving her the answer. Then Ms. Chang, all smiles, responded, confident that everyone else would know the correct answer—and if her answer had been wrong, everyone would have been wrong.

Far different from the rampant individualism in the United States, this example of learning in a collective society was an eye-opening lesson. Both methods have their good points: group behavior is noncompetitive and inclusive, whereas individualism encourages individuals to take initiative and be creative and innovative. This experience motivated me to capture the strengths of both.

Hong Kong's skyline, both on the island and in the new territories, is punctuated by skyscrapers filled with apartments. Laundry is hung on long poles extending from almost every window. The apartments are so tiny that my Chinese friends were reluctant to invite family and friends for dinner. Entertaining is done at restaurants, which are abundant all over.

With some ten million people crunched into a small area, people and cars are everywhere, even in the middle of the night. Only the very rich can afford to import and purchase a car. Parking spaces are at a premium, and are almost impossible to find. Most people use public transportation, which is the envy of the industrially developed world. In traveling to and from school, I never waited more than thirty-five seconds for the subway. When I then climbed the stairs to the street, a bus was waiting. When filled to capacity, the bus would quickly be off and the next bus moved in to take its place. Having consulted for transit companies in the United States, I was most impressed by this effectiveness and efficiency.

The people of Hong Kong appeared to be addicted to gambling. I was told the profits were so enormous they financed the safety net for the poor and disadvantaged. No progressive income tax—a 15 percent across-the-board tax enabled the affluent to become ever richer, that is, if they didn't gamble it away.

Despite the wealth, my Chinese colleagues didn't hide their nervousness as 1997 approached. This was the time when the People's Republic of China was scheduled to take over Hong Kong from Great Britain. Fear was driving thousands of the affluent to flee to Singapore, Australia, and Canada. Some businessmen, seeking to take advantage of the tax structure, placed their families in Vancouver, Canada. Flying back and forth every other weekend—they became known as "astronauts."

Christians were planning "underground" churches, in fear the dreaded Communists would forbid them to attend services—and make the churches over into government institutions. Not much was said about it because the faithful were not certain whom they could trust.

In the spring of 1991, as the academic year drew to a close, the university offered me the position of Dean of the Business School. Shortly afterward, I got word that my father had a stroke.

The thought of my dad dying without me at his bedside was not manageable. At 91, he probably didn't have many years left, and I wanted to share the time remaining. I needed to go home. I began to understand that my values, not "free choice," drive everything I do. I was not free to choose to stay in Hong Kong—I had to go home.

I returned to Baldwin Wallace and, except for short teaching stints in Vietnam, I spent every vacation with my parents until Dad died at 96 on March 1, 1998. Six weeks later, on Easter Sunday Mother joined Dad in eternity. They stayed alive to take care of each other.

After Dad's funeral, Mother said to me, "I don't know why God's keeping me alive." She was in poor health and expected to have died before Dad. I said, "I think I know, Mother." Surprised, she asked, "Why?" "Two reasons, Mom." "First, to save my soul." "Oh-ish!" she muttered, shrugging. "Two," I continued, "To learn patience." "Am I impatient?" she asked in surprise. "Mom, it takes one to know one—and I am very impatient." Two weeks before she died, Mother ceased ordering the nurses to do things, and began to ask, "Am I doing this right?"

CHAPTER 14

May I Return to Vietnam? (June 1987)

In late 1987, I received a message from the Viet My (Vietnamese American Friendship Society, who had been my hosts previously) in North Vietnam inviting me to return to Vietnam and bring with me my comrades who had accompanied me to Vietnam in resisting the war in the '70s. I contacted the people involved and asked them if they'd like to go—*we could have a reunion.* Our assembled group included Bob Willis, Marianne Hamilton, Leonard Hirsch, and Jeffrey Voorhees, along with his wife Marny.

We were different, too, in many ways: Bob Willis was no longer a priest, but was married to a lovely woman named Pat. Marianne Hamilton was still a peace activist, and well respected in the Catholic and peace communities for her local and international leadership. She had co-founded Women Against Military Madness (WAMM), which is an active peace organization for the last 35 years, and stronger than ever. Len Hirsch was divorced and engaged in a lucrative consulting career headquartered in Washington, D.C. (Len had been Organizational Development Consultant in the White House, reporting to Hamilton Jordan, Chief of Staff who reported directly to President Carter, from 1976 to 1980. Just five years before that appointment, he had stood with us at the embassy gate. Only in the U.S., I believe could one protest the nation's policies and still advance to such a high government position!) Jeff Voorhees also had a consulting career and lived in California with his wife, Marny. Marianne was delighted to have another woman along on this trip.

> **We were all curious to learn how peace efforts in Vietnam had developed since the war.**

I had brought along my instant-photo Polaroid SUN camera with electronic flash (which came out in 1983); it was meant to provide amusement and opportunities to share, if nothing else.

A Hospitable Hanoi

> **I remained hopeful that our visit could supply some positive information about Vietnam's rebuilding and needs, and about how U.S. citizens might help in these areas.**

On Friday, June 10, we five, minus Leonard whose flight to Bangkok was further delayed, boarded the plane for Hanoi. No soldiers or military planes marked our arrival at Hanoi, but a blast of hot air that I mistook for the jet engine's exhaust greeted us. How could I have forgotten Hanoi was so hot and humid?

A new airport had been built about 50 kilometers/30 miles outside the city, where members of the Viet My Committee met us with a bouquet of peach blossoms for each of us. Mrs. Nguyen Thi Tinh, a congenial woman, was our interpreter throughout the trip; Mr. Nguyen Van Huynh and Mr. Phan Tuan Phuc shepherded us swiftly through customs and baggage claim and into a waiting van. I was so grateful for the moving air through the half-open windows as the taxi swerved onto a country road heading for the city. The water buffalo were still there, but new, red brick buildings filled the landscape.

Hanoi retained some of the shabby elegance of its French colonial past, but much had become utilitarian, new and bustling. Our skillful driver zigzagged through it all, honking continuously.

As we drove, scenes of rice paddies harvest flashed by, women in conical bamboo hats, water buffalo, and men cutting and binding bundles of rice stalks. Construction seemed to be going on everywhere, mostly small homemade brick dwellings. As before, everywhere people squatted or sat in clusters before tiny hovels. There was still a prevalence of dust and poverty.

The Committee's guesthouse couldn't have been a greater contrast—an old French colonial home with high ceilings, a winding staircase, and formal furnishings, reminding me of the rectories and convents from the 1920s and 1930s.

Our orientation was warm and welcoming; it was evident that our hosts had spent time and effort preparing for us. We would be their guests at no cost to us and, for better or worse, it was a great gift they were offering, and we all knew it.

After a quiet and ample meal, Bob and I thought we'd go for a walk out in the new city—until we found that the gate between high stone walls was chained shut. We were locked in. However, events are not always what they seem, but when requested, the house caretaker happily freed us. After a brief look around, we decided to wait until morning to explore.

Dear Bob, suffering from the humid heat because rooms were not air-conditioned, set out in the wee hours of the morning before the rest of us emerged for breakfast—and managed to get lost. As the hours went by, we began to be annoyed that he hadn't waited for us; then we got worried. We canvassed the streets around our campus and circled the nearby lake twice but saw no sign of him. We finally decided to consult our hosts. At first they were perturbed that he had not followed their suggestions, but they tried to be reassuring.

"We will give him a little more time, shall we? Then we will call in the police to help us." Our hosts, we learned later, were afraid for themselves, as the Vietnamese government might be worried that Bob was an American spy, for whom our hosts would be held responsible. I thought about calling the hospitals but I somehow believed that he would return.

It turned out Bob had taken a wrong turn at a nearby lake, and in a confusion of directions because of his minimal French and no Vietnamese, he found his way back to the lake, only to discover that Hanoi has more than one lake.

He grew increasingly hot and desperate. At one point, he was rescued by a couple of Russian Army soldiers whose faces lit up at Bob's drawing, and invited him to ride along. With many smiles and enthusiastic handshakes, they let him off at the lake—or what he thought was the lake. He strode down the path he thought led to the guesthouse, then another, but no guesthouse appeared. Eventually a friendly cab driver, understanding "Viet My," returned him to a jubilant and relieved Huynh and Phuc, and to us. I told him I thought he'd defected. He quipped, "Even a Communist society can't control you when you're lost." We forgave him of course, and suggested he take a cold bath, poor guy.

Polaroids for Peace

In the midafternoon, we traveled to the countryside past the old airport, to a rug-making cooperative housed in a hot, barnlike structure. The workers were all women weavers, and the products were lovely in colors and design. The work was labor-intensive, the surface was carefully trimmed, using massive handlooms or with large shears. Salaries were based on the number of rugs made. We learned that the Council for Mutual Economic Assistance (COMECON), the economic organization under the leadership of the Soviet bloc, was the marketer and principal customer. Because of the U.S. trade embargo, they had little trade with the West. I assumed that more open trade could better their lives. Walking among the workers, I began using my Polaroid. There was a lot of giggling but the supervisors seemed to approve, and within minutes we had a delighted audience posing and viewing the magic as the film rolled out.

Tinh, our guide, began to talk to me about coming to teach in Vietnam, if ever an embassy were established. Looking at me dubiously, she said, "It's very hard. With an embassy it would be easier. Conditions are bad."

On Sunday, we were chauffeured to 7:00 a.m. mass at the cathedral, Regina Pacis, where Marianne and I had attended Mass in 1972. The façade had nothing of the raw appearance of the newer buildings; it was blackened with the dust of ages. The parking lot was crammed with bicycles and the church was packed, just as in the 1970s, the men on the left, the women on the right. As before, the singing responses were vigorous and haunting, heartfelt and devout.

Outside, a throng of excited kids, many emaciated and hungry, surrounded us, begging. We were not prepared, so our coins didn't go far because we had only a few dong between us. I didn't have my camera because I had deemed it wasn't appropriate to take pictures there. We were hustled toward the van, though not before a teenager purposely bumped into Bob, who had the presence of mind to bow and say, "Excuse me." The young man moved off and stood close by, eyeing us unsmiling.

Bob, Jeff, and Marny were more inclined to believe that the officials had a carefully planned and structured agenda for us, and that Marianne and I were somewhat naïve to identify with them as warm and gracious hosts, anxious to share their culture. She and I perceived the Vietnamese were proud of their progress in postwar rebuilding, and yet humble in showing their needs. The others seemed to notice an undercurrent of anger among some people, which of course would be perfectly normal given what they'd been through because of us. But if such anger were present, it went over my head. *We realized none of us could have the whole truth.*

Why Does the U.S. Still Punish Us?

The next morning, I took some Tai Chi lessons with seniors, beside the lake where a breeze off the 6:00 a.m. waters kept us reasonably refreshed. My body said "thank you" for the exercise. After breakfast we met with Mr. Nguyen Huy, the director of the Economic Institute of Hanoi, a researcher and consultant to the government. A sweet-faced and quiet-spoken man, he was terribly thin, weighed down with the burdens of his nation's poverty.

Mr. Huy said the economic difficulties stemmed from the U.S. embargo, which restricted access to many markets, and from the lack of corporate investments. Agricultural development was limited because of a severe shortage of laborsaving farm implements and raw materials like fertilizers and pesticides. Finally, he thought it was more difficult to mobilize people to rebuild their society than to join together to fight a common enemy in time of war.

On this last point, I could see that years of war and poverty tended to demoralize communities, but what I knew of the spirit and culture of the Vietnamese people led me to internally disagree with Mr. Huy. I didn't blame him for seeing the negatives; after all, he was bombarded with them daily. For me, knowing the people's determination during the war, I believed the same perseverance would see them through these new challenges.

Leonard Hirsch finally arrived that afternoon. He had overslept in Jeff's apartment in San Francisco and missed his plane, which led to further complications.

At the Viet My offices, Marianne and I renewed acquaintances with friends from our past trips. Ly Van Sau, Mme. Nguyen Thi Binh, Nguyen Tran Le, and Mme. Vu Thi Kim Lien. Their English was quite good, and from their experiences in the war and negotiations, they retained an openness of mind. The talk was honest and friendly though often painful, such as, "Why does the U.S. government still punish us so many years after the end of the war?" and "After years of war, millions are crippled and orphaned, and we can't feed our people."

218

We answered as best we could. Our nation was scarred, too, by that conflict, and by the divisions in our political and social systems that stemmed from the Vietnam War. As for the billions in aid President Nixon promised, we sadly gave them our opinion, "It isn't going to come."

Late for an appointment at the Ministry of Education, we hurried over to meet with Mr. Nguyen Chi Linh, the director of the Department of International Cooperation. Education, he told us, was progressing at a better rate than economic development, but shortages impeded advancement. Most children had to share textbooks and writing materials, and many dropped out of school at early ages because of their families' poverty. My colleagues and I left feeling a bit downhearted, troubled that the younger generation faced so many seemingly insurmountable obstacles.

June 14, 1987: Meetings and more meetings. At the Chamber of Commerce, our group sat along one side of an oblong table, Director Luu Van Dat, an elder, and his staff on the other. He explained the recently passed Law on Foreign Investment, which seemed to us potentially exploitative on the part of Western investors. The policy was essentially "open door," with promises that Vietnam would not nationalize industry, would supply an abundant labor force, and make available a wealth of natural resources. We mostly listened, and I felt uneasy. I caught Marianne's eyes, and then Bob's, when Dat mentioned transnational corporations. Dat paused, smiling. "Of course we have suspicions. We are aware there are dangers to our people!" Len was especially eloquent in warning of the dangers of succumbing to capitalism after winning the war. But Dat was willing to risk the dangers because of his country's critical need for management expertise and training from the West.

A nice break on the road to our next meeting was a visit to Ho Chi Minh's home. The property was large, but the house was small and quite simple. Less than thirty yards from his house was a small lake. As we reached the shore, our guide Mrs. Tinh suggested we clap our hands; when we did so, a large school of carp immediately appeared and gazed at us as if we were friends. Mrs. Tinh then explained that each morning when in Hanoi, Ho Chi Minh came down to the lake and clapped his hands; then threw food to the fish—a perfect example of Positive Reinforcement that I used many times in class.

The next stop was more heartening. I had made an appointment with Mr. Tran Quang Huy, head of the Commission of Religious Affairs. Marianne and I knew him from previous international meetings. He recognized Bob from our demonstration at the American Embassy in 1971. He was, in fact, embarrassingly eloquent about its symbolic importance to Vietnam's struggles. Our mutual admiration exchanges slid happily into a broader discussion of the Commission's charge, and we got down to business. The Commission has a delicate job being a liaison with the government and between various religious groups: Catholics, Buddhists, Protestants, Muslims, and adherents to Cao Đài and Hoà Hảo.

Since most of us were Catholics, we talked about how the Church was doing under Communist rule. We were relieved to hear that relations were improving; numbers were growing, and the government seemed to have eased its suspicions that Catholics could not be loyal citizens. However, Huy thought that relations with the Vatican, which still did not formally recognize the Hanoi government, could be better.

Our next appointment was with the Vice Minister of Foreign Affairs, Mr. Nguyen Dy Nien. This meeting took place in an impressive French Colonial-style building where we were greeted warmly but solemnly. He spoke without notes, answering our questions on international relations honestly and directly. He spoke of the Soviet Union, "our good and constant friend"; Cambodia, "Vietnam intervened because of the terrible suffering at the hands of the Khmer Rouge"; China, "the Chinese shell us every day, but we constantly speak with them, asking openly for negotiations rather than conflict."

Vietnam had suffered through five wars since the 1930s, and wanted nothing more than peace. About the U.S. war, Mr. Nien was emphatic, "Wounds remain open on all sides." Their nation had sacrificed immeasurably for independence. "What sacrifices for peace are the U.S. people willing to make?" We left the hall sobered, though having great respect and gratitude for his openness.

The next morning was a long one. At the Ministry of Labor we were ushered into a stark, nearly barren boardroom, quite different from the elegance of the Foreign Ministry. The few decorations included, opposite the doorway, the familiar large portrait of Ho Chi Minh; on the other walls were a faded map of the world, and a single Dutch plate. Bui Tran Giang, the vice director of the section for Invalid and Social Affairs, busied himself with papers and note taking all during our session. The burden of discourse fell to a white-haired man with a prosthetic leg, Mr. Le Binh, who appeared to outrank the other one, at least as spokesman.

This ministry focused on programs for the war-wounded, elderly, and handicapped, as well as those needing jobs in all sectors of society. Also under its purview were women's unions caring for orphans, youth unions helping parents of wounded soldiers, and villages building houses for the wounded and their families.

Many social services seemed to be linked, with an emphasis on postwar trauma recovery. Since part of our inquiry was concerned with healing, we were obliged to bring up return-of-remains. The discussion became more and more painful.

Mr. Binh, in an animated though soft voice, gave the statistics for Vietnamese: 1.5 million wounded, 2 million poisoned by Agent Orange, 4.5 million with stress-related disorders, half a million orphaned, and another half-million prostitutes, drug addicts, and *bui doi*. The term "bui doi" literally translated, means "dirt or dust of life," refers to children (Amerasians) born sometime during the war whose father was an American soldier, and whose mother was Vietnamese. These children, along with their mothers, were the outcasts of Vietnamese society, and were subjects of discrimination everywhere.

> In the face of these statistics, not numbers
> but real people, terribly afflicted people, we were
> laid low. Our words and gestures of empathy,
> even our apologies, seemed banal as the
> dismal facts stood baldly before us.

Our afternoon at the Viet My offices was more pleasant. Our hosts wanted to hear about U.S. political and social life, so we did more talking, less listening. In the evening at a good-bye dinner, conversation continued, and we agreed that cultural exchanges held the most hope for better relations.

On our last morning in Hanoi, a sweltering humid day, we visited a women's union service center. Marny and Marianne had talked with women leaders the day before and received an invitation to tour their place. During the war women fought alongside the men or engaged in war-related, hard labor: They dug shelters, drove trucks, or repaired roads. The director, Mme. Thuy Linh, told us that women now outnumbered men in the poverty-stricken new society, and the thought was that these young women needed to reestablish domestic skills. A surprising challenge. Men returned from the war to find women, because of their hard labor, had lost the habit and desire of beautifying themselves—much to the men's disappointment. The women's union service centers held classes to teach the use of makeup and apparel to enhance their beauty.

After Many Years, Back to Ho Chi Minh City

After waiting a long time, we finally boarded the same Russian jet that brought us to Hanoi, but it seemed blessedly comfortable after an afternoon on hard, hot chairs.

The airport in Ho Chi Minh City (the new name for Saigon) was familiar, although remodeled. The street to downtown was noticeably free of armed soldiers and shelters on each corner, though the same energy was evident. The street swarmed with cars, motorcycles, and bicycles, all in a rush. The French Colonial architecture competed with modern, glass-covered structures, and billboards advertised products, Western consumer-style, instead of block-lettered war slogans.

We stayed at the Rex Hotel. Old-fashioned, it resembled U.S. hotels in the 1920–30s. Our sitting rooms were equipped with a television (showing only government programs), and a small refrigerator. A tea service was laid out with fruit and bottled water—all the comforts of home, if one were of the middle class.

The next day we visited the site of our 1971 protest, which now housed a Soviet oil company. I could scarcely breathe, flooded with memories as we approached the gate. Still formidable, barred and copper-colored, the gates now had steel plates attached from knee-level up. Curious, I walked closer and tried to look in; I pushed the gate, hoping to enter. Two plainclothes Russians quickly blocked my entrance, more effective and less pleasant than the surprised Marine 17 years before. No explanation on my part meant anything.

Bob, Len, Marianne, and I walked around reminiscing and took pictures; then we cut directly across the street to the Viet-My Friendship House, where our old friends, Ngo Cong Duc and Ho Ngoc Nhuan, former deputies and members of the Third Force, welcomed us. Their joy in seeing us shone in their eyes. They seemed scarcely to have changed, except for a sprinkling of gray hairs. The others gathered were an impressive assortment of veterans, politicians, and professors who had struggled for peace, resisting the old regime. Some were younger members of student movements who had been imprisoned over peace protests, like Huyhn Tan Mam, now a doctor and editor of a youth newspaper. There was much talk of our action in 1971, and gratitude on their part. We tried to demur, but it was indeed of important symbolic value to many Vietnamese—and it had been a life changer for us.

At the offices of the Committee of Solidarity of Patriotic Catholics, I brought a present for another associate of those days, Father Minh. He had loaned me his cassock for our priestly protests, and after cherishing it all those years, I returned it, none the worse for sacred wear. He laughed heartily, "I did have another!—and I still have it. Please keep it as a souvenir." I treasure it to this day.

These friends and colleagues fervently wished for more U.S.-Vietnam interchange. The message for peace, they were convinced, would flow most easily through fellow Catholics: people like us; Tom Fox, then editor of the National Catholic Reporter; Dan Berrigan; and Mother Teresa, the blessed internationalist.

Next stop was City Hall, another structure in the colonial deep yellow color with elegant white trim, where we met with the Deputy Mayor Le Qhang Chanh. After a brief hiatus when the electricity failed, we continued the now familiar discussion of human needs and redevelopment. Because Ho Chi Minh City (HCMC) was captured and quickly surrendered its forces, it did not suffer from the Liberation to the extent that other areas did. Here too discussion was on industrial development and the need for investment. I urged the deputy mayor to immediately begin building a subway or a sky train.

"We can't afford that."

I suggested, "Borrow the money or just print it as you are doing now. Otherwise, in twenty years Ho Chi Minh City will be worse than Bangkok or Jakarta because of the city's narrow streets. Public transportation then will cost five times as much."

The deputy mayor simply shrugged. I suspected he was too low in the hierarchy to have influence. My prediction was on the mark. When I visited in 2014, I was informed a sky train and underground transportation were in the works at ten times the 1987 cost.

As for people like us, American and Catholic, we had to tread carefully, too, and earn the government's trust.

The door was opening, certainly, but foreigner's criticism of the new Vietnam was seen as destructive. I assumed we could follow the model of the collective, that is, seek to build unity by working alongside the people and, in faith, explore the possibilities of a new life.

Next day brought a visit to another Liberation institution, the Center for the Rejuvenation of Paralyzed Children, where handicapped children with war and other injuries are raised. They are educated and treated through physical and occupational therapy. A chorus of singing, clapping young people, preschool age to about 20, greeted us as we walked in. Out came my Polaroid, to the delight of the children. Each wanted a picture. Most of them had braces or prostheses on legs or arms. Every age group seemed to be engaged in some form of sewing, building, or repair work, or were in physical therapy, learning to walk and build strength.

What seemed most evident was that even the tiniest of them worked so hard, yet were happy to be doing it.

Later, the impression was strengthened as we visited the New Youth Labor Training Center, which previously had been a Roman Catholic boarding school. The title was a misnomer, as the Center's mission was drug rehabilitation, and the ages served were from 20 to 70, the majority under 40. The drug of choice currently was opium, with some addicted to morphine, valium, or sleeping pills. Before Liberation, ninety percent were heroin addicts. The first phase of the program is to stop the pain during complete withdrawal with the aid of acupuncture, massage, showers, group exercise, and herbal medicines—with the staff and patients' complete acceptance.

An educational component of lectures, videos, and psychological counseling follow for about three months. Then "work and education," job and skill training, goes on for twenty more months. Everywhere in the center, people were working. It seemed a long process to us, but there was evidence throughout that lives were being rebuilt.

The center supported itself with the sales of the patients' woodworking, handmade rice paper, and musical instruments, to name a few. We saw many beautiful examples of craftsmanship.

Next we were invited on a tour of the seminary where we saw the library, chapel, refectory, and the dormitory. Across the way in what used to be the minor seminary, was now used by the government for the education of children. The government promised to return the property to the Church, which they did in the year 2000. It is now a school of theology for lay people.

Before dinner and after an introduction that lauded our actions of 1971, our hosts asked us to speak to the assembled seminarians and priests. Bob described his work as a religious psychotherapist, Marianne her life as a Catholic laywoman and peace activist, and I spoke about priesthood as service to the poor. We tried to answer their heartfelt questions, and they responded with an enchanting hymn in unison, written by one of the students. I felt so much at home.

We returned to the United States loaded with valuable information. Reconciliation was our—and the Vietnamese church's—objective. "Come with us to Vietnam," we said at every opportunity, "Let us end the embargo, normalize relations, trade and visit. Together we can build a better future for our peoples." It was not to happen, however, until some ten years later when Bill Clinton was in the White House.

Patriot: Doan Van Toai

Through Bob Dalton, I met Mr. Toai, who had been a student activist against the war and had traveled to the United States. In 1975 he was working for a bank as the Americans were leaving. During the height of the confusion, he was carrying a couple hundred thousand dollars from one bank to another. He could have escaped and got on a helicopter with all that money, but he was a patriot. When the North Vietnamese marched in, he turned over the money. His hope and expectation was not for a reward, but that they would be open to his ideas on reconstruction of the economy after the war. When he tried to express his views, which contrasted with the ideas of the generals, they instead put him in an education camp for a year. Later he wrote a book called *Vietnamese Gulag* that described his ordeal.

Toai had been a student activist, struggling to bring peace among Vietnamese of differing political persuasions, and he was a severe critic of the corrupt regime of President Thieu. He was deeply loyal to his country, as I was to mine, but our paths to this crucible of conflict were very different. Toai was a native of the Mekong Delta region, born in March 1945, and immersed in regional violence from his earliest days. The ending months of World War II brought no peace to his little village, Cai Von. By March of 1943, the Japanese eliminated or imprisoned the Vichy French who had ruled Vietnam. After the atomic bombs ended the war, French troops returned, but the colony had changed. In September of 1943, Ho Chi Minh declared independence for Vietnam, and another war ensued.

As Toai described it, his village was home to ethnic Khmer, indigenous Cambodians, and tribal battles were common. In addition, a radical sect of Buddhism (Hòa Hảo) was active in the region; the sect had its own army and formed alliances with the French. Naturally, they came in conflict with Vietminh guerillas that led the struggle for Vietnamese independence from French rule.

When Toai was released, he fled Vietnam, going through Cambodia and Thailand to France, then to the United States, where he worked on a Ph.D. The views expressed in his book made him a favorite of the "right" in Vietnam and the U.S. A large percentage of Vietnamese, who had come to the United States when the North Vietnamese moved in, lived in Westminster, California, which came to be called Little Saigon. As time went on, Toai began to write letters to the editor and small articles suggesting that for the good of Vietnam, that people stop regretting the Communists' take-over of their country—and just accept it. Immediately he became the enemy of the "right." One day in the small town of Solano,

California, a man confronted him on the street and shot him point blank. Six bullets went into his body, one into his heart. It was a miracle that medics were able to save his life.

In the next years, Toai demonstrated his skills of persuading U.S. Congressmen and Senators to help Vietnam. He managed to make it possible for Bob Dalton and me, as well as others, to go and teach—and to receive some remuneration. Our earlier contacts had told me, "We're moving toward a free market economy and need to know about marketing, accounting and finance—could you bring over some professors to teach us how to manage a market economy?" I began to do just that. At first the people I contacted needed to pay their own way, as I did—the airplane flight, hotel and food—and we were paid nothing. When I hooked up with Toai and Bob Dalton, who had received money from our government for projects in Vietnam, we at least had our airplane and hotel expense paid for. We worked in that fashion for a number of years; I'd teach during the summer and on winter breaks throughout the 1990s.

The North Vietnamese were immensely fearful. They thought that I worked for the CIA, so I was spied upon all the time and every movement that I made was watched, from 1988 through the next twelve years to year 2000. I learned this in the late '90 when I was accompanied by Ngyen Tran, a Vietnamese man who worked for NASA in Cleveland. He noticed my "shadow." He asked me, "Do you know you're being followed everywhere you go?"

I hadn't paid any attention. The Vietnamese thought in 1972, when we brought out the pilot prisoners, that we were working for the CIA, which was allowing us do this. Nothing could have been further from the truth.

But there was no way I could have changed the minds of the North Vietnamese at the time. People everywhere believe what they want to believe, often going to their graves with their assumptions intact.

Ho Chi Minh City – 1992

Beginning in 1992 I noticed significant changes in Ho Chi Minh City that were a sharp contrast to 1988–1989. After the collapse of the Soviet Union, the favorable trade relations with the USSR and its satellites withered away, to be replaced with a less-controlled "free-market" economy. Beggars and prostitutes returned to the streets, and the dreams of narrowing the gaps between rich and poor began to disappear.

CHAPTER 15

Holy Week in Vietnam (March/April 1994)

At nearly 11 p.m. Thursday, March 18, 1994, I had just finished packing, expecting to leave the next day for Vietnam, when my telephone pierced the silence. Sid Loh, my Thai travel agent in Columbus, Ohio, was on the line. "My travel agent friend in Bangkok wasn't able to get a visa for you to Vietnam," he exclaimed, his voice quivering.

I was shocked and confused. How could that be? I wondered. I'd been a long and loyal friend of Vietnam, even (in some U.S. quarters) infamous, for my efforts to end the war and, lately, for promoting reconciliation between our two countries and an end to the U.S. trade embargo. I'd spent my own money to give Vietnamese people free workshops in business management. The well-received workshops were intended to help Vietnam to manage the transition from a central planning economy to a free-market economy. When President Clinton lifted the U.S. Trade Embargo in February, I shaved my head, demonstrating my personal involvement in the issue.

"Sid!" I said, unintentionally raising my voice, "this cannot be—there must be some mistake! I'm a long-time friend of Vietnam. Tell me what happened."

"I don't know, but your request for a visa has been turned down. Do you want me to cancel your flight?"

"No," I stammered. "I just can't believe they turned me down. Tell me what your travel agent friend said."

I sensed the reluctance in Sid's voice as he answered almost inaudibly, "My friend said you are *on the blacklist*."

"The black list!" I was nearly yelling. "I don't believe it. I'll go to Bangkok and find out what this is all about. If this is true, the Vietnamese will have to tell me to my face that I'm blacklisted." My shattered expectations had turned suddenly to anger.

"I'm so sorry," Sid replied, as if he were at fault. He then gave me the number of his friend's travel agency in Bangkok, and wished me good luck.

I struggled through a restless night. The next day's flight to Bangkok through Tokyo was no better. Normally I'm a cheerful fellow capable of perceiving the positive aspects in most every event. But this news of being refused a visa distressed me no end.

"Don't sweat the small stuff!" I kept repeating to myself, high above the clouds streaking toward Bangkok. "As soon as I arrive I'll fax my friend Dr. Nguyen Tran Xuong (he was the Vice Rector at the University of Economics in Ho Chi Minh City). He will certainly cut through whatever red tape is holding up my visa." I also thought, reassuring myself, I'll fax Father Phan Khac Tu, a member of the People's Assembly (similar to the U.S. House of Representatives). Everything would be fine. It must have been a matter of miscommunication.

My mission this trip was to contact Vietnamese and American businesses in HCMC (old Saigon) and Hanoi, telling them about the Business Certificate Program that Baldwin Wallace College intended to initiate in both cities the next September. Owing to the political and economic conditions in Vietnam, Vietnamese college students and skilled laborers had not been educated in free enterprise and modern management practices. They were not well prepared to work with multinational companies engaging in business in Southeast Asia. Although business and marketing strategies of companies may vary greatly, all companies doing business in Vietnam need well-educated Vietnamese managers—local talent who understand western business practices and intercultural nuances.

Baldwin Wallace intended to establish the Business Certificate Program, and cement a working relationship with the University of Economics in HCMC and with the Vietnam National Institution of Open Learning and Distance Education in Hanoi. The two institutions were to supply classroom space, computer hardware, the recruiting and personal profiles of participants, as well as the management of the TOEFL tests (a test, if one passes, he can take courses in English for credit), since classes would be in English. Helping to arrange housing was also an expectation. Baldwin Wallace would fly in two professors every two months, supply the software and the necessary textbooks, and give the Certificate, plus undergraduate credit.

Before the phone call, thinking about this opportunity to promote the program had filled me with excitement. I felt confident I had the credibility as well as the competence to make it a reality and, in so doing, enable U.S. businesses to connect in Vietnam. I assumed I'd be able to cut through the red tape and make it easier for U.S. businesses to catch up to their competitors from other nations. I fully expected them to recognize the many benefits possible from paying tuition for Vietnamese participants, who would be potential employees.

The phone call was a jolt. I now wondered how I could serve as "the great connector" for U.S. business interests in Vietnam when I couldn't even obtain a visa to enter the country. Despite the positive self-talk and visioning, I worried, fighting feelings of being rejected. At 2 a.m. Sunday morning, I checked into the Nana Hotel in Bangkok, exhausted. Still, sleep did not come easily.

By 9 a.m., I was faxing my Vietnamese friends, Dr. Xuong and Father Phan Khac Tu. I asked them to notify my colleague Bob Dalton and my dear friend Thai Bach Lien of my predicament. Bob and I had been partners with Dr. Patrick Doan Van Toai the last two years in facilitating workshops about free market economies throughout Vietnam. The previous July we had taught at eight different universities in five cities.

Bach Lien Thai was our exceptional translator and interpreter. Although she weighed less than a hundred pounds, when it came to sheer determination and single-mindedness, this wisp of a woman brought to mind a ten-ton truck racing relentlessly downhill. If she'd take on my case, I told myself, we'd surely succeed.

Next I called Jim DeHarpporte, whom I knew when he was a lad in St. Helena's parish. I had not seen him in nearly thirty years. Recently, Jim had been assigned to the Bangkok office of Catholic Relief Services, with responsibilities for Indochina. He'd contacted me after seeing me on videotape the previous January promoting business in Vietnam, and we made plans to meet. That evening Jim and his dear wife took me to dinner, giving comfort as I waited impatiently for replies to my morning faxes. We spent the evening catching up on old times, while enjoying marvelous Thai delicacies.

Next morning, Bob Dalton called me from Ho Chi Minh City. He said he and Bach Lien Thai were working furiously on the visa and that my trying situation had "nothing to do with me personally. The Interior Minister had freaked," Bob explained, "when the embargo was lifted, fearing an onslaught of U.S. spies. Every U.S. passportee was suspect." He added that Father Phan Khac Tu had written a letter in my support to a close friend high up in the immigration department. "Don't lose heart."

At least I wasn't blacklisted. My situation substantiated once more that security police in many nations are suspicious, untrusting, and cautious beyond reason. I was shocked, though, to learn Vietnamese security officials still believed Jane Fonda was a CIA agent. From their narrow frame of reference, they couldn't understand that anyone would be allowed the freedom to do what she did in coming to Vietnam during the war without U.S. government cooperation—and if Jane Fonda was suspect, certainly less significant figures of the antiwar movement were as well.

I tend to err at the opposite end of the trust continuum. Nonetheless, the rest of Monday and all of Tuesday and Wednesday dragged on without response. My spirits were sinking.

Finally, Wednesday night a fax came from Bach Lien announcing that a visa had been secured. I quickly purchased a ticket on Thai Airways for Saturday morning, to be assured of having a seat.

Eager with anticipation I made three trips to the Vietnamese embassy on Thursday to have my passport stamped with the visa— but each time I returned empty-handed. A matronly staffer at the embassy insisted, "Permission had to come directly from Ho Chi Minh City through official channels." She would not accept the faxed statement from Bach Lien, though it certainly looked official. I sent more faxes to Bach Lien. My efforts to call Bob were unsuccessful—he had changed hotels and the new number would not connect, not an unusual occurrence in that city.

Thanks to jet lag, I woke each morning at 3 a.m. I used the early hours to prepare classes scheduled for my return on April 5 and for writing. At 6:30 a.m. I jogged or did group Tai Chi at the lovely Lumpini Park, about a mile from the hotel. Surprisingly, more Chinese than Thais were present. We were all searching, if not for the fountain of youth at least for extended health and calm. Doing yoga in the hotel room also brought peace of mind.

Friday night before dinner I finally spoke via the telephone with Bob and Bach Lien. They assured me the permission for the visa was sent out that afternoon, and I could receive the stamp of approval at the Vietnamese embassy Saturday morning. Bob was leaving for the U.S. Sunday noon but expected to see me before then, promising to fill me in on the details about the refusal.

I planned on getting to the embassy by 9:30 a.m., in order to catch a flight to Ho Chi Minh City Saturday afternoon. I knew catching Thai Air's flight leaving at 10:40 was impossible, but I'd heard Vietnamese Airlines had a plane every day at 2 p.m. and seats would be available, since "cautious folks" preferred Thai Air or Air France. Hope began to fade as I sat waiting at the embassy, my patience being tested again.

To the Westerner, every perceived nerve-wracking issue receives a common Thai response: "No problem," generally followed with a friendly giggle. The Westerner, for his own state of mind, needs to recognize that the giggle is friendly. At 11:30 a.m. with the bright red visa stamped onto my passport, I rushed back to my hotel. The Thai plane had left an hour ago. The travel agent in the hotel lobby insisted that I needed to go to the central Thai ticket office at the Hotel Asia and exchange the ticket to fly with another carrier. Instantly I got in touch with how much I hate rules. Questions buzzed through my head, Can't I just call? No, one must go in person. What about the customer? But I obeyed and imitated Thai behavior rather than the American confrontational style.

I raced across town to the Asia Hotel only to find the airlines office closed for lunch. "Be back at 1:15 p.m.," the sign informed me. *Maybe it was time to giggle.* If I were with a friend, my friend might counsel me to see the humor in the situation. All alone, however, I found nothing to laugh about. I resorted to talking to myself to manage my frustration.

I leaned against the door to be first in line after the lunch break, and tried to focus on the Asian point of view. Usually in the U.S. these things tended to go quite smoothly. Waiting is at a minimum, yet we tend to complain at the least inconvenience. In Asia, the belief prevails that forces in nature and in the environment control human beings. What happens is the way it is supposed to happen. Hence little effort is extended for making change.

Events are more easily accepted.
A more peaceful view, but such behavior is hardly
efficient. Still, the thought calmed me.

At 1:15 p.m. the three-person staff returned. Through laborious translation, I was again informed that the Thai plane had already left and that Sunday and Monday's flights were filled. They could confirm a seat on Tuesday's plane. Exasperated, I asked, "What about Air France?" Unfortunately, its plane was leaving in an hour and a half, not enough time to get back to the hotel, grab my luggage and make it to the airport.

Besides, the Air France ticket office closed at noon on Saturday and would not be open again until Monday. The next plane was not until Monday at 3 p.m. Air Vietnam apparently did not exist for the Thai agent, and my questions about its flights went unanswered. I didn't insist, since she was doing me a favor by rewriting the ticket, plus I had a long line of people waiting behind me.

Back in the taxi, I paid a quick visit to Air Vietnam's ticket office to find it closed until Monday. Apparently I was stuck. I paid the driver $12 for his efforts, and back at the hotel, added up the expenses. The many faxes and long distance phone calls amounted to $119. Seven nights at the hotel, excluding food, came to $280.

My thoughts turned to spending Palm Sunday in Bangkok. Actually, I was growing attracted to the idea. With the kindness of Jim DeHarpporte's family, the city was beginning to grow on me. There was much to learn in Thailand, if I opened my mind and my eyes.

It's amazing what happens when one stops striving to swim against the current.

After Palm Sunday Eucharist, Jim suggested we drive to the airport to see if there were a seat available on the 2 p.m. Air Vietnam flight.

Seat 38A on flight 109 was empty and waiting for me. In bidding me bon voyage, Jim offered to fax Father Tu to see if someone could meet my plane and shepherd me to the Ecumenical Guest House on Tu Xuong Street. His wife invited me to stay with them on my return Easter Sunday, before I left for the States. Thus, nearly a week late but with a joyous heart, I took flight for Vietnam.

After seven days of waiting, the one-hour journey seemed unusually short. Since I arrived only minutes after Jim had sent the fax, I was on my own. I grabbed a meter taxi; surprisingly it measured the cost in U.S. dollars rather than Vietnamese dong, a total of $5.40. I gave the driver a five-dollar bill together with a Vietnamese bill (5,000 dong, about 50 cents) left over from my previous visit, then gave him another 5,000 dong as a tip for his conscientious, safe service. Grinning with pleasure, he eagerly accepted the tip. The next day, exchanging $100 U.S., I received 1,092,000 "dong." It challenged my creativity, as it came in two huge packs of 5,000 dong bills each—I felt very rich indeed as I stuffed the money into my two bulging front pockets.

Sunday night was quiet. The sparsely equipped room in the guesthouse was clean and inviting but had no hot water. However, the cold showers refreshed me, bringing relief from the 90-degree heat. With Monday's dawn the race began: companies to be contacted, appointments to make, dinner with Bach Lien.

Over dinner, she explained that one of two things most likely had happened. Either the Thai travel agency that Sid Loh used somehow lost my visa application, or the Vietnamese agency refused to seek the visa because the Thais were slow in paying their bills for previous visas. Rather than admit the error or failure, the Thai agent told Sid that I was "blacklisted and should not come."

Even with Bach Lien's steel will, it took five days to move the mountain of bureaucracy. Rules are rules. Fearful, no one takes responsibility for a decision but passes the buck to another level. Everything is checked and rechecked. Each official fears the consequences of error or going beyond one's authority.

One gratifying thought was that, as Bach Lien said, "If you had been truly blacklisted, you would not be in Vietnam today or ever."

Tuesday, with the help of a first-year University student, whom I knew only as Lam, I visited the offices of KLM, Dutch Airlines. The Dutch were handling all the recruitment and training of Vietnamese personnel for themselves and Northwest Airlines. The regional manager explained that as a foreign carrier, KLM was unable to hire Vietnamese right off the street. Government rules demand that KLM obtain employees through Vietnam Airlines or through a government employment agency (Forsco).

Looking as though he badly needed a vacation, the manager went on to describe his continuing frustration: "What Vietnam Airlines gives they can bloody well take away." Investing in the training and education of employees, as our Baldwin Wallace program advocates, makes the staff more marketable, tempting Vietnam Airlines to take such individuals back and send them to another carrier, at a higher salary.

"You see," he pointed out, "foreign businesses don't pay the employees directly but, in KLM's case, send the wages to Vietnam Airlines, a government-owned enterprise that keeps 60 percent and pay the workers only 40 percent." Forsco followed the same procedure, he assured me.

I speculated that the policy might be intended to keep workers' salaries at even levels, preventing them from deserting Vietnamese businesses and running off to work for foreigners—or to control inflation. I wanted to see the positive or at least understand the other side. Whatever the reasons, the information put a dent in my expectations. I could see that, if these practices were common, international organizations would have little motivation to send local Vietnamese employees to our certificate program.

We visited several businesses, talking with managers. Most responded positively and promised to get back to me after translating and reflecting on Baldwin Wallace's brochure about training programs.

No time to fret. Turning my attention to Vietnamese firms, I spent Holy Week contacting a dozen or so firms. The meetings were cordial at each organization, but there were no commitments. Bach Lien confided that neither the foreign or Vietnamese businesses were accustomed to invest so heavily in the "people side of enterprise." I was presenting a new concept in Vietnam.

Moreover, Bach Lien argued, "The price of your program *was too high*. Focus on the student consumer, rather than the employer."

She advised, to cut the cost use Vietnamese professors, supervised by Baldwin Wallace's staff. The College could be responsible for the curriculum design, texts, and testing; the Vietnamese could handle the facilitation, and the students would be the beneficiaries.

Deflated, I asked her to describe her ideas in a proposal that I'd take to the dean at Baldwin Wallace. Getting our college's foot in the door, even in a small way, might be advantageous. Once we were accepted, we could move to more extensive programs.

This was hard feedback for me to swallow, and my dream appeared shattered. At the same time, although Bach Lien had never worked nor studied in a non-Communist country, I trusted her judgment of the situation in Vietnam.

Early Thursday morning the Vice Rector of the University of Economics, Dr. Nguyen Than Xuong, called requesting that we meet at 10 a.m. and offered to send a car for me. In early January he had been a guest in my home in Ohio, and on that occasion had met our college's dean. He'd also spoken in Management and Economics classes.

Business finished, now it was time for enjoyment. Plunked on another motorbike, this time Dr. Xuong's, I set off with him for a delicious Vietnamese lunch. He apologized for the restaurant's simplicity, but assured me it had the best food in all of Ho Chi Minh City.

After lunch I visited the HCMC Export Processing Zone. During a tour of a Taiwanese factory, on land set aside for foreign investors, the Director Mr. Nguyen Chon Trung, proudly explained that "export-oriented business will be granted a four-year tax holiday." As yet, he admitted, they had no U.S. investors, asking eagerly, "How can we attract U.S. investors?"

Undaunted by my frustration, he changed the subject and asked how to approach the American investor from the psychological perspective. Still fixated on my Bangkok ordeal, I tried again. "I know the Vietnamese are very patient people. Americans are not. Anything you can do to speed the process will help immensely." I continued, "Americans hate negative surprises. When Vietnamese say "yes," meaning "I understand," Americans usually interpret that to mean agreement. They then expect results from the perceived agreement. When what they expect does not happen, Americans are surprised and become irritated."

"This problem can be solved," I advised. "When you say "yes," simply add, "I understand," or "I agree." The Director nodded, which I interpreted as "understanding." He then expressed interest in cooperating for the success of the Baldwin Wallace educational program and for his investment project, because, he said "the foreign investor here will need educated managers."

I genuinely liked him, his probing questions, openness, and willingness to listen to my diatribe. I think, too, that I identified with him in the huge challenges we both faced. He requested and I agreed to call him when I returned to Vietnam the next August. As we parted, with a twinkle in his eye he urged me to counsel my American investor friends to be more patient with the Vietnamese.

Friday morning's meeting with the University of Economics Rector went surprisingly well. I had feared some difficulty since I'd failed from the beginning to obtain his support for our program. A thoughtful man with friendly eyes, Professor Tien expressed great interest in Baldwin Wallace's International MBA (IMBA) program. He was interested in instituting both the IMBA and the Business Certificate Program.

I suggested that attempting to do the two simultaneously might be overwhelming. He agreed; then suggested we could do a Business Certificate Program first, in preparation for the IMBA, saying that perhaps the process would serve as a possible weeding out of the less capable. He described the Business Certificate Program as a "short course," but I didn't understand him clearly.

I was encouraged when he assured me that program graduates would not be taken away from companies that paid their tuition. "The participant employees and their employers will be asked to sign a statement," he offered, "promising to remain with the sponsoring company for at least two years." Then he asked, "Is the Baldwin Wallace proposal open to amendments?"

Obviously pleased with my "of course" response, the Rector asked if I had time that day to work with a University Committee on a joint proposal, since he knew of my scheduled departure on Sunday.

Anxious to obtain the University's commitment, I answered, "Yes." An interesting way to spend Good Friday afternoon, I thought, facetiously, wishing I could go to the liturgy instead. Once we sat down, it was immediately obvious that they were worried that the cost of the Certificate Program would threaten its very success, and sought opportunities to limit the price.

I did my best to explain that many foreign companies expected—it was in their self-interest—to invest in their employees' education because the work of competent employees paid rich dividends. But my Vietnamese colleagues remained skeptical. I sensed that my arguments weren't registering. Retreating, I asked the committee to write a proposal describing what they envisioned would work, and promised to champion their ideas with the Dean Mark Collier the next week. With that, Dr. Xuong commissioned the chair of the Business Department to write the proposal, and for Bach Lien to translate.

**The proposal arrived Saturday evening as promised.
A quick reading demonstrated to me once again
*how difficult intercultural communication is.***

Apparently my friends objected to the cost because they thought the entire program was simply 60 hours, whereas I thought I'd communicated that each course had 60 class hours. I concluded that with the Dean's help we could save the project—we'd clarify the issues and fax a proposal that would be approved.

Later that evening, I was invited to concelebrate with Bishop Lam at the Easter Vigil in the Notre Dame Cathedral—a profound

and special time for me. The Cathedral was packed, people literally standing in the aisles for a ceremony that lasted nearly two
and a half hours, witnessing to a people's faith that had withstood
decades of communism. How appropriate, I reflected, to end my
mission celebrating the Resurrection.

In the end, Vietnam's Economic University declined Baldwin
Wallace's proposal, considering it too expensive. Our president
Neal Malicky accepted the result, suggesting that our idea was
ahead of the curve.

> "Not my will but thine be done Lord" came to mind
> as I reflected on the result. In addition, my sports
> experiences reminded me, "You can't win them all."

CHAPTER 16

Teaching Opportunity in Thailand (2002)

Assumption University

U ntil the Clinton Administration reestablished diplomatic relations with unified Vietnam in 1995, the easiest way to receive a visa to enter Vietnam was through the Vietnamese Embassy in Bangkok, Thailand. It took three or four days each time, which afforded me the pleasant opportunity to explore, not only Bangkok but also other areas of the country. I traveled throughout Thailand during the late 1980s and '90s.

I felt welcomed everywhere in Thailand. The Thai people, 65 million strong, exhibited a genuine curiosity for internationalists. Happy faces greeted me everywhere. On the sky train, which had replaced the streetcars of the '70s, young Thais, both female and male, would compete to be the first to leap up and give their seats to a mother entering with small children.

I was given the same courtesy, based on my age. At first, surprised and embarrassed, my tendency was to resist. I quickly acquiesced, however, remembering from childhood that to accept acts of kindness and other gifts was a sign of gratitude, even if the gesture wasn't treasured. In Thai culture, moreover, *refusal* causes both the giver and the receiver to lose face. Thus accepting a seat allowed the young Thais to experience the joy of showing unconditional kindness.

On each visit, I noticed many universities, more than in Indochina or even China. The bright neon signs advertising the universities caught my attention and imagination. I wondered what it would be like to facilitate the learning of Thai students, compared with other students in Asia and the States. I grew more and more interested, but simply dropping by and announcing my availability didn't seem appropriate.

In the summer of 2001, after I'd presented a paper on organizational change at an Organization Development (OD) conference held just north of Chicago, another OD consultant approached me. She shared her teaching experience at Assumption University, operated by the Brothers of St. Gabriel. Teaching abroad had brought her intellectual stimulation and joy; she liked Asian students.

The school, however, wanted international professors to teach full semesters (12 weeks) each time. To be absent that long, she confessed, meant losing some or all of her business clients. Companies expect an almost-instant response to a perceived need, thus she could risk being away a short time, but not twelve weeks.

For some ten years, I had been teaching intensive three-week courses in Vietnam and China for Southern California University for Professional Students (SCUPS). She asked if she might participate in this intriguing academic effort so I shared Dean Doan Van Toai's address, and sent him a letter of recommendation. The Dean coordinated my Asia classes. But alas, he needed finance and accounting professors, rather than organizational behaviorists.

As I was about to receive a sabbatical leave, I was free to teach a whole semester in Thailand. I asked her if she might give me a contact at Assumption University. She did, and shortly thereafter, I made contact with Dr. Vinai and explained my availability beginning in January 2002, and my eagerness to teach Organizational Behavior in Assumption's Master in Business Administration program.

I didn't reveal my priesthood, because I didn't want the decision-makers at this Catholic institution to feel the least bit obligated to accept me because I was a cleric. Also, I had learned that U.S. students accepted my credibility more when I stressed my business rather than cleric background. Because most of what I teach is countercultural, that is, contrary to what Asian students already hold fast—I need as much trust and willingness to consider new leadership and management ideas as I could muster.

Dean Dr. Vinai responded positively. I arrived at Assumption University shortly after the New Year in 2002. Because Assumption was the first and only English teaching institution of higher learning in Thailand, it had the reputation among many academics and the traditional elite of being the Harvard or Oxford of Thailand.

Thai alumni went on to become successful government officials and business leaders, largely owing to their competence in English, the language of choice in politics and business (much to the consternation of the French). The Thai alumni in turn sent their own sons and daughters to Assumption. Neighboring countries such as China and the Philippines followed suit.

In my first class meeting, I customarily organize students into five-person study teams, careful to maintain a balance of gender and nationality. Strong study habits and self-discipline, plus the ability to plan ahead, were an early benefit, especially for the Thai students as the Chinese taught their teammates how to study.

Despite their collective background, working in teams was a new experience for all, and they relished the opportunity.

Thai students place a high value on face-saving (*rak sa nah*), that is, taking care to not cause themselves *or others* embarrassment. For them it is a value that supersedes honesty. A Thai student can never give negative verbal or written feedback, even if solicited. When I ask how they like the course, and if there is anything I can do better, the answer is always: "The course is just fine and nothing could make it better." Hence, the only way I can learn how Thai students actually view the learning experience is to observe their behavior.

Participants who enjoy and appreciate the relevance of my facilitation arrive early for class (despite onerous traffic) and stay to the finish, often asking additional questions. Those less enthused arrive late for class, and leave early, or they simply miss class.

Thais almost never say "No." Such negativity would be an embarrassment to themselves and to others; one would lose face. This behavior extends to doing business in Thailand. For example, if approaching a Thai firm with a proposal to produce 1,000 widgets, a wise business owner will investigate the proposer's background of capability, because the proposer would lose face if he or she admitted they lacked the necessary expertise.

Because the focus of MBA learning was to become effective business leaders in Asia, my facilitating of student learning did not deal with religious matters. Belief in God at this moment in their lives had little relevance. The Buddhist saying is relevant, "When the student is ready, the teacher will appear." As a behavioral scientist who was (secretly) a priest, I attended to the way students' upbringing influenced their mental models and behaviors. Content with enabling them to be ethical businesspersons, I perceived I was preparing good ground in which eventually the Christian faith could bear fruit.

The Dean made no effort to get to know me personally, nor as far as I could determine, any of the other international professors. I assumed from his behavior that, if he had his way, he would prefer Thai faculty; diversity didn't appear to be a high value. He managed the Business Department from a distance and made it "all business." He made no reference to his spiritual life or religion, which I thought odd, given he was a member of a religious order.

Dean Vinai assigned me two large classes, one in the daytime (about 45 students) and one in the evening (over 50 students) of mostly Thai students who worked during the day. I was greatly pleased with the growth of one particular study team. Their final research paper was so well done that I helped them analyze the data and facilitated the paper's publication in an academic journal.

Burapha University

Near the end of the semester, one of the Assumption professors who, like most others, moonlighted at another university in order to provide for his family, informed me that Burapha University was about to inaugurate an English doctoral program in Business Administration (DBA). They were seeking to hire an international professor with a doctoral degree to head up the program. Would I be interested in the position? Eager for a new challenge and an opportunity to influence business professors in behavioral science, I responded, "Yes."

A meeting was arranged with Burapha's Academic Dean Dr. Suda Suwannapirom and her young associate Dr. Adisak Chandprapalert. The dean's intelligence and entrepreneurial spirit impressed me, and I also trusted her associate, who proved to be very supportive whenever he was available.

From the outset it was clear they were eager to have me sign on, despite my limitations (unskilled in statistics, with a dislike for technology). Although the pay was minimal—25,000 baht per month, $700 U.S. dollars (my rent was 20,000 baht per month)—I was expected to work only four days per month. This schedule suggested they wanted a rubber stamp rather than a leader.

"Could I join the last four days of one month with the first four days of the next month?" I asked. They acquiesced. I readily agreed, showing off my weakness because it was such a joy to experience being wanted and needed.

During the next eight years I dedicated myself to developing a credible doctoral program, arriving in early January each year and remaining into May. I then returned for two weeks in August and another two weeks in November.

To accommodate the two weeks in November, I had to arrange for a substitute teacher to cover one of my classes at Baldwin Wallace because I continued to teach Micro Organizational Behavior in the Executive MBA program during the fall. During the period of absence from Thailand, I guided operations via the

Internet, which process resulted in my overcoming some of my aversion to technology.

One of my major objectives was to enable Thai professors, staff, and students to gain respect for behavioral science in regard to organizational leadership. Working in the classroom and modeling behavior outside, I was determined to have my Asian friends appreciate the role that awareness of emotions plays in being competent, effective leaders. I achieved the goal only slightly.

I face almost the same challenge with American executives, but far less so with Brazilians. The Brazilians readily understand that thoughts affect the way we feel and emotions influence our thinking. I always point out (to the dismay of my American and Asian students) that, without self-awareness when grading papers, my tiredness negatively impacts a student's grade. Feelings of joy have the opposite effect.

When in Bangkok, I held monthly board meetings in order to continue to influence the process and to encourage the organization to work as a team. Suda must have approved; periodic raises topped off at 40,000 baht ($1,400 U.S.) per month, plus an additional 100,000 baht for each course I facilitated. Of course, my apartment rent also skyrocketed to 35,000 baht per month, absorbing much of my raise.

As at Assumption University, acceptance into the program required participants to be able to speak, read, and write English. Nevertheless, because English was their second language, the dissertations became a major challenge. Many were reluctant to get an English tutor or editor, despite my pleas. I did all I could to help, but it put great pressure on my time and patience as it often required correcting the English to figure out what was being communicated.

Later, I came to understand this was a cultural expectation of one's teacher who, in turn, receives a love as for a parent. In addition, although the doctoral students demonstrated competence in mathematics and statistics, once the data was compiled, the students found it a major challenge to analyze the data in order to understand the implications of their research.

I found myself working with each DBA candidate in much the same way my beloved professor Don Wolfe, my dissertation mentor fifty years before, assisted me. My advisees and I labored diligently and seemingly forever. In the end, I was proud of the students' efforts and achievements.

Moving On

With a change of presidents at the university in 2011, a new academic dean was appointed to replace Dr. Suda, who herself had been a candidate for president. A policy change ensued. I was informed that, if I wanted to remain an administrator, I would need to live in Thailand fulltime. Nonetheless, I couldn't quarrel with the new policy itself; it made good sense to have administrators present fulltime. So I retired. Yet I continued to return to Thailand each winter, until 2015, attracted by the friendly, easy-going culture of *mai pen rai*, "Everything is okay, don't worry," reminiscent of my days in Berkeley in the 1960s, and a newly found love of solitude.

Many of the challenges I've faced throughout my lifetime are still very much with me. I'm still searching for inner peace, for creative relationships with others, and for the experience of God. Therefore, a major reason I'm drawn to Thailand each winter is friendships I've developed with the Thai people, and with internationalists.

Thailand's Political Turmoil

On September 19, 2006, a nonviolent coup d'état occurred in Thailand while the democratically elected Prime Minister, Thaksin Shinawatra, was in New York City to address the United Nations. His victory in 2001, and re-election in 2005 by an even larger margin, signaled the political rise of the country's poor, long-silenced rural majority located mostly in the northeast part of the nation. Thaksin, himself a billionaire in the telecommunications industry, said he believed that by helping the poor help themselves—via government-invested tax monies—ultimately the whole country would benefit, including the affluent.

Having visited the northeast both before and after Thaksin's election, I found the difference between the time before his election and afterward remarkable.

The infrastructure improved measurably. Newly paved roads and new school buildings with more teachers were clearly in evidence. Many more people were eating in restaurants and shopping. By 2006, I was told that universal health care was in effect. Now, not only the affluent could receive the services of doctors and dentists, but the poor as well.

The profound improvements the population experienced in the northeast were also felt among the taxi drivers, manual workers, and small business people in Bangkok who credited Thaksin. All of these situations combined to give Thaksin an overwhelming re-election. From the point of view of others, Thaksin was accused of corruption and secreting money in his maid and driver's names. In his enemy's eyes, he began to show contempt for the 1997 Constitution, which gave Thailand a shot at real democracy in action. According to a friend, Ed Vargo, Thaksin had no grasp of the kind of compromise democracy needs, any more than did his opposition leader Suthep. Thaksin was accused of dismantling a structure involving local people from the South that were dealing with the insurgency there, in favor of central control—the insurgency took on new life, and we had the horror of the Tak Bai massacre. The demonstration was in Southern Thailand city of Tak Bai, protesting the detention of six men. Police shot seven people, plus 78 more died in transit to a prison camp because they suffocated on overcrowded trucks. Thai newspapers took on the character of the media in the U.S.—a steady flow of photos of Thaksin.

In my view, Thaksin's mistake was to send in the military, as President Bush did in Iraq.

I ask myself, why such hatred of Prime Minister Thaksin Shinawatra? A major reason, I suspect, is on account of the sex trade. It is big business in Thailand, bringing in huge profits. When the U.S. pulled out of Vietnam, the Thai sex industry faced a cut in profits, since no more U.S. soldiers were descending on Bangkok or Pattaya for rest and recreation (R&R). A rescue package was nevertheless close at hand. The sex business, an unofficial partnership with the tourist industry and the government, developed a plan to attract tourists (as clients) to replace military personnel. As millions came, principally from Japan, Europe, and the United States, young, beautiful, submissive, and cheap Thai girls were needed. Where to find them? The obvious place was northeast Thailand where poverty is rampant. Girls and young women were easily available from poor, actually destitute, families who were barely surviving. After 25 years of exploiting the poor in that region, the profiteers saw Prime Minister Thaksin pouring money into the northeast, raising the standard of living and making the trafficking of women more difficult and more expensive. No wonder those profiting from commercial sex were enraged.

The military moved to delegitimize Thaksin's government with a coup, and the country's Supreme Court banned his Thai Rak political party. His political enemies, who controlled the judiciary, tried and convicted him in absentia. Thaksin has been living in exile since the trial, largely in Dubai, with sojourns to Britain, Germany, Montenegro, and Nicaragua.

Shortly after the trial in 2007, the Asian depression struck. Thailand's economy went into a tailspin. Buildings stood abandoned, half-finished, becoming terrible eyesores. The constitution was rewritten, allowing 73 senators to be appointed rather than elected, which seemed anti-democratic to me. The international community intensified its pressure on the military regime to return the nation to its democratic ideals if it expected further foreign investments. Reluctantly, the military held an election. Thaksin's colleague and supporter, Samak Sundaravej, was elected prime minister, a big setback for the military.

Before long, the political opposition representing the affluent and elite took to the streets in protest. To stand in solidarity, they wore Yellow Shirts. In short order, they moved their demonstration to the airport, occupying the beautiful new facility that Thaksin had championed and made operational ahead of schedule to the amazement of thousands. For this success he was accused of corruption—his enemies argued that Thaksin couldn't have achieved it without being corrupt.

The Yellow Shirt's airport occupation brought passenger and freight transportation to a halt. First the Prime Minister Samak ordered the police chief, and then the top army general, to disperse the demonstrators. Neither complied. Nothing happened.

I was in Bangkok at the time (2008) for my November visit. Beyond surprised, I was shocked—not even food and water had been cut off from the demonstrators, which would have forced them to nonviolently vacate the airport. Fearful of not being able to get out of Thailand to fulfill my course responsibilities at Baldwin Wallace University, I considered making a mad dash by rental car to Malaysia or possibly Phnom Penh, Cambodia.

Other people had already thought of that, and planes were full with backed-up reservations. It could be weeks before getting a seat. Thankfully, a Northwest Airlines employee that I'd become friendly over the years, told me about an airport built by the Americans during the Vietnam War that had been abandoned. The airport was resurrected, enabling Northwest Airlines to continue in business. A long cab ride, a quick takeoff, with a stop in Hong Kong, got me to the United States, breathless, just in time for class.

Back in Thailand, Prime Minister Samak, lacking control, capitulated and resigned. The military regime appointed Abhisit Vejjajiva, who claimed to be impartial, as prime minister. He was hardly impartial, however, and his policies favored the traditional elite and affluent, the Yellow Shirts.

In 2010, demonstrators wearing red shirts, members of the Pheu Thai political party, who are a direct descendant of Thaksin's Rak Thai party, took to the streets in protest. Most Red Shirts are working-class Thais—the social activists who believe that the people of Thailand deserve a political and judicial system that ensures universal human rights and justice. They include employees in industries and services such as restaurants and hotels, unregistered laborers, farmers, taxi drivers, and the poor. Although it is difficult to give an exact figure of the total number of Red Shirts, there are millions, and their supporters number in the tens of millions.

Instead of occupying the airport, these demonstrators congregated around five-star hotels and upscale department stores. Tourist business plummeted, and the new prime minister, pressured by the business community, called out the army. Strikingly unusual for Thailand, the nonviolent protest turned violent, and dozens of people were killed.

Ultimately an asset-freeze ended the political unrest.

Once again, the people of Thailand and the international community demanded that democratic elections be held. The military regime finally agreed in 2011. Thaksin's younger sister, Yingluck Shinawatra, a longtime executive in her brother's communications firm, threw her hat into the ring. A member of the Pheu Thai party, she was elected prime minister with a considerable parliamentary majority. Opponents grumbled that her criminal brother would now be running the government from Dubai, with Yingluck merely a figurehead.

Despite doubts, Yingluck handled the leadership responsibilities well. She received high marks for the way she managed the terrible floods in 2012, especially protecting Bangkok. The economy continued to improve, and tourists were beginning to return in high numbers.

In October 2013, however, Yingluck apparently made a fatal mistake. She proposed an amnesty law that would pardon opposition leaders, including her military-appointed predecessor Abhisit and his deputy minister Suthep Thaungsuban. Both were facing murder charges for the killing of a Red Shirt demonstrator in 2010. In addition, the amnesty would free the jailed protestors from that event, and enable her brother Thaksin to return freely to Thailand.

Believing in forgiveness, I greeted her proposition with utmost joy. I prayed it would heal the rift between the two parties, which I assumed was her intention. She further sought a constitutional amendment that would make the senate, 73 of whose members are appointed, a fully elected body. This democratic move made total sense to me; I applauded her effort to extend democracy.

It was too, too much, however, for her political opponents, members of the People's Democratic Reform Council (PDRC). Hatred for her and her brother Thaksin that was beyond my imagination erupted and launched a wave of street protests.

In an effort to defuse the situation, Yingluck dissolved the parliament and called for a parliamentary election on February 2, 2014. Immediately her proposal was rejected. The PDRC threatened to bring down the government. The U.S. State Department warned Americans not to travel to Thailand. U.S. citizens already in the country were urged to stock up on food and bottled water and to remain indoors, avoiding the streets.

Ignoring the warning, I arrived in Bangkok on January 22, 2014. After locating an apartment, I went searching for the demonstrators. I found Yellow Shirts in eight major thoroughfares obstructing city traffic. I was surprised to see that the majority were women ages 45 to 60; few students were in evidence. Wisely, Yingluck didn't call out the police or army to remove the protestors. Instead, the police were ordered to protect the Yellow Shirt demonstrators; this action pleased me no end.

When I was a protestor against the Vietnam War, we made our point nonviolently, and then went home. There was no intention to bring down the U.S. government. My heart sank at the broadcast intent to not only bring down the government, but to hurt the tourist industry and all who depended on it for survival.

The protestors camped out at eight city intersections, and the protests dragged on into the third month. They were supplied with showers, portable toilets, washing machines, a medical center, nightly entertainment, and a host of security guards. The demonstrators demanded that Prime Minister Yingluck step down, and that a council and "neutral" prime minister be appointed. Appointed by whom? Well, the military as before.

Voters on February 2, eager to elect a new parliament, were blocked by protestors at 11 percent of the voting stations where they threatened and attacked voters, preventing them from voting. As expected, not enough votes were achieved to convene a new parliament.

> **I prayed that Thailand would not break out into a civil war and go the way of Syria and the Ukraine.**

As I moved about the city, I saw that Thailand had changed virtually overnight. Smiles had disappeared, replaced by angry or stoic faces. I heard personal attacks of vile racist, sexist, dehumanizing insults hurled across the political divide. Everywhere, "face-breaking" had replaced "face-saving." Political leaders, to my surprise, remained silent as their followers engaged in uncharacteristic behavior; they didn't seem to realize that the equal standing of all citizens was being threatened as political enemies verbally attacked each other.

I suppose my surprise was unwarranted. What disturbs me, however, is the fear that average Thais are manifesting. Losing trust in one another, they dare not admit or discuss their political preferences. Instead of smiling at strangers or rushing to get up and give their seats to old folks or women with children, eyes are locked down on the floor or on their iPhones and iPads, with wires dangling from their ears. *Trusting behavior has given way to terror.*

What Would I Do if Asked to Help Thailand?

Lying on my bed in my Thai apartment, gazing up at the dark ceiling on the last day of February, I wondered, "What would I do if I were asked to help Thailand?" I began to imagine a process leading to compromise.

To start with, if I were called to help as an Organizational Development Consultant, I'd visit the Yellow Shirts and then the

Red Shirts. I'd actively listen to each, and then I would listen some more. Next, I would return to visit the Yellow Shirts in their headquarters (all who would be willing to meet) and listen even more, followed by my listening again to the Red Shirts.

Each time, I would listen intently, identifying with each group. I would try to understand their concerns, their fears. I'd endeavor to discover their motivation, and seek to feel what they're feeling. I would acknowledge and sincerely share their suffering. Then I would feed back to them what I perceived I heard, so they could verify whether I truly understood them—my intent would be to understand each group and gain their trust by becoming as one with them as possible.

Next, I'd take a risk. I'd request that each group, in turn, determine among themselves: "What are the fears and concerns that motivate you to behave the way you do? Not *what* you do, but rather your perception of *why* you do it." I'd ask each group to record their perceptions. I'd ask them to do their best to put themselves in the skins of the Thai people in the other group, to seek to understand what the concerns, fears, and motivations might be which lead them to behave as they do. Again, I'd ask them to record their findings.

Most important, I would then request that each group do their best to describe how the other group perceives themselves—that is, what they assume are the other group's concerns, motivations, even fears, if the other group was honest enough to admit them. And again, record the data.

In the end, both groups would have recorded a picture of how they:

1. Perceive our own concerns, fears, and motivations.

2. Assume the other group perceives theirs to be.

3. Guess how the other group perceives themselves.

4. Guess how the other group perceives us.

I would bring the two groups together in one location. Taking turns, each would present in the order above. Presentations would be made without allowing interruption or questions for clarity.

After all eight presentations had been given, I would invite them to ask questions of the other group, *for clarification only*. Then, taking turns, each side would make statements to clarify how they understood the other group's presentations and what they liked about it. Once everyone understood how his or her perceptions compared with how the other group understood the situation, each group would retire on its own and prepare a plan that they envision both groups would accept. Then both groups again would come together to present their vision, followed by dialogue leading to a final vision containing the best elements of both.

Finally, the two groups, having become one group through their agreed-upon vision, would develop an action plan to implement their common vision. My overall intent is for open and respectful dialogue, followed by thoughtful informed deliberation resulting in competent and determined resolution and/or a viable compromise.

"Would this all work?" I asked and then answered myself. "I don't actually know. It's worth a try." I kept remembering the screaming epithets and grenades hurled at children. I posted my process design on an Internet group (LinkedIn) and received two favorable responses, one from an American and one from a Thai. Nothing else.

My time being up, I left Thailand on April 21 with sadness and regrets. Disappointed, I realized I was not in a place where I was able to be of assistance. I concluded that if the Yellow Shirts prevail, I shall fly away with no wish to return.

As Suthep predicted, a week after my departure the (affluent-controlled) courts handed down a series of decisions favorable to the anti-government movement. A number of judges and top government officials handling cases against the government had long-standing antagonistic relationships not only with the prime minister, but also with her party and her family. This conflict diminished public faith in the credibility of the judiciary branch.

On Friday, May 7, 2014, Thailand confronted fresh turmoil and uncertainty after a court (with charges of corruption) ordered, as expected, the country's prime minister and nine of her top ministers to stand down. It was the third time in seven years the elites had forced out a government associated with former premier Thaksin Shinawatra.

Supporters of deposed Yingluck called for a huge rally Saturday, May 17, to protest the ruling by the Constitutional Court, which exercised powers laid out in the constitution the military government wrote after the 2006 coup. Meanwhile, the pro-government group rallied in support of the caretaker government on Aksa Road in Bangkok's western outskirts. They remained there in place. Although the protester groups were separated, they made the military nervous lest they come together and fight.

The leader of the anti-government protesters, Suthep Thaugsuban, told his followers to stage a "final offensive" on Friday, May 16, to achieve their goal of fully ousting the government.

On May 20, the top Thai general declared martial law and invited leaders of both warring sides to come together in an effort to reach a compromise, hosted by the army. With no success after two days, the general lost patience, seized power and arrested all the leaders. He then appointed himself interim prime minister and established a junta called National Council for Peace and Order (NCPO) to govern the nation. He has given no sign that he intends to appoint a neutral person to be Thailand's prime minister or to hold elections.

The prime minister's idea of democracy apparently involves the creation of an unelected congress and a reduction of the role of elected politicians. The royalist elite and their middle-class supporters in Bangkok and the upper south of the nation seemed pleased with the move.

People in the rest of Thailand, most of whom voted consistently for pro-Thaksin political parties in every election since 2001, are alarmed, some threatening revolution. Thankfully, few guns are available in the country, limiting the amount of violence likely to transpire.

The King of Thailand, Bhumibol Adulyadej, turned 87 on Friday, December 5, 2015. Because of his age and health concerns, members of the Thai establishment worried about the future of the monarchy. Several months after the military coup in May, the political elite appeared to be constructing a constitutional infrastructure intended to guarantee their power for the foreseeable future. The King died in October 2016.

Hearing from my friends in Thailand, sadness fills my heart as I continue to pray for them and for Thailand. A society with Thailand's traditions of openness and popular participation, I suspect, will not be reversed. An improved democracy will eventually be Thailand's fate; the sooner, the better. I visualize it in prayer.

CHAPTER 17

Responding to a World Under Threat (2005)

Heading to Palestine in July 2005

I joined the Michigan Peace Team delegation for peace and solidarity for Palestine. The Patriarch Irenaios Skopelitis of Jerusalem's Orthodox Church invited this team of three nuns and four priests—David Smith, Leo Anderson, Peter Doherty and me—to become human shields between the Palestinians and the Jewish settlers as the latter departed from Gaza.

I'd last been in Israel/Palestine in 1982 when I took a group of Baldwin Wallace students on a tour of Israel and Egypt. The Palestinians' sufferings were apparent to me, but in the years since 1982, their hopes for a better life had been dashed again and again.

Flying from Minnesota to Holland, I slept most of the trip. I was exhausted from getting everything possible done before we left. Somehow air travel, especially trips for a political purpose, invoked in me a foreboding urgency, a pressure to put my affairs in order. It wasn't prescience because I had no inkling of what lay before me.

As we got off the plane in Tel Aviv, the capital of Israel, armed soldiers greeted us. We passed through immigration, simply stating that we'd come as religious tourists. We spent an hour searching for a phone in Tel Aviv to call the Michigan Peace Team to let them know we'd landed safely and were on our way to Ecce Homo convent in Jerusalem.

A bearded older man overheard us and offered to take us to Ecce Homo, a familiar place (he claimed), for 220 shekels (over $62). After a side excursion to a moneychanger, we followed him to a van. Suddenly a younger fellow appeared and the elder said good-bye, startling us with his abrupt departure. The young driver ushered us in beside an older couple already seated, and with the driver's girlfriend sitting beside him, we took off on a swift and bouncy ride to Jerusalem, 36 miles from Tel Aviv.

Once in Jerusalem, the driver failed to understand our suggestions and drove in circles, unable to find the Lion's Gate. Finally giving up, he decided to drop the couple at the Ambassador Hotel, but then they refused to pay the amount the driver asked. The driver then advised us to transfer to a nearby cab whose driver said he knew how to get to Ecce Homo.

At Ecce Homo

Our troubles weren't over. Arriving finally at Ecce Homo at 3:30 a.m., even with all our pounding, cab horn blaring, and shouting, we couldn't rouse the doorkeeper for what seemed an hour. My friend Father David Smith said he was willing to sleep on the steps, but the doorkeeper finally appeared, and the first day of our journey to the land of Jesus came to an end.

Our rooms faced the loudspeakers of the minaret/tower a half-block away, giving Smith, he reported, "An excellent opportunity to savor the 4:30 a.m. call to prayer." I was less spiritually attuned this day, out for the count. Church bells woke us both around 8 a.m., and we made our way to the breakfast room. The Ecce Homo convent is a cross between a working Christian community and a hotel, billed as a quiet place for pilgrims to rest from the crowds. In the Muslim quarter, it fronts on the Via Dolorosa, the path on which Jesus carried his cross to Calvary. We ended the day with dinner on the roof, talking theology and politics with another volunteer couple.

Peace was possible, we agreed, but if the peoples of the land were to benefit from the Gaza withdrawal, a way must be found for Israelis and Palestinians to live together.

Unfortunately, on our arrival we learned the withdrawal from Gaza had been delayed by a month, reportedly to avoid the Jewish holiday of Simhat Torah. At this critical juncture, the task of the Michigan Peace Team was to witness to the living conditions and emotional state of the Palestinians and, where possible in our meetings, to enhance their skills in negotiating for better treatment from the Israeli government.

Entering Gaza

On the fourth of July, David and I packed up and took a taxi to Eretz, the checkpoint into Gaza. In the evening, I wrote in my journal that the Israelis were "quite nice," but thorough, as they checked our papers and looked through our suitcases. Our later experiences at checkpoints were less agreeable.

Many Palestinians feared that the withdrawal of the Jewish settlers would bring greater danger, since it's easier to attack a population if your own people aren't among them. And of course they were correct, as history demonstrated. Soon Israel was attacking Gaza by land, sea, and air. Not even children playing on the beach were safe.

By 11:30, we were through the area. Another taxi driver approached us, requesting 50 shekels for a drive to Gaza City. We called our contact, Manuel Musallam, the pastor at Holy Family Church, who gave the man directions.

After two more telephone calls to get more directions, we pulled up at the Latin School, built through the pastor's initiative twelve years before, when, at the request of the Latin Patriarch, he had gone to Gaza to serve a congregation of 200 Catholics. Now he could not leave because he was *a man without a country*. From 1967 to the present, he was unable to obtain official papers (passport), so, he said, "I am not legal anywhere and if I leave Gaza, I won't be able to get back, or stay anywhere else."

The pastor is a heavy man, in failing health and had difficulty walking, but he was outgoing and friendly. He talked with us at length in his office, serving us drinks and shawarma sandwiches, which were delightfully—to me, not David—spicy. The pastor seemed lonely, and was grateful we'd come to see him. The only priest in the Gaza Strip, he had built and continued to run two schools, with about 1,100 students, most of them Muslims. He pleaded with the Patriarch for a priest to assist him, but none would agree to come. They were afraid; it was too dangerous. Even retired cardinals in Jerusalem refused to visit because of the danger. My heart ached for him. He had no priest to hear his confession or give him the sacrament of the sick, should he become ill.

In the evening, we traveled about five miles to Holy Family church for mass. The church was named "Holy Family" because the Catholics here believe it was the place to which as refugees that Mary, Joseph, and Jesus fled to escape King Herod's soldiers. At the time, Gaza was part of Egypt.

After everyone had left the improvised gathering, David purified some water and we shared cheese and crackers from my suitcase. As we reflected on the days' experiences, as lovely and warm as they'd been, we couldn't help drawing physical comparisons between the Israeli and Gaza settings. How damaged and dreary the Gaza streets were, unfinished gray structures among ancient buildings and rubble, and how Israel's new buildings sparkled with beautiful yellow stone.

Our plans for meeting the rest of our delegation were for all of us to gather and stay in Rafah, on the southern border with Egypt, in apartments previously inhabited by the International Solidarity Movement (ISM). Previous ISM members included Rachel Corrie, killed by a bulldozer while trying to protect a Palestinian home. Rachel had come to Gaza as part of a Sister Cities project. On March 16, 2003, she was crushed to death after a standoff between two bulldozers and eight ISM activists. Wearing a bright orange fluorescent jacket, she was run over by the bulldozer that she believed was about to demolish her friend's family house. We would be visiting the area where she was killed.

Although the pastor was eager to have David and me stay in Gaza City to help him, the team believed our presence was needed more in Rafah, where there were regular confrontations between Gazans and the occupying Israeli army.

Then, shortly after 10 p.m., we received a phone call from Michigan, reminding us that we were supposed to call to report our safe arrival in Gaza. We were embarrassed; it was our responsibility to report in each evening. This reporting was a far cry from our actions in Vietnam, when people heard nothing from us for weeks at a time. In those days, family and friends had only newspaper articles (none too complimentary) to go by. Mobile phones were quite an advantage, I concluded—an impression that was strengthened a few weeks later.

David and I took a cab to Rafah, driving easily though the Abu Holi checkpoint, which seemed to be empty of guards. At the Amman-Cairo Bank, we called team members on my cellphone. They came out from the apartment to meet us, only a quarter block away—as soon as they came out of the apartment, shopkeepers pointed us out. Everyone seemed to know *what we were doing there*.

The Wall of Rafah

After leaving our baggage, we went to visit Block O, a strip of land where the Israeli Defense Force had demolished houses to clear out an area along the wall with Egypt. The Palestinians called the area a "sea of death." The year before, Israel had invaded Rafah in Operation Rainbow to "clear terrorist infrastructure," and to kill militants responsible for earlier deaths of Israeli soldiers. Human Rights Watch claimed that over 1,500 houses were destroyed to create this large buffer zone between the wall and Palestinian houses, displacing around 16,000 people.

Israel refers to the strip of land between Rafah and Egypt as the "Philadelphia Road" or "Pink Area," a mile-long swath of broken concrete, splintered wood, and twisted metal, the remains of bulldozed or bombed houses and buildings that fronted the steel or concrete wall that separates Gazan Rafah from Egyptian Rafah.

In the Gaza strip, of the 1.5 million Palestinians, 73 per cent were in eight refugee camps.

These refugees were from Palestinian villages in what became Israel, driven out by the war of 1947–48. Only seventeen primary health care clinics were operating, eleven of them in the camps. These were the bare and inadequate statistics we were given as background. Everywhere was devastation. In Rafah that July, no other Westerners could be seen, not even journalists.

We had our first sight of the Wall, about fourteen feet tall and unadorned except for a looming gun tower just on the other side. We were cautioned not to go closer than about 500 yards. We couldn't see anyone there but felt their presence and their eyes upon us.

Samir, friend of our translator, Mido, invited us to meet his family at his home nearby, about 800 yards from the Wall. His house was intact except for numerous pockmarks from bullets. There, David pulled out his violin and we sang, "We Shall Overcome," as a number of children gathered.

> **Our presence seemed to be a special day for everyone, the music and clapping a vivid contrast to the bleak surroundings—in fact, *a deliberate refusal to surrender to despair.***

Next day, we spent an hour or so arranging our apartment space, moving beds and chairs. Our hosts had brought in four beds, two storage shelf units, and a washing machine. David, who is well over six feet, opted for a bed without head and footboards. Later, we walked the neighborhood. We found the local store for daily provisions, such as yogurt, mango juice, cheese, and pita bread. Most mornings for the next three weeks began similarly, with meditation—yoga and prayers; a trip to the local store (one of us); and a light breakfast of pita bread, sometimes jam, and tea or coffee. One of the priests was often the cook. That first morning, walking to the ATM machine at the bank to withdraw our allotment, I made a point to greet everyone, men, women, and children along the way. Everyone responded with, "Welcome!"

Visualizing the Future

As our Gaza team met in those early days, we were determined to establish long-term and short-term goals—we'd be there a little less than a month, and the needs were dire and enduring. Once the settlers and Israeli army had withdrawn, we longed to see the Gazans as self-sufficient as possible. Rather than wringing their hands over the situation, the Palestinians could have an opportunity for greatness. If they were able to feed and improve the quality of life for their people using their ingenuity and creativity, life could be not only sustainable, but also meaningful.

Self-sufficiency would be imperative, a strategic advantage; the less dependent they were on outside resources—developing their own material and human assets—the stronger they would be. They would employ their own people. (Unemployment in Rafah in 2005 was 60 percent.)

In the short term, the community could develop internal leadership among young people, with the assistance of volunteer facilitators like our team. Their present leadership would draw in young leaders from all the diverse parties, to work together for the wellbeing of Gaza. The Michigan Peace Team had outlined several steps we could take toward this objective:

1. Be present, listen to their stories, hear their pain with empathy and compassion, play with the children, and earn their trust.

2. Locate and invite to meetings young representatives from different neighborhoods in Rafah.

3. Discover what our presence can do to support their becoming self-sufficient. Our goal was to work ourselves out of a job.

4. Establish regular communication via the Internet with these leaders, and stay current on happenings, informing them of our activities in the States.

5. Return annually for the next three years.

6. Our purpose in Gaza was to support them and to admire their ability to stand proudly, relying only on their own strengths and resources.

This was our vision, and in our interchanges with the people of Gaza, we held to it. And, through all the subsequent ravages and terror, we still do. However, I do feel guilty because it has been over thirteen years—and we have not returned. My heart hurts for our friend, the lone priest in Gaza City.

Friday, July 8, was a holy day for the Palestinians, so we also spent it in prayer and rest, and later the five of us had mass together in the apartment. Fida, our translator, brought a special fish dinner, reminiscent of Sunday dinners in my childhood. She shared with us her dilemma of being the sole person employed in her family, thus responsible for their wellbeing.

We began to brainstorm about hiring her, engaging her to make films about Rafah, Gaza, and Palestinian culture because filmmaking was her area of expertise. A possible topic, I suggested, could continue until the end of August, when the Israeli settlers' homes would be demolished.

We asked our friends whether they would prefer that Israel spare the settlers' homes, which could be used for Palestinians. They said they preferred the homes be destroyed, since they were not well designed for Palestinian use. Most Palestinian families had eight to ten children, and therefore wanting houses of maximum capacity on minimum land space. The Israeli homes were for families of two or three children and were designed to occupy (or "redeem") a maximum of land with a minimum of people.

Fida also wanted to document the plight of women, how they managed day-to-day during the Occupation after so many family men had been killed—how women raised their children. Much could be delineated about educating children. NOTE: She did in fact make such films: in 2013, she toured the U.S. with her 2010 film called "Where Should the Birds Fly?" about the 2008–2009 Israeli attack on Gaza.

On that day we also prayed at the gun tower nearby, and David played his violin for the neighbor children. My camera quit functioning, so I began to use the new camera we brought from a local Palestinian photographer.

In the evening we met with a medical doctor, a tall thin man with a moustache, whose home had been destroyed by an Israeli bulldozer—the very bulldozer that took Rachel Corrie's life.

The site in 2005 was designated a "Security Zone," and if the doctor stepped on this private land, he would bring gunfire from the border guard towers. His and other wrecked homes in the area were to be relocated in Deir Al Balah, a Palestinian city in the central Gaza Strip and the administrative capital of the Deir el-Balah Governorate. Rachel Corrie's words, "This has to stop!" echoed in my ears as I listened to the doctor.

The doctor invited us to stay at his makeshift home, to live with him rather than in the apartment—perhaps it would have been better if we had. We were taken aback, though, because we knew he'd moved eight times. He said that when we internationals came, the residents felt safe, but when we leave, soldiers come at night over and over. Rachel and her friends had stayed with the doctor's family as the tanks surrounded the house each evening, and they crawled on hands and knees, out of sight of the windows, to go to the bathroom during the night. Once Rachel was dead and the internationals gone, the soldiers destroyed the house.

The doctor told us the story of the day Rachel was killed. Only he and members of the International Solidarity Movement had seen what really happened: "I saw everything. I saw her standing in front of the bulldozer. The driver saw her; he couldn't help but see her. Rachel was wearing one of her team's bright orange tops and she shouted 'Stop! Stop! Stop!' but the bulldozer kept advancing; it pushed up dirt that she was standing on, so that she was looking straight at the driver. All who witnessed it agree that the 'dozer pushed the dirt over Rachel, burying her.'"

His words and the horrific images have stayed with me to this day. The Israeli government has never acknowledged any responsibility for the killing.

Holy Family Church

Early Sunday, July 10, we four priests and our guide and translator, took two taxis to Gaza City for mass in Father Manuel Musallam's

Holy Family Church. He asked us to concelebrate, which we happily did, and to say a few words about our mission. Each of us spoke of our love for the Palestinian people, and our determination to tell of their suffering once we were back home.

I spoke of the Holy Family's flight from Bethlehem, and from Herod's murderous threats to kill Jesus because of his jealousy and fear. Tradition had it that they traveled to Gaza, which was then part of Egypt. "They may have walked on this very ground, making it sacred. God blesses Gaza in a special way. In the spirit of Pope John Paul," I said, kneeling, and I bent down and kissed the floor of the church. At the kiss of peace before Holy Communion, Father gave us a warm welcome and expressed his gratitude for our presence.

After mass we were invited to visit the convent of Mother Teresa's Missionary Sisters of Charity where they served us sweets and a cold drink. We stayed to talk with the dozen or so handicapped or disturbed children and ten elderly women the sisters cared for, paying special attention to each child and blessing them. David prayed charismatic healing over a child and three elderly women. The sisters took advantage of being able to go to confession with someone other than Father Musallam.

In the afternoon we met with Director General of Al Mezam Center for Human Rights to talk about the Michigan Peace Team's work, and to learn how Palestinian human rights were addressed. "Our group documents rights violations," he said, "such as confiscation of property and humiliations at checkpoints, where people often wait for days." The Rights group's biggest challenge internationally was the lack of recognition of the occupation; at Oslo, the international community was not ready to say, "End the occupation." Even after the withdrawal, the control of persons and goods at the border would remain. "There is no way to export our products. Sixty to seventy percent of people in Gaza are living beneath the poverty line!" The lack of opportunity was definitely more emotionally damaging than among the poor I'd seen in Asia. The Palestinians had experienced many of the benefits of a wealthy society, so they harbored anger at its depletion.

We spoke of opportunities that might be inherent in the situation. A strategic advantage would be using their ingenuity to become self-sufficient, avoiding the huge debts in which other developing nations were drowning. In the end, the Director General listened intently and reflected on the possibilities. The day had grown late, so we raced back to Rafah, where the men collapsed for a time because we were exhausted—although the women paid another pastoral call to a woman's group nearby.

Most evenings we gathered in our apartment, amid the children's shouts echoing up and down the stairways, as we debriefed the day's happenings and meditated on the scripture for the coming day. The practice was an inspiration for us all. I was so grateful for the gifts our team shared—David's discernment and his stories about the effectiveness of nonviolence; Peter's wit, often keeping us in stitches with puns; Liz's gentle encouragement and compassion for the Palestinians; and Lou's generosity in shopping and preparing our meals, especially breakfasts. He was the first up in the morning, praying while heating coffee—and he managed our "common pot," the money we each contributed and drew from for daily expenses. Just a bunch of socialists, obviously. We called in each evening to the Michigan team, taking turns reporting on the day's activities; someone there carried an emergency phone 24 hours a day, in case of critical need.

Universally, people on the streets called out to us, "Welcome!" and young boys would ask our names, though they didn't seem to understand what they were asking, perhaps having heard "What is your name?" spoken by adults. Their frequent response when we'd stop was to ask, "Money?" stretching out their hands. We'd say, "No money," smiling, but they would continue. They were surprisingly multi-lingual, asking, "Kesef? Argent? Haben sie Geld? Monee?" Parents familiar with foreigners encouraged their small children to be friendly, and the children even gave us a hug or kiss if the adults were with them. On one occasion, when our door was open, a pair of teenagers asked to come in, bringing a gift of soda, and, since they were studying English, stayed to practice their skills.

Muwasse

On July 11, we attempted to enter Muwasse, meaning "low wetlands," a Palestinian section of Rafah by the sea that was cut off from the rest of Gaza by the Israeli settlements. We had prepared some questions for the Muwasse residents as they waited at the Israeli checkpoint to work or to attend school in Rafah. This was the southernmost section of the Gaza Strip, which stretches from the Egyptian border in Rafah to Khan Yunis. About 9,000 to 10,000 people lived in this area, isolated by the Israeli settlements, mostly located along the coastline. If we could get answers from the residents, it would help us understand the situation.

The first entryway we approached was closed and no longer being used. We spoke there with a man who is a football player and architect with three wives and 26 children, all of who lived by the entrance. I asked him how he remembered their names, and he joked, "Easy, I just shout 'Mohammed!' and they all show up." We all broke out in laughter. I never thought to ask him, "What about the girls?"

He had a question of his own, deeply challenging us as we began to interview him: "What did we do that caused the U.S. to give money to Israel for guns and tanks to shoot at us? The U.S. gives us wheat to bake bread, but gives Israelis guns and tanks to kill us. Why?" We could not offer answers. He showed us his bullet wound, and told us he'd been without work for five years. In 1948 he'd been forced to relocate to Gaza. From 2000 through 2004, the Israelis had shot repeatedly at his house. His house was riddled with bullet holes on the outside, although he had managed to fix up the inside. When I asked him what projects he would like to see developed, he said, "Tourism."

This man was an engineer who had helped build 90 percent of the new settlements. If it were possible, he would like to live side-by-side with Israelis. "We are cousins," he declared. "Why do they kill us? Now they destroy the buildings I helped construct." His voice was hoarse, and his passion clear in his gestures. He knew the settlers thought that in giving up the land "given to them by God," they were being unfaithful. Yet they were removing water, and sand for glass making, from the area, with the intention of selling it back to the Palestinians. He believed that selling the water would eventually pay for offshore oil the Israelis would need.

We then drove past Khan Yunis to the second entryway, the Amtofah checkpoint where people crossed between Emossi and Muwasse. It also was closed to us, but we were able to videotape interviews with Palestinians there who were attempting to get home. Our translator asked David and Lou to stand between her and the Israel watchtower, so she could film without being seen or shot. We then stopped at a Palestinian police office to formally request entry to Muwasse. The Palestinian official phoned the request in to the Israeli office where it would be considered. Permission was refused.

We got into conversation with the Palestinian police about the checkpoint. There, a mother of a very sick 9-month-old child called on the phone for help to take him to the hospital in Emossi. She'd been waiting for three hours at the checkpoint. The hospital called and said if she wasn't permitted through, the hospital could send a doctor from Emossi to tend to the child. We waited to see if the doctor would be allowed to cross over to attend to the child. Nothing happened. Finally we left, heavy-hearted.

On July 12, our translator took us to a boys' school, a summer school, where the youth were awaiting the scores of their Baccalaureate exams. We attempted to teach them baseball. They were quick learners, but we experienced our first casualty. Lou was pitching, and I tried to hit a ball into the outfield—instead, the ball took an errant bounce on the pavement, smack into Lou's nose. It bled profusely but fortunately not for long; I felt awful. After that fiasco, the Gazans weren't really attracted to the game. Nonetheless, we left the balls and bats that I had brought from the U.S. with the school. Lou went to the apartment to rest, while we went to visit our translator's neighborhood of Keshta. Instead of resting, Lou spent the time washing his clothes because we had brought few extra clothes, and the heat took its toll on what we had.

Our translator showed us where her home had been—it was now a pile of rubble. Again, children poured in from around the area as though we were Pied Pipers. David serenaded all on his violin as we tossed balls and played Frisbee. Peter made them laugh with his juggling talents and clowning. Other than the children, we didn't meet her neighbors; she didn't take us to visit friends in the area, not even her aunts, with whom Liz had resided.

I was so surprised at the extent of competition among the children. They were so anxious to play and enjoy themselves, but it was difficult for them to share with one another. They fought over the ball or Frisbee most of the time. Throwing to each other seemed a new idea for them. Instead, each child would throw the Frisbee back to me. I grew frustrated because I so wanted them to entertain each other with the toy, but had no success. In the demolished areas, they seemed happy to receive the candy we offered them, but before long the older ones confiscated it—whether it had to be given to older people, or sold, I didn't know. The experience differed from that in Thailand where the older children made certain each received his/her share. Children who lived in our apartment building would *not* take the candy but simply said, "Shukran," "Thank you."

We'd been invited to our other translator's home for dinner, and we arrived around 2 p.m. The conversation, of course, turned to politics, for which I was grateful. For the Palestinians, it was impossible to think beyond the Israeli occupation, even though they were currently most worried about the settlers' and soldiers' withdrawal. In an effort to be a catalyst for planning for the future, I asked, "What do you think you can do to help Palestinians to work for the good of the nation, Gaza, and the West Bank?" The question was prompted by our observation of the children's individualistic behavior earlier. I was hoping they'd conclude (as I had) that their future depended on their joining together, not to battle the Israelis, but to defeat them financially by working together. Unfortunately, we didn't get a clear answer.

The most religious women are covered from head to toe, all but their eyes, by a "burqa." In many Muslim nations, and even outside, this covering demonstrates deep faith in Islam, although reasons may vary. Traditional families fear that, with democracy, will come the degeneration of their culture—and that young women will not want to wear traditional dress (similar to what happened to Roman Catholic nuns after Vatican II). Men are expected not to speak to a woman on the street, for fear of beginning a process that could lead to infidelity. For similar reasons, alcohol is forbidden, for the good of the people.

These cultural norms reminded me of the restrictions of Catholic teachings in my youth, claiming that sexual thoughts were sins against God; kissing a girl for more than a second, or repeatedly, was a sin against God; all such restrictions were designed to prevent infidelity and harmful behavior to one's partner and children. In my youth, "dangerous" activities permitted to adults were forbidden to children. I concluded the result was intended—to treat believers like the children they were perceived to be.

Our female translator covered her face except her eyes. She explained that it helped give *her* confidence to speak. By December 2007, when David briefly visited Gaza again, she had abandoned the face covering.

After dinner, Lou taught our translator's sister how to play games of solitaire; he knew at least six. An uncle entered into a theological discussion with David. He sought to convince us that, since there is only one God, and Allah has no son, therefore Jesus couldn't be God. The uncle's assumptions were that we knew little about Islam, and that if Americans could only learn more about their religion, we would not treat them so badly, and Americans would come to love Palestinians. I agreed with his basic point.

And the greatest obstacle to understanding each
other is both perceiving that the way each sees reality
is the way it is. Hence, if one sees reality differently,
one is obviously wrong. Dialogue comes to a halt when
one views the other as absolutely wrong.

Demolished Homes

We met with a member of the Demolished Houses Group, made
up of representatives (volunteers) from each of the thirteen areas
where houses had been demolished. The group had rebuilt 600
dwellings—still, 2,700 families needed homes. He had been living
under the seats of the football/soccer stadium with a family of ten
people since 2002 when his house was demolished. With no work,
they live off his savings from his former work as a petroleum technician and welder.

"During bombardment," he told us, "many young people came
from America and Europe, and stayed in my house, sleeping there
when we were in danger of demolition. Our situation is better than
before—we can sleep at night. Before, tanks were shooting much of
the night; children were terrified, some in shock, night after night."

"What do you hope for, now?" I asked, because I constantly
sought to encourage people to think positively.

"Nothing gives us hope here! Nobody cares," he lamented.

My heart sank. I assured him that thousands of people all over
the world did indeed care about him and his people. I'm afraid I
was not convincing. I could see in his whole demeanor the message, "Show me."

As we approached our apartment, we could hear music. Just
outside the building, we came upon a street party, where a huge
crowd of perhaps 500 men had gathered—and not a single woman.

Our driver took us in hand and guided us through a maze of young men to seats of honor near the front.

A Hallowed Site: Remembering Rachel

The next morning, we visited the site where Rachel Corrie was killed, to offer mass there and pray for peace. We dearly hoped that the soldiers at the nearby gun tower wouldn't shoot at us. Our translator arrived promptly at 9 a.m. to conduct us to the area. On the spot, as nearly as we could determine, we set up a make-shift altar and offered Holy Mass for Rachel and the Palestinians and Internationals who'd been martyred in Gaza and on the West Bank. Children gathered, quiet for the most part. Fida also filmed. In a short homily, I suggested that Rachel was a saint and martyr, laying down her life for her friends—we prayed for her and the Palestinians, and we prayed *to* them, asking them to intercede for us at the throne of God.

Afterward, we went to the Life Makers Center (Rachel Corrie Center) founded by Fida Qishta, our translator. The first four floors were dedicated to women's health, the fifth floor to grade school children suffering from Post-Traumatic Stress Disorder. The Center, run by the Union of Health Work Committee, cares for some 90 children. A women's gym serves 50 women a day; psychologists see about 1000 women a week, and a single gynecologist sees between 35 and 45 a day. More people are able to come at night, after their work.

In some haste we left to visit Demolished Houses Group's office, so we could film an interview with him about Rachel's last days. She'd stayed in the home next door to his, the doctor's home. When the tanks came in the night, she would stand in front of the house with a bullhorn to tell the Israelis not to damage the house because there were women and children staying there.

"Why kill her?" Mahmoud exclaimed, his voice recorded in the notes of our colleague David. "They could have taken her away—they could have taken her bullhorn." He then asked to speak on the film directly to Rachel's family. He spoke from his heart to tell them, "I am a father also. I know your feeling. I am very sorry about what happened. Please raise your heads. Your daughter—we love—no one can take her place." He then had some words for the American people: "I invite you to be beside us in our houses. Try to stand here with us. See for yourselves. We don't hate the American people. The information you receive about us is not the reality."

The Future of Palestine

We bid Sister Liz Walters goodbye, as she was leaving for Jerusalem early the next morning. We four priests then visited a man who lived in an isolated house, the last home standing in his neighborhood about 100 meters from the Wall. Peter had stayed with him two years previously, when tanks surrounded the house. A man of about 65 with a trim white beard, he was dressed all in white, including a white hat. He knew our translator well enough to tease her on her strength, which he likened to an Israeli tank.

> **I continue to seek to go beyond complaints and find approaches that bring about change.**

When I asked him about his views for the future of the country, he remarked, "There is no democracy here in Gaza, *or* in America." I believe the Israelis will leave, but they will remain in control and continue the checkpoints, 'leaving us in prison.' We even have to beg the Israelis for salt."

"What can the Palestinians do about it?" I queried.

"We need to remove the Palestinian Authority and have an honest election."

"What are you doing to make that happen?" I pressed him.

"For now, we are waiting. We want to see what the Palestinian Authority will do after the Israelis leave. If President Bush (George

W.) will leave us alone, all will be better." He went on to say that people in the U.S. should organize to stop Bush, and if they did that, "we will do the same here." Further he thought, "The Israeli soldiers' main motivation for demolishing houses is to make people suffer, and thereby maintain control," but he had no love for the Palestinian Authority. He did like Hamas, believing they were more religious, less secular.

"What did Ahmed Yassin (cofounder of Hamas) do that the Israelis killed him?" he mourned. Yassin, a quadriplegic from a boyhood accident, was assassinated the previous year, when an Israeli helicopter gunship fired a missile at him as he was wheeled from morning prayers.

"Most people in Gaza support Hamas," the man emphasized, "because they know that Hamas helps the poor survive." He was very disappointed in Arafat, who had done little or nothing for the people of Gaza since 1988. "And Bush will take credit for the settlers and soldiers' leaving, but it means nothing if our people cannot leave here, have passports, see others," he complained, throwing his arms up in desperation.

I asked again, "What projects could Palestinians do after the settlers leave?"

He said, "Not much." Whereupon our interpreter entered into an argument with him that the Palestinians could build their own factories and so on. From their interchange I concluded that she at least had internalized the idea of self-sufficiency we'd been proposing. Peter wondered whether employees might own a factory, but supposed the plants would be too small to compete with large companies. One of us suggested that people could begin small and develop as the products and services met the needs of Palestinians. Our host didn't appear convinced, but seeds of possibilities were sown.

Later, we met with a group from the University Graduates Association of Rafah, a two-year-old program funded by organizations such as World Vision. Their purpose, among other services, is to develop skills and find jobs for graduates. The leaders, a staff of six representatives like Ahmed seemed tied to the idea that outside assistance would be needed to lift Gazans from poverty. At least two and sometimes three conversations seemed to be going on at once, so eager were people to be heard, but I was gratified that everyone attended to this one issue: self-reliance. Our interpreters were an immense help in this instance.

On the way home, we encountered another marriage celebration. Again, the festivities included a street dance with drums, electronic organs, and an electric guitar. As we danced, one of the young men grabbed me from behind and placed me on his shoulders as he gyrated to the music. Another strong young Palestinian lifted Peter. We waved our hands above our heads, trying to keep time until we were rescued and shown chairs for us to rest. Many dancers sported rifles, intermittently firing live bullets into the air above their heads, literally celebrating with "fireworks." Others snapped photos, to the glee of young boys excited to be in the pictures. Although we made our escape around midnight, we suffered another casualty: Peter's right leg had some sort of injury, causing him considerable pain.

The next day at the cyber café, we encountered a Palestinian journalist who offered to set up a meeting with some of the leadership in Rafah. He shared information about present business practices: The Palestinians, for example, manage a small plant making designer jeans, which can be shipped only through Israel, and Israel takes most of the profit. The jeans' label says, "Made in Israel." The journalist owned farmland, growing carnations, which he sold for pennies to Israeli merchants, who in turn sold them for ten times the amount. These common practices added to feelings of resentment among the Gazans.

In response, we encourage him to envision cottage industries that produce goods for their own people, not for the Israelis. After the journalist left, we continued the discussion with Rachel Corrie's friend about this change of thinking, focusing on independence. The conversation led to his belief in the possibility of Israel and Palestine existing side-by-side in the future, but he was worried

stopped, but showed no signs of retreating. Continued orders from the tower went unheeded. More shots.

After two hours of witnessing the standoff, we returned to the apartment. An hour after we'd left, several people were wounded as trucks and cars crashed through the checkpoint, and a boy of fifteen was killed. We later learned that the move had been coordinated with Palestinians entering from the Gaza City side. During the night we could hear stepped-up shooting and mortar fire.

Appreciative Inquiry Approach: Discover, Dream, Design, Deliver

Two days later, we held our scheduled workshop for young activists at the Rachel Corrie Life Makers Center. We were up early, before 6 a.m., for the usual cold shower and breakfast of pita and jelly, hot coffee and juice. We headed out about 8:30, but most participants didn't arrive until 10:00. We spent the time preparing flip charts in English and Arabic and reviewing the methodology among the interpreters and ourselves. Approximately sixteen young people came.

We followed the *Appreciative Inquiry Approach*, believing that this organizational development methodology would elicit the group's own strengths and ideas. We determined not to impose our own ideas, or even our hopes, on the participants. Appreciative Inquiry starts with the belief that every group (or organization), and each person in it, has positive aspects or gifts that can be built on.

**Questions in this *Discovery phase* include:
"What's good about what we are doing presently?"
"What has been working?"**

Our plan for the *Discovery phase* was to begin with having two people tell stories to one another about their successes in life—and

286

watching the smiles begin and grow was a joy. Then each person introduced his or her partner to another pair, telling the partners' stories. Afterward, the four reflected on how they felt having another person recount the internal strengths that had enabled them to be successful. To conclude this first step, the whole group listed the qualities and characteristics present in the team they were building.

Now empowered, they tackled the *Dream phase*: We asked them *to imagine* the Gaza they wanted after the settlers and army withdrew. This exercise seemed terribly difficult at first, almost as though their imaginations had been crippled by the relentless daily deprivation and humiliations, the struggle just to survive. With the help of David, Lou, and Peter, they gradually warmed to the possibilities of a future for Gaza, and with it, wonder began to fill their eyes.

The next task, *Design phase,* was the most difficult, requiring *specific plans to make the dream a reality.* One man wanted to raise funds from Palestinians and others living abroad to build a factory; others pictured beginning cottage industries, making small items. Time ran out; in fact, we went overtime and made plans with the group to meet again the next day at the Rachel Corrie Life Makers Center. I thought one of the best ideas brought forth was for the Gazans to print their own money and cease using the Israeli money. However, before we could design active steps to make it happen, time became an issue, along with low energy. We concluded with music from David, Irish revolutionary tunes and "We Shall Overcome," with an added verse, "End the Occupation."

In the evening we four went for a stroll in order to debrief the day's events and get away from the apartment. We'd received a message from Sister Liz suggesting that our rooms might be bugged. Her questioning at the border checkpoint led her to think the Israelis knew more about our group than we realized, so we took this bugging possibility seriously.

We ended our day, as usual, with prayers and the scripture reading for the next day. Our prayers included thanksgiving for the young Palestinians we'd been with that day—and we made a point of praying for the Israeli soldiers we see every day.

On July 21, we returned to the Life Makers Center at 9 a.m. Eight women and four men showed up, five of the group were repeats from the previous day. Because some of the participants were familiar with the workshop format, we moved quickly through the Discovery part. Then Peter and David shared their dreams for Gaza, and I read the combined Dream from the day before.

The group divided into teams of eight, with us sitting in with the teams, to plan for the future—after withdrawal of soldiers and settlers. Each team set three goals that were "specific, measurable, attainable, relevant, and time-phased." Everyone, including us, made personal commitments to work to fulfill the group's goals. We four priests committed to remain in contact through email and give them feedback. My only disappointment was that the group did not tackle getting rid of the shekel. As long as the Gazans used Israeli coinage, I feared they would continue to be dominated by their oppressors.

We were excited to see other hopeful signs in our companions, especially our two translators who had been part of the workshop each day. Everyone thought seeds had been sown, and that we would learn of the fruit in coming months. Had we had more time to begin the action phase, the project might have persisted.

Time to Reflect

On Friday, we spent more time in reflection and review than we had in past weeks. It was the feast day of St. Mary Magdalene, and we celebrated the Eucharist in her memory. Writing in our journals, reading on the computer about the current situation here and everywhere, we prepared our hearts for when the team members separate, which would happen on Sunday.

I brooded over the patriarchy and misogyny endemic in this culture that so repressed women, kept them enshrouded in dark garments from head to toe, and allowed little contact with men.

Perhaps there were some benefits, but I couldn't see many, and was troubled. A cure for this malady is freely available. It's equality! In the cyber café we often noticed many young men gaping at obvious pornography. Also obvious in the culture was the equation of manhood with the number of children the men fathered.

If something changed, and the sexes were encouraged to mingle, and women could wear what they wanted, what would happen? A young man and woman can't even be together unless one's father sits between them. I suspected young people found a way around this forbidding rule, but it wouldn't be easy.

Emerging from the cyber café, I ran into another good friend of Rachel Corrie. She had slept at his home for many nights. He currently served in the Palestinian army, though he detested war. Questioning me about our presence in Gaza, he expressed curiosity about the priesthood and religious life. He was intrigued with the idea that God came from heaven to teach us how to be happy, not only in paradise, but in this life, which is my continual assertion. Smiling, he invited us to lunch with him at his home, "I want to hear more of the Jesus story." David and I thought we could take him up on his invitation next week, after our schedule cleared.

On Saturday, we revisited Khan Yunis and Liberal Arts University. We divided into pairs, David and Lou in one room, and Peter and me in a second. Then Peter and I, at his suggestion, hosted fifteen students each for a question-and-answer session. The students were intensely engaged. The young people peppered us with questions about U.S. policy, of course. "Why is the U.S. supporting the Occupation? Israelis keep occupying our country, destroying our homes, making it difficult to travel anywhere, and taking the best land. What is motivating the U.S. to do this?"

They continued: "Palestinians who visit your country return and say Americans are good people, friendly and welcoming. Is it the propaganda that causes Americans to support the U.S. government's support of the government of Israel? Also, most of us speak English. Why don't Americans learn to speak Arabic? Is there something wrong with us?"

Peter and I struggled to respond. Sorrowfully, we had quite a few inadequate answers, or none. The best we could offer is that the average U.S. citizen is ignorant of what is going on in Gaza and on the West Bank.

In the office of the University's Director, Kathrene, and her assistant Ebal, we had an animated discussion about our single status; the assistant was astounded to learn that at our age, the four of us weren't married. Such a thing was incomprehensible to her. She lectured us, claiming that Mohammed taught that Allah's will was for everyone to be married and have children. She insisted we explain how our status was not abnormal.

My response was that every woman I'd loved would insist that I love only her to the *exclusion* of all others, and I couldn't, as a priest, do that, because I loved them all; I loved women *inclusively*. My arguments didn't faze her. She continued to extol the meaningfulness of marriage.

Peter's request that she note how happy the four of us were, even though we didn't have wives, made little difference. He persevered: "We wouldn't be able to come here and risk our lives in solidarity with the Palestinian people if we had wives and children back in the U.S. to care for." He added that many people remain single for reasons besides a religious one. "A dedicated scientist, for example, might remain unmarried, to focus on his work."

Ebal shook her head, smiling at his specious reasoning. David offered that some have Allah first in their lives, and this relationship is primary, even above having a wife. None of our explanations came close to denting her belief. Certainly she was unhappy with us. She was like some dogmatic Christians, who behave the same way in an argument—anyone who does not believe their way is simply wrong.

A phone call from Omar in the Governor's office invited us to stop at the Elkarama Center for Culture and Arts for a tour and a show featuring Arabic traditional music. Most of the musicians were volunteers, and rehearsals were catch-as-catch-can, before and after work. The ancient stringed and wind instruments combined to make music that took our breath away.

Haunting and lyrical, the songs were Arabic traditional, based on poetry, or they were specifically Palestinian, played for occasions both formal and daily, such as work songs, weddings, or songs of praise to the beloved and to Allah.

We were blessed to be there in the moment, because the next days would bring experiences that threatened to erase from our memories such pleasant hours.

Abducted!

On July 24, a feeling of sadness crept over me in the early hours of the morning as I contemplated the separation of our collegial team because Lou and Peter would go on from Gaza City to Jerusalem, then back to the United States. Our team had become quite close during our time together. Moreover, more work needed to be done. It seemed we had just begun, scratched the surface, as it were. If we stayed another month, we would be able to be the human shields we had intended to be while the settlers were being removed from Gaza.

The electricity had cut off about 6 a.m. No surprise. Gazans were used to it. Presumably the Israelis did so simply to irritate the people and to remind them who was in control. Lou had been up since 5 a.m., heating water for coffee, so we were able to begin our day with a bit of warmth. Not that we needed heat because lacking air-conditioning, we regularly opened our door to the hall to catch a breath of air.

Abruptly, about 7 a.m., two armed men appeared in the doorway, both in their twenties and wearing military fatigues, one very tall, armed with a pistol holstered at his side, while the shorter man had a rifle strapped to his back. "We are police!" a heavily accented voice declared. Not alarmed, I welcomed them from my place at the table across the room, eager to reach out in a friendly manner to everyone, including the police. We'd just finished our pita-bread breakfast. I pointed to what was left, apologizing for the remnants, and invited them to come in, have a chair and break bread with us: "Join us," I exclaimed enthusiastically.

The taller man responded only by eyeing Lou, closest to him and said, "Come here!"

"I *am* here," Lou smartly said, staying seated. The man then advanced toward me, speaking quietly but with authority, "I'd like to speak to you out in the hallway." I didn't think anything of it—of course I would come, trusting the police meant only good things, and that they needed our help. I wanted to make it obvious that we were there to support the people of Gaza. I rose from my chair as he approached. He gently placed his hand on my shoulder, which seemed a friendly gesture, and the two of us walked back toward the doorway. As I reached the entrance and stepped into the hall, I was startled to see two more armed men in fatigues, hiding from view on either side of the doorway. Automatically, I held my breath.

The tall man whispered in my ear, "Do what I say, and you won't get hurt." At that, he threw a hood over my head and hurried me down the steps to my left. I had all I could do to concentrate on my feet, seeing them through the bottom of the hood, fearful I might stumble and break an ankle. Our female translator chased after us, screaming objections in Arabic, but was ignored.

Once outside they hustled me to a waiting car. A hand firmly guided my hooded head down to keep it from clunking on the car roof and then pushed me into the back seat. With the tall man and his accomplice on each side of me, the other two jumped in the front seats and the car sped off.

Immediately, the big guy shoved my head down into his lap, so no one on the outside could get a glimpse of a hooded person in the back seat, while at the same time warning me to do what I was told if I wanted to live. I had no intention of struggling.

The drive didn't take very long. They couldn't have gone far; they seemed to drive around a bit, perhaps to get me disoriented and in case anyone was following. Then the car came to an abrupt stop. I was warned again, "Don't try to escape or cry out or I'll be forced to shoot you." Almost dragged out of the car, I was quickly led down what seemed a stony path beside a fence that appeared to be on my left. I was brought directly into a room and told, "Sit on the bed" as a hand guided me around and pressed down on my shoulder.

"Don't worry, we won't hurt you. Just do what I say," he warned me again. The words somehow didn't ring true, and thoughts of this being the beginning of my life's end consumed me. I heard much whispering going on over by the door, perhaps with some-one outside. After a moment, as if they had forgotten something, I was softly ordered to stand, suggesting they were being careful not to be overheard. Two people searched me, looking for I don't know what. They didn't take my wallet or my rosary beads, only my phone. Their manner struck me as unprofessional, as if they were frisking a person for the first time. It added to my fear, think-ing amateurs were likely to do something stupid (to me) that they would regret afterward. Someone pushed me gently back onto the bed. More whispering followed.

The door opened after a soft knock, and I was aware of a new person entering the room. Approaching the bed, he declared in a low, commanding voice, "I'm going to film you making four state-ments. Give your name, your profession, and say you work for the CIA and the Israeli Army."

I objected, "That would be a lie, I neither work for the CIA nor the Israeli Army."

"Say it anyway or I'll shoot you," he retorted. He then quickly left, apparently expecting me to do as I was instructed. His voice sounded familiar. Within five minutes he returned. Someone removed my hood. It was a guard, now hooded.

Facing me was the hooded man; only his eyes were visible. He held up a phone in his right hand to capture me and my words.

"State your name and profession," he ordered in a soft voice; again I was disturbed by something familiar in his speech.

"My name is Harry Bury and I am a professor from the United States," I said. I didn't admit to being a priest.

"Who do you work for?"

"The CIA," I stated, trying to smile broadly, trying not to look credible. I consciously stopped. He impatiently motioned with his left hand for me to continue. I faked not understanding. He whispered, "Say you work for the Israeli Army."

"Oh," I said, seeking to be obedient but as unbelievable as I could, "I work for the Israeli Army." Internally I rationalized that no one in the United States would believe such a lie; they would understand I was speaking under duress. Later, I was told by the guard that my admission was not for American news, but to influence other Palestinians. It was designed to show Abbas and his government on the West Bank that the Gazans were strong enough to snatch and hold an international in broad daylight—and thus were not to be ignored.

He seemed satisfied, and ordered the guard to replace the hood on my head and left the room. I sat quietly. The voices of children playing in the distance caught my attention. After a short time, a voice stated, "You can remove your hood so you can breathe better." I snatched it gratefully from my head while quickly scanning the room. I noticed he had removed his hood as well. Armed with a pistol at his belt, this rather chunky man sat in the only chair, a good ten paces from me.

Taking stock of my surroundings, which were meager, rustic, but quite clean, I reached the conclusion the room was ordinarily unoccupied, making it an adequate hiding place. The door from which I'd entered was to my left. Farther left was a large curtainless window. Bars for decoration, rather than protection, kept the window from being used as an exit. If necessary, I thought to myself, I could probably kick them out. No bathroom was evident. A couple of prayer mats lay on the floor. Slowly I reached for my rosary lodged in the left front pocket of my jeans.

"What are you doing?" he asked nervously.

"It's my prayer beads." I announced, knowing that similar beads were used by Muslims in prayer. He noticeably relaxed.

Mentally and prayerfully, I began to prepare for being shot to death. I wasn't grieving about it. It didn't occur to me how the event would bring pain to my family and friends. I simply talked to myself, "I guess this is how God intends for me to die." I then prayed, "Please, God, don't let them torture me. You know I am a coward when it comes to pain."

Obviously, I was afraid, because I never thought to question what my abductors had ordered me to do, even lying that I worked for the CIA and the Israeli Army. Only later, safe in the United Stated did I feel guilty and wished I had refused to lie.

Yes, it is easier to be courageous when one is *not* in danger.

I prayed in silence. Finishing my rosary and returning it to my pocket, I ventured a question. "Are you the police?" including him with the others.

"No."

I paused; then asked, "Are you the Israelis?"

"No!" he stated loudly as if angered by the accusation.

"Who are you? And what's this about?" I persisted.

"I've been shot four times," he answered as though eager to explain, pointing to places on his legs and his upper body. "Can't get any medicine, the hospitals don't have enough medicine." He went on, looking distraught, "We hardly get enough food, the schools don't have books."

He was not only blaming the Israelis, he was blaming Abbas, the leader of the Palestinians on the West Bank. He continued, "Abbas gets money from American and the other Arab countries, but he doesn't share it with the people of Gaza. It's as though we don't exist."

"I'm sorry," I offered sincerely.

Perceiving he was understood, he added, "There are a million and a half Palestinians in Gaza. Only Hamas is giving us food and medicine, not enough, but without it we would be lost. It is Hamas doing it. If there were an election in Gaza today, Hamas would win."

I found his claim informative. Sure enough, a year later, no surprise to me, Hamas easily carried the election. The United States, however, rejected the democratic results because Hamas ostensibly refuses to recognize the Israeli state.

"Why do Americans help the Israelis occupy Palestine?" he asked, as if I knew the answer.

I responded regretfully, "I believe the American people don't know what is happening to the Palestinian people."

"They have television! They should know!"

"They don't get the whole truth on television."

He shook his head. "They have Al-Jazeera, other Arab television!" When I told him Americans don't get those stations, he was surprised and could not believe it.

He emphasized that he and his companions were not angry with me (or other Americans they'd met), but were angry with the West Bank Palestinian government, which treated them little better than the Israelis did. He was upset that the Jewish settlers were receiving new houses in Israel while Gaza houses were continually being demolished. "Palestinian homes are being destroyed and nothing is done for them—either by the Israelis or their own government. We are homeless or living in makeshift shacks with no running water or toilets."

By now, I'd seen enough of their situation to know he was accurate, and my heart went out to him. If asked, I would have been willing to help my captors. A knock on the door sent him scrambling, pistol in hand. I turned away in an attempt to cooperate, and strained to hear a brief conversation at the entrance. The speaker didn't enter. Returning to my side, my guard hooded me again, this time with two hoods, effectively blinding me, and then he handed me my phone, saying, "We're taking you to another place." His words made sense to me; I'd read about other captives being moved from place to place to avoid being discovered. He took my arm and we stumbled together along a rough path to a paved street a short distance away. He stopped, leaned toward me and whispered in my ear, "Go home!" I heard footsteps running away.

Unbelieving, I slowly pulled off the hoods, dropping them to the pavement. I looked around; my street was deserted but I could see cars crossing at either end blocks away. I was more or less in the middle—nothing was recognizable, but once more I was aware of children's voices. Turning right, I headed in their direction, which took me to the corner and then to the left. I didn't recognize any landmarks. The signs were all in Arabic. I hurried toward the voices, and came upon a walled-in playground area of a school.

Kids were playing, running around and yelling. I walked up to three young men sitting on folding chairs, leaning against the wall of the building, and asked, anxiously, "Anyone speak English?" They looked at me, perplexed. One got up and hurried away, apparently to find someone who could speak English.

Surveying the scene, I thought of my phone. Anxiously, I pulled it from my pocket, pressed one of the buttons, and lo and behold, I was talking to Mary, our emergency contact in Michigan. She was as surprised as I was, because my friends had reported my abduction. Within minutes Mary had me in touch with my colleagues and our female translator at the police station.

By this time, the errand runner had come back with an English speaker, so when the police asked me where I was, I could tell them. The authorities sent a car over to take me to the police station, where I made my report and where I was reunited with the others. I was surprised the police did not take me back to the place where I was released in order to find and examine the room in which I was held. Seemed the obvious thing to do if they were intent on catching my abductors.

The governor called and asked me to come over. When we arrived in less than an hour, he was quick to apologize for what happened to me, and promised the abductors would be caught. Upon leaving, we persuaded everyone that the six of us should go together to the bank, not take a taxi but walk, to demonstrate we were safe and not afraid. All went well, and we picked up some dinner.

Afterward, as we celebrated the Eucharist together, we were interrupted several times by well-wishers who dropped by our apartment to express their sympathy and renewed support. They implied I did the right thing. Obviously the word had spread throughout Rafah. In our meditations, we prayed for all sides in this terrible conflict.

Must We Leave?

The next day, David and I decided to continue our normal routines and commitments. We returned to the Rachel Corrie Life Maker Center for the workshop series on community organizing. The nine participants came up with two projects toward making their dream a reality—an IT company, and training in computer use and programming. I was pleased with their goals, yet disappointed that getting rid of the shekel was not a priority. Perhaps, they perceived it was too great a task for them to be successful. If I were to return to Palestine today, I would raise the issue once again. Refusing to use the shekel, I believe, would be far more potent than missiles—and nonviolent.

We then visited the "Children's Parliament," a summer camp using the airport as a facility for their meetings. The children entertained us with song, first the girls, then the boys.

Peter and Lou had gone to the closed Abu Holi checkpoint; if it opened any time during the day, they'd go through to Gaza City. Alas, like the Palestinians, they spent the day sweltering in the hot sun and then returned exasperated and worn out. When I heard about their ordeal, I felt anguish. Still, I realized Palestinians went through this treatment every day of their lives. Who were we to think we were different? We had no more idea than the Palestinians did about when the checkpoint would be opened. We discussed contacting our Congress people to put pressure on Israel to stop this unjust practice. I wanted to contact Representative Dennis Kucinich from my district in Cleveland. I thought maybe if our personal plight was on the Monday evening news, it would call attention to the larger injustice. Peter insisted we first contact Michigan Peace Team to learn their thoughts on the matter.

Peter and Lou were scheduled to leave by plane shortly, so they were anxious, and would go the moment the Abu Holi checkpoint was open. Until then, we were trapped in Gaza, where the situation seemed to be getting worse. We had remained in close contact with the support staff in Michigan and with our Palestinian friends. Further, I was becoming more and more agitated as I was being urged, even ordered, to remain silent about my abduction. My plea was that these oppressed people were trying to alert the world about the extent of their suffering. So few seemed to know. Peter and the advisors in Michigan were afraid the mention of my abduction would affect the Palestinians adversely in the eyes of Americans.

David and I were inclined to stay. When we consulted with our translators, they said they felt responsible for us, and advised we should leave. They worried for our safety outside the apartment, warning us to keep the door closed. They echoed recent reports that Ariel Sharon, the Israeli prime minister, was threatening an invasion of Gaza, and our translators expressed concern that if the checkpoint remained closed, we'd miss our plane back to the States.

Suddenly, at 6:50 p.m., the female translator called to say the Israelis notified the Palestinian Authority (police) that the checkpoint at Abu Holi would be open from 7–9 p.m. She urged all of us to go. Lou and Peter had not unpacked their bags; they were ready, but I remained upset. It seemed the Israelis controlled us (and the Palestinians) like puppets. Nonetheless, we gave in. We literally threw our clothes in the bags, hurrying to reach the checkpoint before 9 p.m. The speed of our taxi, swerving through traffic with its horn blaring, unnerved me. I didn't think we'd arrive in one piece.

Thankfully, we did arrive shortly after 8 p.m. Abu Holi still hadn't opened, and cars were lined up for blocks. We began to wonder if it would open at all, and imagined driving back to the apartment in the dead of night. Then just before 9:00 p.m. the checkpoint opened. Cars and trucks rushed forward to get through, fearful the Israelis might close it at any moment. Horns blew, tempers flared. But by 9:30 we were through and on our way to Gaza City and the Holy Family Parish, where we spent the night. The next day, we drove to Eretz checkpoint. Our translators (and friends), had not left our sides, and wouldn't until we were safely out of Gaza, saying, "We are family now." We felt sad; we would miss them very much.

We didn't know what we were going to run into when we left Gaza and were in the hands of the Israelis. But nothing was said. Our bags were not examined, except by the x-ray machine. We got through. Peter and Lou headed for Tel Aviv Airport and on to the United States. David and I went back to Jerusalem. Rested, the next day we found a bus that took us the six miles from Jerusalem to Bethlehem.

Visiting Bethlehem

Once through the checkpoint, we started walking down the street in Bethlehem. A taxi driver drove up and wanted us to go with him. We kept saying no, saying we were just going to the Church of the Nativity. He kept insisting until finally we gave in and got in "Eddie's Taxi." Then he invited us to come to his house. He seemed kind; we couldn't say no. Besides we were trapped in his car. Once there, Eddie and his wife treated us to grapes and watermelon and talked with us about their experience, about how the Israelis controlled the water and electricity. "They bill us exorbitantly. If people don't pay, they are cut off. No water, no electricity."

Eddie promised us a tour to the Wall and perhaps to talk to Israeli soldiers, but time was slipping away. He finally shepherded us to the booths near the Church of the Nativity. People in the booths sold religious goods to tourists. In recent years, Israelis began bussing in pilgrims, and then out again to go back to Jerusalem. We were told that the hotels and residents were no longer able to make a decent living selling these religious goods because no one was allowed to stay the night. We heard again stories of residents trying to visit relatives or do business in Jerusalem, and being turned back, refused exit. One man complained that whereas as a child he would visit Jerusalem weekly with his father, now it had been five years since he had been to Jerusalem. Similar to the Gazans, the Palestinians living in Bethlehem experience being in prison, with no idea when it will ever end. After a brief stop at "St. Joseph's Store of Religious Objects," where David bought a cross, we arrived at the Church of the Nativity. We paid Eddie, who requested more "for his children," and we agreed without objection.

The church was riddled with bullet holes. No evidence of daily mass. We needed to descend into the basement to see the place where Jesus was rumored to have been born. Guided by a monk, it too looked like a battleground between the Orthodox and the Roman Catholics. It was hard to pray. I was eager to leave because I was not moved by this experience.

Once back in Jerusalem, on July 28, David and I went to St. George Episcopal Cathedral to see Mordechai Vanunu, the Israeli (born in Morocco) technician and whistle-blower who revealed details of Israel's nuclear weapons program to the British press in 1986. Thanks to Vanunu, many people understand that Israel has nuclear weapons—but the nation has never admitted it. Vanunu was kidnapped in Rome and imprisoned in Israel, where he lives to this day. According to the conditions of his probation, he is not allowed to leave the country or speak with foreigners. Yet he agreed to speak secretly to David and me. Similar to me, he is apt at breaking laws.

On Christmas Day, 2013, Mordechai Vanunu, inside an Israeli courtroom, appealed to the Israeli High Court, "I don't want to live in Israel," he declared. "I cannot live here as a convicted spy, a traitor, an enemy and a Christian," he said in English, having vowed not to speak Hebrew until he is allowed to leave Israel. On December 29, 2013, the court rejected his petition, on the grounds that he continues to possess information that could jeopardize Israel's national security.

I was struck by his slight but athletic stature. He told us he swims every day and, grinning, said he "eats low on the food chain." His mind, like his body, was well-toned and his speech incisive. When we asked him, "How can we help?" he urged us to invite and encourage Christians to come to Palestine and support Palestinian Christians by staying at their hotels and buying their goods, while also giving them emotional and spiritual sustenance. His advice underscored what we'd heard about Israeli economic constraints—the oppressive control—of all aspects of life in Palestine.

Vanunu recently compared his actions to those of US National Security Agency whistleblower Edward Snowden. "Snowden is the best example of what I did 25 years ago—when the government breaks the law and tramples on human rights, people talk. That's what he did, he speaks for everyone, and that's what I did—I spoke for everyone."

On a Bus to Hebron

After we left Vanunu, David and I found a bus for Hebron, where he'd promised to play his violin at a checkpoint separating the settlers in Hebron from the Palestinians. There we agreed to meet with a dozen International Solidarity Movement representatives, holding signs stating, "Music is a passport, may it open the way"; "Soldiers, music is the instrument of peace, your weapon is the cause of hatred"; and similar messages.

David played, and I sang and danced as children joined in. More Israeli soldiers showed up. I tried to engage them in dialogue but my words and smiles were met with stern faces and stony stares. After about an hour, we moved to another checkpoint, with similar results.

We then went to Hebron's Old City, a microcosm of Israel's policy of forced evictions and separation, where rows of shops that once catered to tourists are now closed. Ancient passageways shouted of history, but mostly in my imagination. I wished the walls would inform my understanding of the peoples who lived and suffered here long ago, and now.

We made our way to the Ibrahimi Mosque, which contained the tombs of Abraham and Sarah. Bordering the Tomb of the Patriarch, fifteen houses had been destroyed the previous year, 2004. The families had been evicted so an Israeli-only bypass road could be built to link settlements. The mosque had separate sides, one for the Israelis and the other for Muslims and Christians. Our entrance contained another checkpoint. Israeli soldiers forbade David to bring his violin inside and also counted his medicine bottles, to ensure he didn't have something to harm other visitors. We mildly complimented the soldiers for their consideration of the pilgrims. Our remarks were met with sarcastic smiles, or so it seemed to me.

Abraham's tomb was lodged behind glass, preventing anyone from touching it. I prayed quietly for his descendants. The day and its sights seemed long and emotionally draining. By late afternoon we were happy to climb aboard a van to Jerusalem, Ecce Homo, a warm shower, and a meaningful Eucharist, our Last Supper in the Holy Land.

Conclusion

My thoughts often return to Gaza. What do I think is the future of this land? What do I think we accomplished in our short time there—more than 13 years ago now—and with our continued contact?

The settlers and soldiers departed from the Gaza Strip the next month, August-September 2005, amid anger, grief, and violence. Since the 2005 withdrawal, Israel continues to control Gaza's airspace and sea space, effectively enclosing and walling the land. Although in the January 2006 elections, Hamas won a plurality of the total vote, the Israeli government, the United States, and the European Union (EU) refused to recognize its right to govern the Palestinian Authority. Direct aid to the Palestinian government was cut off, political disorder and economic stagnation continue.

The Michigan Peace Team, now renamed the Meta Peace Team, continues to be active in the Holy Land. Our work laid much of the groundwork for slow but positive progress toward peace. Besides facilitating the Gazans to become as independent of the Israeli government as possible, even to the extent of doing away with the shekel and printing their own money, we committed ourselves to work to change public opinion worldwide. To implement printing their own money, however, seemed beyond their imagination. They reacted similarly to many people giving advice, even when solicited, with numerous reasons why it wouldn't work. Nevertheless, I was satisfied that we were able to facilitate Gazans and West Bank Palestinians in visualizing what they believed was good for themselves, not what Americans like me determined was in their best interests.

> **NOTE:** The Gaza Strip is a self-governing territory that borders Egypt for 6.8 miles on the southwest and Israel on the east and north for a 32-mile border. The people are ethnic Arab, and the majority are Muslim. This area is very improverished. Israel has ruled this area since 1967—but withdrew its troops in 2005. Israel, however, still has tight restrictions on trade. The country has 40 percent unemployment and almost 40 percent of its people live below poverty.

The key for the Palestinians is unity. As long as disaffection persists between the followers of Abbas and those of Hamas, it contributes to Israel's benefit. Being divided only adds to disorganization and ineffectiveness. *One vision, one community*—I so hoped that ideal would be a legacy of our presence. As Jesus said, and Abraham Lincoln quoted in regard to slavery, "A house divided against itself cannot stand."

On leaving, we determined to communicate what we learned and experienced on the ground in Israel, the West Bank, and especially in Gaza, as my story is endeavoring to do. Whenever I can, I encourage internationalists to go and get their "boots dirty" in the land of Jesus by mingling with people on both sides of the great divide. They will discern, as we did, that besides the extremists in each group, a far greater number of Muslims and Jews have compassion for one another and hold out a hope once more for "a land flowing with milk and honey," in which both are living together free of fear as sisters and brothers.

In the meantime, David has been active in the movement, both in the United States and abroad, to encourage divestment and boycotts of Israel, similar to what was effective in ending apartheid in South Africa. This message has begun to resonate with trade unions, churches, universities and international companies who perceive Israel as violating the human rights of Palestinians.

In January 2014, for example, a Dutch pension giant announced publicly that it was divesting from Israel's five largest banks. Their action was taken because of the Israeli government's intention to build 1,400 new homes on the West Bank for Israeli settlers, together with its continuing colonization, administrative restrictions, land confiscation, and Palestinian home demolitions. All of this was designed to completely discourage Palestinians so that they leave Israel, the West Bank and Gaza, and seek refuge in Jordan and other neighboring countries.

In April of 2014, Fatah and Hamas forged a unity agreement that established a new government of technocrats unaffiliated with either party. The unity agreement not only undercut Israel's claim that it cannot negotiate with a divided Palestine, but also threatened Israel's long-term goal of dividing Gaza from the West Bank and pursuing its destructive policies in both regions.

Terror returned in late summer of 2014 as we continued to pray for Palestine and Israel. Palestinian rockets motivated far more damaging Israeli attacks. We cannot pray for things to return to "normal," as Professor Noam Chomsky writes, "For Gaza, the norm is a miserable existence under a cruel and destructive siege that Israel administers to permit bare survival but nothing more." Assaults on the Gaza strip have been periodic but regular over the past decade, "the relentless siege and savage attacks punctuated by episodes of 'mowing the lawn,' to borrow Israel's cheery expression for its periodic exercises in shooting fish in a pond as part of what it calls a 'war of defense.'"

Hence, the siege continues, with its tragic consequences for human life and health. But with the latest carnage, U.S. and international support for Israel's oppressive policy shows signs of weakening. As author Noam Chomsky points out in his 2010 book, *Gaza in Crisis: Reflections on Israel's War Against the Palestinians*, that U.S. law requires that "no security assistance may be provided to any country the government of which engages in a consistent pattern of gross violations of internationally recognized human rights" and many are demanding that Washington observe its own laws and cut off military aid to Israel—so far, to no avail.

My greatest desire is that because of our brief presence in Gaza, the West Bank and Israel would encourage Palestinians not to lose hope but to resist injustices with strategies of nonviolence. We gave them examples of Gandhi's and Mandela's strategies as well as those of Martin Luther King, Jr., while facilitating the Palestinians to come up with their own nonviolent approaches, which would empower them to persevere with courage, proud and happy in the land of their ancestors.

CHAPTER 18

Vietnam Revisited (2014)

Prison Reform

Vietnam still calls to my heart and mind. In late November 2013, my old friend Charlie Sullivan emailed me with a request. He is founder of Citizens United for Rehabilitation of Errants (CURE), an organization that periodically hosts the International Conference on Human Rights & Criminal Justice Reform. As mentioned in a previous chapter, their sixth conference was scheduled in Bangkok, Thailand, in early March of 2014.

Two Vietnam veterans, famous photojournalist Alan Pogue, who focused on social justice, and *National Geographic* writer Mike Rodriguez, planned to do a story on Vietnam's prisons, and possibly visit areas where they had served during the war.

Charlie asked that I use my Vietnamese connections to receive permission from the Vietnam government for the two of them to photograph the prisons, and for me to guide the two veterans to visit places where they had been some forty years previously. Charlie suggested about a ten-day trip immediately following the conference in Bangkok.

I had agreed earlier to attend and speak on prison reform at the conference. The Thai government had granted conferees permission to visit a women's prison in Bangkok that showcased the exemplary work that Princess Maha Chakri Sirindhorn had done for incarcerated women in Thailand.

Wishing to be of assistance in Vietnam, I emailed old Vietnamese friends in business, the Church, education, and the government, asking their help in getting the government's permission to visit and photograph the prisons in Vietnam. A travel agent and two retired government officials confessed they were unable to do as I requested. Alas, I received no replies from the others. Complete silence. I wondered if they'd even received my emails. So, I repeated my request. Still no response. In December I sent Charlie the sad news.

Charlie persisted. In hopes of last-minute success, he contacted members of the U.S. House of Representatives and the Vietnamese Embassy in Washington, D.C. I agreed to stay involved, but thought that getting into a Vietnamese prison was nearly hopeless.

Ho Chi Minh City (HCMC)

Arriving in Bangkok for the conference in March, Alan Pogue was eager to again try our luck at getting into at least one prison in Vietnam. Two participants at the conference promised to contact the U.S. Consulate in Ho Chi Minh City (HCMC) to arrange an appointment for us with a consulate official.

"At the very least," one said, "you might accompany a consulate official to a jail when he tries to intervene on behalf of an American citizen who has gotten in trouble with the law." That sounded feasible; I'd received similar services in Saigon in 1971 when twice arrested for demonstrating against the war—once outside the U.S. Embassy gate.

Without total assurance that we would get into a prison, journalist Mike Rodriquez decided not to risk it. Alan thought it was worth a try. The two of us flew to Vietnam on our own nickel as I'd done many times, and again we stayed at a hotel for $20 a night, $200 for the ten days, which was $50 less than the round trip flight from Bangkok.

We contacted the Red Cross in HCMC. One of those helping us at the Bangkok conference said the Red Cross was doing significant prison work in Laos and quite possibly were involved in similar efforts in Vietnam. Alan located the Red Cross on his computer, getting their address and phone number. On the phone, through a translator, a Red Cross staff member asked for an official letter of our "intent and purpose" written by the organization we represented. Charlie immediately sent a letter from Washington, D.C., confirming our mission. Even with more red tape, we received no response.

Alan also contacted American Veterans Against the War in Vietnam at their office in Ho Chi Minh City, who promised to call back. They never did. I contacted a Vietnamese businessman close to government leadership, and a day later he apologized for not being able to assist us. Apparently no one wanted to risk contacting the Communist government regarding this sensitive issue. I concluded people making our request were afraid because of being placed on a list of persons who might be denied future requests for Vietnamese government assistance.

As a backup plan, I suggested to Alan that we visit the Anh Linh Free School for street children, which was effective in preventing many kids from following their parents and relatives into prison. Thanks to Jerri Hirsch, I had visited the school every time I was in Vietnam in the previous ten years, riding on the back of motorbikes belonging to friends Nguyen Thao (earlier chapter) and her sister Nguyen Trang.

Off we went, Alan with his sack of equipment on back of a Trang's bike and me following on a Sister Cam Thuy's smaller bike. Sister Cam, a past principal, and Sister Kim Ngoc, the present principal of Anh Linh School, joyfully received us. Alan busied himself with photographing the children as they were taking tests, eating lunch, and at recreation. I interviewed a boy whose parents were both in jail. His father, whom he hadn't seen since he was six years old, had died just the day before; thus my interview became a counseling intervention.

I spoke with another lad who had quit Anh Linh School, gone back to the streets, was arrested, and put in prison. Finally released, unlike his brother who went back to prison, he realized his errors and was now working as a tattoo artist and helping out at Anh Linh whenever he could. He realized that learning to read and write at the school had enabled him to now have his own business. My questions to him about prison life bore no results, since his answers were vague and unclear.

Bridges to Learning, which Jerri Hirsch and Bob MacMurdo founded in Minneapolis, Minnesota, supports Anh Linh School. Thanks to them, 231 children through grade 9 are nourished in ways beyond the meals they receive, and the children wear their blue-and-white uniforms with pride. They receive the support, values, and education needed to withstand the pressures of returning to the imagined freedom of the streets, and are building a future in which they can be proud. Bridges to Learning was born, enabling more and more children to be served, and has just helped the nuns to open a new school.

Vietnamese Women and the Church

Once in Vietnam, I learned why Father Huynh Cong Minh, my priest friend from Vietnam War days, hadn't answered my prison-request email. He'd just had surgery in France and was in recovery. He returned to Vietnam shortly after Alan and I arrived in Ho Chi Minh City. By the time I was able to visit with him, it was too late for him to arrange for us to get into a prison. However, he took me to meet a group of Vietnamese—six women, two young men, and a priest who in the 1960s had been a Young Christian Workers (YCW) chaplain.

Once seated at table for lunch in one of the women's homes, I immediately asked the group, "What do you think is the future of the Catholic Church in Vietnam?" It was as if I'd opened a Pandora's box. One woman after another poured out her feelings of disappointment with the institutional church. "If the church was a purely human organization, it would have no future here," the women exclaimed in English, speaking almost as one. "Only because of the Holy Spirit will it survive."

Startled, I asked, "Why do you say that?"

Each in her own way, the women responded: "The church is too legalistic, focusing on laws and rules and regulations. The priests are not with the people. They don't understand what we are experiencing. Many foreign priests' homilies use examples alien to Vietnamese life."

**Pope Francis' words came to me:
"Move away from a church that locks itself up
in small things, in small-minded rules."**

One of the young men spoke up. "My friends get up on Sunday mornings as if to go to mass, but really to escape the anger of their parents. When they get to the church, they don't go in. They sit outside eating ice cream until mass is over." I thought: These are exactly the young people the Church needs in order to have a real stake in the future of the Church and the country.

I turned back to the women as the other two priests remained silent. Secretly I rejoiced that the priests were the beneficiaries of such honesty. I said, "Give me some specific examples, like this young man did, of what you mean when you say the church is too legalistic."

As I listened to all their sincere comments and complaints, sadness filled me. What harm we clerics were doing by antagonizing women because women have the greatest influence on the faith of the young. We are failing to engage our strongest allies.

On the Sunday following, while vesting for mass at the Notre Dame Cathedral, I shared the above information with another American priest. He is currently teaching English in the Catholic seminary in Ho Chi Minh City. He replied, "Oh, yes, the priests here think and act like they're the kings of the village.

"Oh my goodness," I said, "it sounds like the church in America at the time I was ordained in 1955!"

Father Minh then said to the women, "Don't wait for the archbishop or the priests to lead you. Gather together a small group of like-minded people, including non-Catholics. Dialogue together about what needs to be done in YCW fashion: observe, judge, and act—to make things better for your neighbors in Ho Chi Minh City."

I thought: what a great idea. Being a resident-led group (which I like to reframe as a team), they would have a low level of bureaucracy and be very flexible. If they managed to attract "young advisors" in the 15-to-21-year-old bracket who would then stimulate social action by showing the adults how to engage young people in community life, local decision-making, and improving services, the women's discouragement would change into hopefulness.

Further, the youth showcasing their work on social media would spread the word and invite other groups to engage in similar activities in Vietnam and in other countries. I envision them installing a sense of intergenerational purpose with leaders of all ages.

The priest urged the women to use the *"doi dien"* (face-to-face) process and *"dung day"* (stand up), and, to not lose heart. Because the women had been active leaders in the church when they were young, they were willing to take his suggestions under consideration. I sat quietly listening, agreeing with his vision of change coming from the bottom up and not from the top down.

Pope Francis would be open to it also, having said as much: "I prefer a church which is bruised, hurting and dirty because it has been out on the streets, rather than a church which is unhealthy from being confined and from clinging to its own security."

I pictured neighborhood-sized units of citizens small enough to enable local people to meet regularly and work out together everyday community issues—small yet representing all the elements of the neighborhood. I perceived it as a strategy to overcome apathy and the feeling of anonymity of "we don't count and nobody cares for us, and there's not much we can do about it."

I thought the priest was suggesting real participation in which neighbors acquire a sense of belonging, a sense of dignity, a sense of self-confidence, and a realization of what mature adults can achieve—and that no one is going to meet their challenges except themselves. This is a step toward realizing their power.

Third Force Once Again

The next day Father Minh invited me to another luncheon, this time to meet old members of the Third Force (Catholics in the south 50 years ago who opposed the South Vietnamese government, whom they perceived to be a puppet regime of America). The eight men in the room represented a group of sixty who continue to meet four times a year. Among them was Nguyen Dinh Dau, the 94-year-old Vietnamese historian and friend of Tom Fox, whose home I visited on my first trip to Vietnam in June 1971.

After joy-filled introductions followed by affectionate fond remembrances of the old days, we began to talk seriously. When I asked, "What is life like for you in Vietnam today?" I was met with a spirit of frustration and cynicism.

Most of those present were Vietnamese nationalists who acted nonviolently to free their country—first from the French colonizers and then from American influence in the late sixties and early seventies. They still retained great admiration for Ho Chi Minh, who in their minds was not a Communist at heart, but had turned to the Communists for help after the Second World War, when America supported the French colonialists in order to secure France's cooperation with the U.S. interests in Europe.

After Ho Chi Minh's death, the Communist element of the revolution/civil war took control. Today these Third Force Veterans see little difference between the present authoritarian government and that of the American-puppet South Vietnamese regime of the 1960s and 70s. Behind their words, I heard dashed hopes and expectations—feelings of having been betrayed. This time, however, gone was the energy to do anything about the present situation.

"The Communist system isn't fair, the rules of the game, as under Thieu, don't apply to the people at the top. Not one Catholic has been appointed to a leadership position in any government institution or business or hospital, you name it." The men seemed to have given up hope that the situation in the country would change. Each perceived that they had little influence in society and voiced fearfulness for their future and that of their children and grandchildren. It seemed like a cloud of depression blanketed the room.

One person spoke up half jokingly, "We need you to come back and chain yourself to the U.S. Embassy gate again." Sensing the seriousness of the moment, I shook my head and said, "A new generation is here; we cannot use old tactics." Surprised at my own sense of ownership for the situation, I went on, "We need to pray and put our heads together and come up with new strategies for the 21st century. Let's use our imaginations." My urging raised little enthusiasm.

Before I left, one man told me he had been a major in the South Vietnamese Army and had been trained at the School of the Americas near Atlanta, Georgia. He said Colin Powell and Saddam Hussein were also in the same class with him, "but I outranked Saddam because he was only a captain; he was friendly and smart." This was news to me, and would probably be news to most of the American people that the despised Saddam Hussein was trained by our military. No wonder there was little objection to his murder—because "too much" information would have come out if he had been tried by the international court.

An English Newspaper in Vietnam

As we continued our discussion, a new idea emerged. Vietnamese people continue to obtain much of their news from the written press. Literally hundreds of newspapers are published throughout the country, yet not a single one is in the English language. I suggested that the old Third Force rise again to publish an English-language newspaper. Working in solidarity, Third Force folks, who at present are somewhat divided, would further the paper's goal to decrease the gap between the Church and the Communist government, much as the group had done during the war.

The unstated policy would be to publish articles that describe only positive actions of the government, the Catholic Church, Protestant churches, the Buddhists, and other religious institutions. Examples might be presentations of the work the Quakers are doing with prosthetic in the north, the success of the nuns of Notre Dame with the street children at Anh Linh Free School, and the fine work Father Tu is doing with handicapped persons. Another could be the ecumenical free clinic based at Tam Tong Mieu Temple in HCMC with staff members from followers of Buddhism, Catholicism, Minh Ly Dao, and Cao Dai, who volunteer at the clinic. In addition, Koto International, a social-profit organization founded and managed by Jimmy Pham in 1999, educates street children in Hanoi and HCMC to become cooks and restaurateurs.

Articles would also describe the effectiveness and efficiency of government hospitals, especially the excellent care given to Agent-Orange patients. Other areas of news could be the government's success in improving Vietnam's infrastructure and overcoming homelessness and drug addiction. I'd be especially interested in the government's positive efforts at prison reform, and the successful use of monies the U.S. Government is providing to reduce and treat AIDS/HIV among prisoners.

More than an effort at good public relations, the paper would also evidence a sincere determination to give hope to the Vietnamese people in highlighting the actual good being accomplished in society—who is doing it and how. Once established, the paper would go online. Given the international popularity of social media, the hope is that the paper would help mobilize large numbers of young Vietnamese to promote the common good—perhaps even interest the young people who are missing Mass.

Slowly but surely the newspaper would move to what the Third Force envisions: A healthy and flourishing Vietnamese Society. The paper holds the promise of creating a culture that resists and replaces focus on what is wrong and negative, in order to focus on what is right and positive, and to teach the next generation the value of joyfully seeking the common good.

Perhaps in the beginning, to save money, this new endeavor might rent the printing press of the Catholic paper, *The Catholic and the Nation*. The newspaper could also provide additional employment.

Although the word "Catholic" will not appear in the title of the newspaper, government leaders would be aware that Catholic laity are behind the editorial policy. Gradually, the intent is that government fear of the Catholic Church would dissipate and the government's trust in the Church would also grow. Catholics would then be entrusted with positions of leadership. In turn, leaders in the Church would become less antagonistic toward the Communist government, which itself is motivated by fear. The Church would become more understanding and accept that the government, like all human institutions, is not perfect and needs support to gain the confidence to reform itself. Publishing stories in which Communists and religious people work together toward the common good would go far to minimize the existing polarization in Vietnam. It's worth a try.

Maybe because of this radical reversal of philosophy in a Vietnamese newspaper, the young people of Vietnam will come back to the faith as they see the many challenges and opportunities open to them through the religious groups working together with the government to make things better for everyone. It could touch the minds and hearts of a new generation. That is what I visualize.

CHAPTER 19

Another Mission: Twin Cities Nonviolent

"Throughout my life, I have always hated to hear anyone trying to justify violence."

—Harry Bury

Living in Minnesota – Byrne Residence

My new permanent home at the Byrne residence, a home for retired priests, began with intensity in late June 2014. With sadness, I had sold my home of 34 years in Berea, Ohio. No longer enjoying the financial or emotional blessings of teaching at Baldwin Wallace University—and deep in debt from seeking to help the poor both here and abroad, I needed to move back to Minnesota, where I began some 45 years ago.

Living at the Byrne residence among my fellow priests has been a "cum si cum sa" experience. I love and respect each one of them. My intent in coming was to do everything I could to make their lives as joyful and painless as possible. I find it meaningful to continue this work.

A major joy and blessing for me is to participate at daily Eucharist with one another taking turns presiding. Having the Chapel just fifty steps from my apartment is a rich blessing.

I'm finally coming to realize that a life
connected to Jesus results in a life that loves more,
forgives more, and gives more. Through Jesus,
we stay connected with God and one another.

The Association of US Catholic Priests (AUSCP)

The last week in June 2015 another mission became apparent. Donald Cozzins, a dear priest friend and author, was to receive the award for achievement for promoting the spirit of Vatican II, which would be given at the AUSCP annual meeting in St. Louis, Missouri. He asked me to introduce him. I felt honored and was eager to do so. It was the fourth year of the Association's existence whose purpose is to continue the work toward implementation of the Second Vatican Council (1962–1965). I found the meeting to be a breath of fresh air, an opportunity to share with common minds and hearts, ideas and actions that are dear to me. I eagerly joined the Association.

At the 2016 Association meeting in Chicago, a priest, Bernie Survil, asked me to head the committee on nonviolence for the organization. I made every effort to decline. I cited little knowledge of the computer, explaining my ignorance and need for secretaries when I was a professor, and how they handled the technology for me. He brushed this excuse aside, saying he would take care of this inadequacy on my part. I further claimed to be too old, suggesting that such an effort would be better managed by a younger priest. He was quick to point out that at our meeting with some 180 priests, only one was under age fifty. In the end, he persuaded me to accept the responsibility.

I was not wise enough to ask, since he would be doing the secretarial labor, what were his expectations of what I would be doing. I did request not to have the title of chair of the committee, but simply facilitator.

Twin Cities Nonviolent

Hardly a week later, shortly after July 4, I received a phone call from John Dear, a renowned priest and author of many books on nonviolence and a dear friend of the recently deceased Jesuit priest, Daniel Berrigan. John asked if I would work to create an environment in which the Twin Cities (St. Paul and Minneapolis) would become nonviolent cities.

I had never met or spoken with John before. He mentioned that Carbondale, Illinois, has become a nonviolent city, the only one so far in the United States, and promised to send me the ten steps used to achieve this marvelous reality. I, in turn, could implement the ten steps in making St. Paul and Minneapolis nonviolent cities.

> The two incidents occurring so close in time suggested to me that God's providence was here at work. How could I say "No!"

Asking the Archbishop

I made a call to the new Archbishop of St. Paul and Minneapolis, Bernard Hebda, asking for an appointment. His secretary explained, "The Archbishop likes to know what is the topic or purpose of the meeting." I readily explained that I would like the Archbishop to declare the Twin Cities "nonviolent cities." She expressed delight with the idea.

I received an appointment with the Archbishop the very next week. A month before I had met the Archbishop at a meeting of priests, and gave him a copy of my recent book, *An Invitation to Think and Feel Differently in the New Millennium*. In few-and-far-between meetings with past archbishops, I was ushered into the office where I waited for the archbishop to arrive. Notably this time, the Archbishop came out, greeted me personally and then cordially escorted me to his office. I noticed he was carrying my book in his right hand. Upon reaching his office and sitting down together at a small table, I said, "I see you have my book. Have you had a chance to examine it?"

The Archbishop replied, "I've had an opportunity to look it over and intend to read it completely on my vacation." He then thanked me again for giving it to him. Internally, I was aware of feelings of gratitude that he was willing to consider reading my book, hoping also for his feedback. Quickly, assuming his time was limited, I launched into the purpose of my visit. "My hope is that you will call a news conference and declare the Twin Cities nonviolent cities," I said with some trepidation.

It was a step beyond John Dear's request, applying self-fulfilling prophecy theory that "the expectation of an event tends to cause it to happen." When we envision an event occurring, seeing it with our mind's eye, the event tends to actually happen. Anticipating his question of how this challenge could be done, I shared with him the ten steps that I understood Carbondale, Illinois, used to become a nonviolent city. The Archbishop carefully examined this information, as I summarized each page in handing it to him. He seemed to showed genuine interest in the possibility.

I volunteered to assist him in making his declaration a reality, and suggested using the latest cutting-edge organizational development theory, "Appreciative Inquiry," as our theoretical model.

The Archbishop listened attentively as I explain the four-"D" approach: "Discovery, Dream, Design, and Deliver."

"A steering committee," I continued, "would first discover what is already occurring in the Twin Cities that is contributing to a nonviolent environment. For example, organizations such as Minnesota Alliance of Peacemakers, Every Church a Peace Church, Black Lives Matter, Women against Military Madness (WAMM), to name a few."

I went on, "The committee would dream in the spirit of Martin Luther King, what the Twin Cities would look like and what would be happening, when the Twin Cities are actually free from violence."

"Next," I added, "the committee would design a strategic plan toward making the dream a reality. Delivery would follow in which the committee would serve as a catalyst for activities, and along with volunteer cohorts, would act to achieve our dream, our mission." I emphasized two further points. Declaring the Twin Cities free from violence would activate the self-fulfilling prophecy theory causing us to act as though nonviolence were already a reality and, secondly, "speaking with vehemence," it needs to be a bottom up, not a top-down approach. Ideas and actions need to come from people in the trenches, so to speak. I see our mission as a coming together of the community in dialogue, every voice matters, leading to greater peace rather than discord."

The Archbishop responded, "We could use this kind of approach in the church and elsewhere." I immediately felt supported. He then asked, "Do you know a Father Eric Rutton?"

"No," I confessed, and explained that I have been away from the archdiocese, teaching in Cleveland and elsewhere in the world for the last forty-five years. The archbishop seemed surprised. Grateful feelings pulsated through my body, since his surprise suggested to me that he had not consulted my personnel file prior to our meeting.

I also concluded that he understood the nonviolent mission for he explained, "Father Rutton knows more about ecumenism (working with other religions) than perhaps any other priest in the archdiocese." My heart jumped. Clearly he realized that if this (our) mission were to be successful, we will need all religious faith leaders to work together.

Before departing, I stressed that the moment is here to motivate a critical mass of people in the Twin Cities to get involved in creating systemic structures that would measurably limit violence in our area.

In our Twin Cities of Minneapolis/St. Paul, we've had several incidents of people of color being shot by police.

"People are ready for it." I exclaimed. I was thinking of Philando Castile, a person of color who recently was fatally shot during a traffic stop by a St. Anthony police officer in a St. Paul suburb.

The officer fired seven shots in rapid succession into his body as the Philando sat behind the wheel in his car. The victim's girlfriend captured the tragedy on her iPhone. All Americans viewed it on television and especially people in the Twin Cities.

Shortly before that, a young person of color, Jamar Clark, had been gunned down by another policeman in North Minneapolis. Black Lives Matter protesters were out in force demonstrating, calling for justice, making the point, "When all lives matter, black lives will matter."

The Archbishop nodded in agreement. He then seemed to caution me to keep the mission local. I believe we must not only remove guns from the streets in our cities, we desperately need a moral commitment to the banning of nuclear weapons and the abolition of war. I'm committed to working for a less dangerous, morally responsible global future. Still, I heard the Archbishop's counsel, "one step at a time."

After a pause, I went on to suggest that if he led this effort of freeing the Twin Cities from violence, it would go a long way towards restoring the church's credibility locally in moral matters. The damage done from the pedophile crisis and the assumed condemnation of gays and gay marriage might be mitigated if the church strongly and publicly led this endeavor in creating a safe environment for all the people in the Twin Cities and suburbs.

As he rose from his chair signaling our meeting was concluding, the Archbishop's facial expression told me this was not his primary issue. It was the principle of nonviolence that hit home for him. He offered to call Father Rutton and asked that I also call him. Implied, I assumed that after he and I met, we were both to get back to the Archbishop with our thoughts.

Meeting Father Rutton

To give the Archbishop time to telephone him, I waited a week before seeking to contact the priest. When I finally made it through to him, we set up a lunch meeting. Over lunch, I shared the mission and the ten steps to make the Twin Cities nonviolent that John Dear had sent to me. Rutton showed genuine interest, and carefully took notes. After he had a chance to study the materials I supplied, he promised to get back to me. My expectation was I would hear from him shortly. Time passed. I waited impatiently. After two weeks, I finally called him. He expressed the wish to consult with someone at the Minnesota Catholic Conference (MCC). This made total sense, as the MCC has connections with the Minnesota Council of Churches representing most of the other churches in the state. I asked if I could attend the meeting, and he happily agreed.

In the meantime, I contacted Bill Keatts of "Discussions That Encounter"—a four-person group against racism inaugurated by Bill and the Reverend Arthur Agnew, pastor of Bethesda Missionary Baptist Church. Along with an Episcopalian Lou Schon, and a Baptist, Rasalyn Sampson, we instituted the rudiments of our non-violent steering committee. Together we committed to each bring five nonviolence activists to a meeting at St. Frances Cabrini Church on January 12, 2017.

Our newly formed committee agreed not to advertise the meeting in order to avoid naysayers who might tell us why our mission will never work. We are interested in people who are already convinced of the necessity of creating a nonviolent community, and who possess the time, energy, and motivation to devote to its achievement—and are idealistic enough to make a try at the impossible. I was encouraged by our initial team, and expectations are running high.

In February 2018, we met with representatives of all the peace organizations we know to plan a week of nonviolence in the fall.

Announcing...Our Upcoming Twin Cities Nonviolent Event (TCNV) – September 21–30, 2018

Our intervention to create an environment in which the Twin Cities of Minneapolis and Saint Paul, Minnesota, can become free from violence is moving slowly along. Preparations are being made to initiate Ten Days of Nonviolence in the fall of 2018, beginning on September 21st, International Peace Day.

At least thirty peace organizations in the Twin Cities have shown interest in participating by presenting what they are doing to promote peace and to make the Twin Cities a safer place to live and bring up children.

When I was a youngster, I hitched hiked nearly every summer day to go swimming in the Camden pool about ten miles from home. My parents never worried about my safety. Similarly, we children were free to play outside after our evening meal, as it was getting dark, again with parents trusting that we were safe.

Our intention, therefore, is to create an environment in which people are not afraid to move around the cities in all neighborhoods and downtown areas, day or night, without being concerned for their safety. We intend not only to challenge the unjust and oppressive social structures that create violence, but also promote peace with justice, equality and dignity for all. Hence, not only do we perceive that people are safe, but that they also have opportunities to grow and develop into people that can make valuable contributions to the Twin Cities.

Organizations that are joining are not only working for reasonable gun regulations, eliminating war, militarism, racism, and the like, but also organizations that are eliminating homelessness, creating high-quality jobs, helping persons coming out of prison to find a place to live and a good job—and similar efforts.

Many of these organizations have been working all alone, unaware that their counterparts' work is congruent with their own. Our meeting together is enabling them to know of each other and build relationships, thus increasing each organization's effectiveness. Author Robert Hall, in his book, *This Land of Strangers*, writes: "The truth is, relationships are the most valuable and value-creating resource of any society. They are our lifeline to survive, grow, and thrive."

Our vision of the Twin Cities becoming free from violence is designed to be a self-fulfilling prophecy.

At future meetings, we are hoping to hear the different ideas and approaches that participants intend to present in September, in terms of lectures, workshops, artistic renditions and the like, all demonstrating actual work being done to create an environment in the Twin Cities in which people can feel safe and free to grow and develop.

I am hoping and praying that most of the religions, schools, government officials, including the police, and even gang members, will be involved. Our committee will coordinate and publicize the activities. Stay tuned!

The United States Bishops Annual Meeting

In mid-November 2016, the bishops of the United States held their annual meeting in Baltimore. Pax Christi, a peace organization within the Catholic Church and the Association of US Catholic Priests (AUSCP) were hosting for twelve bishops, a "simple supper" of soup and bread in the spirit of Pope Francis at St. Vincent de Paul Parish the night of November 15.

This supper was just two miles from the hotel where the bishops were meeting, so we hoped to attract as many bishops as we could. Our program focused on PTSD suffered by United States military personnel in wars. Videos that were witness of ill soldiers demonstrated that PTSD was caused not only by participating in actual conflict, but most especially by the shooting and killing of children and women intentionally or unintentionally during armed conflict. I found it hard to watch.

The previous April, Catholic charities gathered in Vatican City at a conference sponsored by the pontifical Council for Justice and Peace. At the conclusion, they declared, "There is no just war." Their declaration went on, "The time has come for our church to be a loving witness and invest far greater human resources in promoting a spirituality and practice of nonviolence and in forming communities in effective nonviolent practices."

At the AUSCP previous June meeting, our organization supported the Vatican's "Just Peace" declaration. Taking a clear stand for creative and gospel nonviolence, we agreed that too often the "just war" theory has been used to endorse, rather than prevent war.

Suggesting that a just war is possible undermines the moral imperative to develop tools and capacities for the nonviolent transformation of violence.

This has been my lifetime goal. Oh, if only this support had happened during the Vietnam War. I'm Thanking God, however, that it is happening now. I'm grateful to God beyond words.

Washington, D.C.

April 6, 2017 was an overcast rainy day. Exactly hundred years ago on this day, the United States entered World War I, the war to end all wars. The day before, I arrived in Washington at the invitation of my fellow priest, Bernie Survil, to participate in a seminar on nonviolence at Catholic University.

The previous February, I assisted in drafting a letter to Archbishop Timothy Broglio from the Association of the US Catholic Priests (AUSCP). We pledged our prayers and our willingness to assist in this important trust. As well, we made the request that, in his new position, he would replace "Just War Theory" with "Just Peace Theory," which recently received the blessing of Pope Francis.

On March 14, 2017, I wrote personally to the Archbishop stating that Bernie Survil and I would be in Washington on April 6 and requested we might visit with him at his office. If that were not possible, perhaps we could speak with one of his auxiliary bishops or staff members. If that were not doable, maybe he would be kind enough to suggest another date for a meeting with him.

April 4, 2017

A day before flying to Washington, I received the Archbishop's reply stating that neither he nor his auxiliary bishops would be in Washington on April 6. He added that his "meager staff" was "also occupied" on that day. No mention was made of a future date.

On the morning of April 6 at the Dorothy Day House in Washington, as a number of us gathered to further prepare for the afternoon seminar, someone mentioned there was a daily noon mass at Archbishop Broglio's office building (The Edwin Cardinal O'Brien Pastoral Center). I telephoned the Pastoral Center, gave my name and that I was a priest of the Archdiocese of St. Paul asking to participate in the noon mass. The secretary put me through to the vicar general, Monsignor John Foster. I made the same request. He asked if I would like to stay for lunch afterward, to which I gratefully agreed.

Upon arriving at the Pastoral Center, slightly before 11:30 a.m., I found the door to be locked. Pulling and then pushing on the door, frustrated I waved and knocked to get the attention of the receptionist whom I could barely view through to the door window. Finally, she waved back, which I interpreted as "please wait."

After some minutes a tall priest appeared, opened the door, and stood in the entrance. I gave my name and said, "I have come for mass." He announced, "The Archbishop called and said I *was not to let you in*."

Dumbfounded, I spoke meekly, "Why, what is this about? How come?"

"I don't know," he replied, "he even got me out of a meeting to tell me."

Still shocked, I managed to ask, "What is your name?" He soundly stated, "Monsignor John Foster."

Reaching for my briefcase at my feet, I started to ask, "Can I leave some materials," but before I could finish my question, the Monsignor, moving his hand from side to side, clearly said "No."

Silence followed. I did not know what to say. Then, as if an afterthought, he added, "If you wish to go to mass, there is a noon mass at the shrine."

I don't recall saying good-bye. Feeling dismissed, I trudged off in the rain back to the seminar on the Catholic University campus. More amazed than angry, my thoughts wandered to Pope Francis and his request that people enter into dialogue, talk to each other, rather than fight with each other. I wondered, "How can dialogue happen when we priests cannot even talk to each other?"

**It occurred to me that thinking
differently is a threat causing fear.**

Later in April, I mailed the intended information to the Archbishop's office stating there must have been some misunderstanding for my not being able to participate in the noon mass.

The Archbishop responded, thanking me in a personal note for the information. He added that "to celebrate mass at the pastoral center," I would need to make a written request ahead of time, together with "a copy of the customary letter of good standing from your archdiocese."

I doubt that was the real reason for the refusal, given the vicar general's initial invitation inviting me to lunch.

CHAPTER 20

The End is the Beginning

**"Too much is about getting even (justice).
It's important to get inside what it takes to bring
about peace in the world—not only in theory but also in
practice. That's what I've lived."**

– Harry Bury

Transformative Change

At the beginning of every course, I suggested to my students that *to learn is to change*. "If you haven't changed your behavior by the end of this course, then you haven't learned, and I have failed and should not be paid. The more you've changed, the more you've learned, and the more pay I should receive." I noticed students smiling as I make this statement.

**"Change is always a risk. But, it is also a risk
not to change. Even a greater risk, I think."**

– Cardinal Walter Kasper

Over my lifetime I came to discover that I needed to change a lot if I were going to be a witness to the gospel message of Jesus, that is, bring peace on earth. In the process, I have become a different person, both a person I've never been, and a person I've always been. My transformation doesn't nullify my past but rather builds upon it.

I didn't change alone. It happened with and because of others, many of whom I've mentioned in my story. Also, change required "opportunity"—such as invitations to the Pentagon, to Gaza in the Holy Land and to Vietnam—without which I could not have changed to the degree that I have.

My transformation can be considered from four perspectives: What I've discovered physically, intellectually, emotionally, and spiritually.

1) Physical Discoveries

Good health and enormous energy throughout my life have been a blessing. Other than the normal childhood illnesses, from which I recovered quickly, only four challenges occurred.

First, during a 1995 physical exam, my doctor discovered a tumor on my prostate that turned out to be cancer. Because of my good health at age 65, he counseled an aggressive approach, explaining that prostate cancer patients who are over 70 and in poor health usually die from some other malady, because prostate cancer tends to grow slowly. I did extensive research and picked what to me was the best treatment option. I am alive to prove it worked.

Second, in the summer of 2006, a horrendous nosebleed that wouldn't quit woke me in the middle of the night. Lying on my back trying to control the blood flow, I had trouble breathing. Frightened, I realized I couldn't drive to the hospital, so I called 911.

In Emergency Receiving, I was told that a new technology for treating nosebleeds was a balloon. In retrospect, I realized it was probably the first time the resident physician had done the procedure; scar tissue damage was excessive and nearly closed my right nostril. Two surgical efforts over the next year proved unsuccessful. At present, I can barely breathe out of the right nostril. Further, I have lost much of my ability to smell and taste.

A third medical challenge happened when I was diagnosed with glaucoma, a disease of the eyes. However, my eye doctor said, "Don't worry. If you place the eye drops I prescribe in your eyes every day, I guarantee you will not go blind." While grateful for his encouragement, I was surprised at his certainty.

I asked, "Doctor, how much do the eye drops cost?"

"It's a hundred dollars a bottle. But you will not have to pay that much because you have insurance."

"How long does a bottle of the medicine last, Doctor?

"One month."

I pursued it, "What happens to people who do not have insurance?" My question was met with silence. Immediately, I pictured in my mind's eye scads of blind people begging on the streets of Bangkok, Thailand. Now I understood. They had no money or insurance.

The fourth challenge came at age 85, when the pain in my right hip made it difficult for me to walk. On examination, I learned serious arthritis was the culprit. Surgery was advised. I went ahead. Today I can walk without pain, but I can no longer run and play racquetball—a small price for being pain free.

Overall, I had no complaints about my treatments except this one important thing: if when the staff came into my room, they saw themselves in the bed, and treated me in the way they would have liked to be treated. With this thought, in the hospital's request for feedback, I urged for more training for the staff to value and show more empathy.

In each of these challenges, my visualizing overcoming cancer, managing glaucoma, and dealing with arthritis has enhanced the experience. With affirmations, I visualized being well with God's help—and miracles happened.

Interesting that when my dentist found no cavities for years, he said, "I don't know what you are doing, but keep it up." Never have I been asked what my secret has been to achieve a healthy life.

For all my surgeries, my dear friend of almost 45 years, Nancy Nelson, drove me to the hospital, and then nursed me back to health.

She was ever present, serving as both listener and questioner to make sure the right procedures took place. I'm forever grateful for her kindness and care. All patients need an advocate, someone who asks lots of questions of the doctors and nurses—someone determined and fearless like Nancy.

Genetics have played a major role in my good health throughout life. Mom and Dad lived to be 91 and 96 respectively, dying within just six weeks of each other in 1998. My Carmelite sister is nearly 84, and my brother has made it to 81.

Another secret to a healthy old age is regular stretching exercises. At first Tai Chi, and now Yoga, became a daily practice. If I could influence early childhood education in the United States and throughout the world, I would advocate stretching exercises for children in a manner that would become habit-forming for life. It needs to be the goal of all gym classes.

A month at Pritikin Longevity Center in California with friend Bill Carlson (Nancy Nelson's husband) in 1987 taught me another key to high-quality health: a diet of mostly fresh fruits and vegetables—a diet that Michelle Obama advocates as she seeks to improve the diet and exercise of the nation's children. In addition, my dog Mickey took me for a 30-minute walk every day, no matter the weather.

Had my parents made these health discoveries, I suspect it would have added immensely to the quality of their later lives. These health discoveries have been transforming for me.

2) Intellectual Discoveries

My story of transformative intellectual growth is found in my recent book, *An Invitation to Think and Feel Differently in the New Millennium*. In it, I wanted to address the underlying theological, spiritual, cultural, and political issues alive and transforming in our world community today. My intent wasn't to give answers, only to raise questions about what could happen if a critical mass of people continues to change fundamental assumptions.

Certain questions addressed are:

- What are the spiritual and secular foundations for an ethics of social justice for the common good? This inquiry is of high value to me.

- How do we move from the politics of fear and blame—which I observe in Thailand, Vietnam, China, Palestine, Israel, the United States, and countless other countries—toward a politics of values that affirm both human life and human dignity, with effective implementation?

- How do we enjoy—in the church, corporations, community, and government—the benefits of centralization, while, at the same time, encourage and realize genuine subsidiarity and solidarity?

Socialization

It seems that our behavior is essentially influenced by our socialization. It may be called conditioning, programming, even "brainwashing." Our view of how the world works is based largely on our particular culture and upbringing. Our understanding, though, isn't chiseled in stone; our mental models never stop changing. They continue to emerge and evolve because of friends, schooling, religious practice, media, travel, personal experiences, and more. People reared in China perceive reality quite differently from those reared in Nigeria. Bostonians perceive the world differently from Texans. However, if a Texan should move to Boston, some changes in perception are apt to happen.

I assume that the way people view reality in one culture is not wrong, but simply different from the way others perceive it in another culture. The older we get, the less likely we are to change our programmed conceptions, and thus, the more we behave in a routine and habitual manner.

Our socialization or programming leads to many unconscious, fundamental assumptions about life. For example: we may assume some people are evil, and/or, we may assume that facts, as we perceive them, are completely certain. These assumptions lead to further assumed judgments such as: some people are evil and deserve to be punished for justice's sake. Many assume this point of view (this assumption) is absolutely certain and feel hate and fear toward those judged to be evil. Behavior follows, to build more prisons to house these "evil" people, no matter the cost, because safety (one's top value) is paramount. Too often, torture, as in solitary confinement, is practiced to teach these "evil ones" a lesson.

Our programmed beliefs, attitudes, and values become ever stronger because we look for evidence that confirms how we already view the world. It often takes a significant emotional event to influence us to even begin to question our programmed mental models, much less change our minds and think and feel differently about highly valued issues. Thus, I conclude, one is rarely motivated to significantly change one's own behavior, only doing so when convinced it's in one's self-interest. Instead, one sleepwalks through life, behaving routinely and out of habit, convinced that the way one views reality *is the way it is, without question.*

Through study and extraordinary life experiences, I've come to change four fundamental, unconscious assumptions about reality— a mental model that continues to evolve.

• First Assumption

I've learned to assume that we are all in the process of discovering; no one is completely certain about any person, idea, or event. No scientist claims that something is empirically true, but rather ascribes high probability. Yet, the average individual usually insists that the way he or she views something is certainly the way it is, and often seeks to convince others of its certainty. If the individual is unsuccessful, his dissenter with his or her ideas is often dismissed. Once one is certain about an issue, listening to another view tends to be a waste of time and energy. Unaware, the individual is claiming infallibility. "I'm absolutely right and I know I am absolutely right." Clearly, if others disagree, they are wrong!

How many "bosses," even bishops, have we all endured who assert they are right about something, often demanding absolute obedience and eliminating the possibility of dialogue? When one feels passionately about an issue, one may even be willing to kill those who disagree, as manifested in wars throughout history.

Author of the 1971 *Rules for Radicals: A Pragmatic Primer for Realistic Radicals*, and famous community organizer, Saul Alinski, agreed, writing "If you think you've got an inside track to absolute truth, you become doctrinaire, humorless and intellectually constipated. The greatest crimes in history have been perpetrated by such religious and political and racial fanatics."

If a critical mass of people terminated this assumption of being certain, and assumed we could be wrong about any issue, we would be more likely to listen— not for purposes of refuting, but to understand and learn from those who disagree with us.

Cultivating an open mind, we are more likely to change our mind and, therefore, our programming. Our behavior, I assume, would contribute to peace in our families, communities, organizations, and nations. For example, people in one culture would not be upset if a woman in another culture wears clothing covering her body from head to toe.

• Second Assumption

> I've learned to assume that nothing in life
> is absolutely good, and nothing is absolutely bad;
> both good and bad exist in each and every
> situation, event, and person.

As a consequence, I assume that it is in the self-interest of all to desist from our current practice of focusing on the "bad," naming it a problem, and trying to fix it. We have a society that looks for problems, and, as a result, we reward problem-solvers who concentrate almost entirely on the negative. So much attention to what is bad or wrong takes the joy out of living—for many, life itself becomes a problem. Pope John XXIII characterized persons of that ilk as "prophets of doom," and Pope Francis refers to them as "sourpusses."

My life experience has led me to discover that our time and energy is better served if we attend to what is good in every person's behavior, event, and situation. I've learned to appreciate others, and find value in what occurs, by observing the positive. When I'm most attentive, I quit complaining, blaming, and condemning others, and myself, and begin to celebrate the good and positive events, situations, and people in my life. Removing from my vocabulary the very word "problem" has been an effective first step for me. Rather than use the word "problem," instead I speak of "challenges" and "opportunities." I can imagine a critical mass of people on this earth refusing to see problems, and instead, start seeing challenges and opportunities, which then would result in less complaining and considerably more joy, happiness, and creativity. And yes, positive change.

Further vocabulary changes based on this optimistic view of reality are the removal of such expressions as, "I have to," "I must," even "I choose" in both my thinking and speaking. I now think and say, "I get to," "I want to," "I need to," and "I'm determined to." The result: I perceive I am in control of my life, and not controlled by others or events. I am my own person, intelligent enough to look after myself, and not be a victim of others or of life circumstances. It feels good.

Moreover, I no longer say "that's true," or "yes," but rather, "I agree," indicating I am not in possession of the truth, in accordance with the first Assumption. Facts, in my opinion, are simply perceptions. Hence, I say and write, "I perceive," rather than "I know."

• Third Assumption

I've learned to assume that we are all one; we aren't separate from each other. While our senses may suggest otherwise, I've learned *not* to trust them completely. For centuries our senses informed us that the earth was flat and wood is solid. Instead of assuming that we are all separate from each other, therefore, *why not assume we are all one*? Not only would this make our life on earth more productive and hopeful, it would also make it far more exciting, energizing, and engaging.

According to God's revelation through St. Paul, Christians believe we are all one in Christ, that Christ is the head and we are all the members. Jesus himself claimed to be the vine, and we are the branches. We are not autonomous beings, but differ only in our functions and the roles we play, similar to the hand and the foot of one's body. In so being, we image the oneness of the Father, Son, and Holy Spirit.

I can imagine a critical mass of the earth's inhabitants assuming *we are all one people*. Once this idea is internalized, we realize what is good for others needs to be good for us, and vice-versa, otherwise, it isn't any good at all.

> Then, competition as a way of life dies,
> and cooperation replaces it. War is not even
> considered because to kill another is to kill oneself.
> Peace results.

• Fourth Assumption

Lastly, I've learned to assume there are no evil or good people in the world—simply people acting in their perceived self-interest. I can't imagine any sane person getting up in the morning bent on doing evil. Evil we do, but not intentionally. I assume one rationalizes, believing one has good reasons for the murders one commits, the harm one does.

When the United States Air Force deliberately dropped two atomic bombs on the Japanese people in 1945, President Truman and the pilots themselves assumed they were performing a meritorious action. The Japanese people, however, had a far different perception as they watched their children being vaporized.

Loving parents are able to make a distinction between their children and their children's behavior. Although they are upset with their children's negative behavior, the parents don't condemn their children, but rather continue to love them no matter what they do. I'm learning to do the same with people who seek to hurt me—and others.

> I very much wish and pray that my government
> will change and act similarly. They may be upset
> with foreign governments, but not condemn
> them, and instead use empathy in an
> effort to understand their motivation.

338

Although I may view certain behaviors of individuals or nations, including my own, to be unacceptable—even downright evil—I intend to love the person or the national people. I assume they are doing the best they can in accordance with what they understand. They may very well be ignorant, but not evil.

I can imagine a critical mass of people worldwide assuming *war is not the answer*, assuming individuals who break society's laws act out of ignorance. A just societal response is neither revenge nor punishment, but rather rehabilitation through education. I understand that the original intention of the United Nations communication was to separate the warring parties, bring them into dialogue, facilitating a dialogue that would lead to compromise and peace. Unfortunately, out of fear, five nations—U.S., England, France, Russia, and China—opted for a veto that resulted in the United Nations being largely impotent when it comes to preventing wars.

If a society has yet to discover methods for rehabilitating errants (a.k.a. criminals, another term that needs to be reframed) such as pedophiles or murderers, in the future I trust society will not blame individual errants. Society needs to take responsibility for not knowing how to rehabilitate them—much the same as the medical profession doesn't blame the cancer patient for their lack of knowledge on how to cure said patient's cancer. In both situations, I trust society will invest in further research, so that both cancer patients and lawbreakers, together with their victims, can be healed and find peace.

In the meantime, may we make every effort to treat the errant persons as kindly as we can and seek to enable them to understand that changing their behavior is in their long-term self-interest.

This is a transformative discovery for me, hardly envisioned as a young priest emerging from the seminary over 60 years ago. I took it for granted that the appropriate consequence for "criminal" behavior was punishment, described as justice. However, having viewed and experienced continual crime and punishment has changed my mind. While these people do bad things, they are not criminals, but mistaken, and so should not be punished but "educated."

> When a critical mass of people discover, internalize, and act on these four fundamental assumptions, I believe individuals, families, organizations, and nations will take a major step toward peace in our beloved ravaged world.

3) Emotional Discoveries

"Awareness, awareness, awareness…" urged the Indian Jesuit priest Anthony de Mello.

I'm finally becoming aware of not only what I'm thinking and doing, but especially what I'm feeling in the present moment. I never gave feelings much thought while growing up. If you had asked me, "What are you feeling?" I'd answer with a thought. For example, "I feel that my mother isn't doing very well." Actually, I wasn't "feeling that," I was "thinking that." I now assume in retrospect that my actual feeling was anxiety because my mother was ill.

Graduate school at Case Western Reserve University, particularly the T-group (sensitivity training) experience and the Gestalt Institute of Cleveland provided the environment in which I made this transformative discovery, a discovery *that* enabled me to begin to have open and honest relationships with men and women. Through exercise after exercise, I learned to feel, be aware of feelings, and appreciate feelings as special gifts from God. I began to get in touch with the affective side of my personality. Hence, I learned to pay attention, appreciate, and be affectionate.

I learned that no bad feelings exist. Benefits arise from feeling sad, cold, hot, hungry, fearful, and even angry. There is a time and place for every feeling.

No one can cause me to laugh, I now assume. I determine that something someone says is funny, and almost instantaneously I want to laugh, and I do. No one can *make* me angry. They might do something with which I disagree. I then determine the best thing for me to do is be angry. *I always do what I want.* The key, therefore, is wanting what is spiritually, emotionally, intellectually, and physically good for me, in accordance with my evolving socialized values.

If I'm not experiencing feelings of happiness, no way do I permit myself to blame people, or the weather, or the government, or anything else outside myself. I'm responsible for whether I feel happy or not. It makes no sense to empower another—or the weather—to upset me.

If I were to allow someone else to bring unhappiness upon me, I'd be giving away the power and control over my own life that God gave me. Not to accept this gift of power and control would signify a lack of gratitude to God.

When I experience feelings of unhappiness, I look not outside but inside myself to determine what I'm doing that brings unhappy feelings into the picture. Unlike the comic Red Skelton (on radio and TV from 1937–1971), I refuse to claim, "The devil made me do it."

From Anthony de Mello, Indian-born Jesuit priest and psychotherapist, a spiritual teacher, writer and public speaker, and from personal experience, I've learned a technique that has been transformative—namely, I observe everything inside me and around me as much as possible, and as if it were happening to someone else. My "I" watches my "Me" think, feel, and act. My "I" then determines whether or not Harry J. Bury wants to continue Me's behaviors in the present moment.

341

My "I" for example, notices how my "Me" responds as Harry converses with a friend over lunch. When "I" conclude that "Me" is failing to actively listen to my friend and is thinking about what to say next, my "I" directs my "Me" to listen in an active manner (because active listening is a high value of mine) and my "Me" obeys. When I'm under attack, however, it is difficult for my "I" to control my "Me's" behavior. Without thinking, failing in awareness, I resort to childish, even primitive programming. I verbally strike out mistakenly without awareness of my violent behavior. Afterward, I regret my action. I call this behavior a sin.

Human behavior was presented to me at an early age as a "deficit model," which was described as *a problem*. I was socialized to believe people are broken and need to be fixed, or screwed up and need to be straightened out. Humans in need of fixing are those who do not follow the rules. Those equipped for the task of fixing people are at the top of the hierarchy. Blind obedience stands as a high value. Just listen to your "superiors," I was told, and do what they tell you, and you'll do fine both in this life and the next. Much of what I heard was "Don'ts," which outnumbered "Do's" by a long shot. "Don't do drugs, don't drink and drive, don't eat too fast, and on and on.

Once one is labeled psychotic, neurotic, a crook, or another unfavorable description, it is difficult if not impossible to outlive the judgment. Often, blame follows those who are labeled pedophiles, alcoholics, drug addicts—all stereotypes, and all perceived to deserve punishment as a deterrent to their negative behavior. It's important to distinguish between the person—and the person's behaviors.

It is almost impossible to have empathy and compassion if I do not listen to the other person, and if I do not ask questions. Each person is on a development path and the journey is about integration, development, and wholeness. Some get stuck at a low level and need a jumpstart to get going again. Often, only being loved unconditionally does the trick.

The renowned psychologist Abraham Maslow seems to agree. In 1964 he wrote that psychology tends to focus on mental illness at the expense of mental health, so he began to study people who are self-actualized—persons motivated to learn and understand, to appreciate and enjoy beauty, and to do what they were created to do and be in life.

Self-actualization means becoming our authentic selves as we realize our potential, and to transform and transcend ourselves. We connect to something beyond ego; this attitude encourages others to share in the search for fulfillment.

Other positive psychologists, especially Martin Seligman, famous for his theory of "learned helplessness," enabled me to become ever more optimistic about humanity. His research efforts focused on what makes life worth living. He examined human strengths rather than weaknesses. I became entranced. I came to understand and internalized that the good life on earth is not simply the absence of dysfunction, but requires its own understanding, particularly through experience and feeling. The "heart" for Seligman matters more than the "head." Critical thinking is important, which I previously understood, but I now discovered that even more significant is unconditional caring, and how a person verbalizes one's caring.

One's sharing of feelings isn't the result of genetics; it is learned behavior. I found this idea "good news." I finally began to understand Jesus and the "good news" of the gospel. So, I set out to learn, fortified by past experience. Although an introvert, I observed the positive results from the extrovert behavior of my seminary classmate, Frank Reynolds, and imitated him with satisfying success. I watched how his outgoing, attentive behavior toward each person in a room brought delight to the faces of all. I thought to myself, "I can do this too." And I strove to imitate him, although it was a slow, gradual transformation.

I focus now on being aware of my feelings, and am determined to be happy. I use self-affirmations and visualization to manifest happiness in my life. I avoid complaining. Making every effort to increase positive emotions, I've come to experience happiness and wellbeing daily. I experience gentle re-enforcers by reading comments made by people like Abraham Lincoln, who said:

"Most people are as happy as they make up their minds to be."

Discovering how to make myself happy was a transformative event for me, marred only by my failure to pass along this skill to many others. It is amazing how this idea and this behavior are resisted. I'm grateful for the learning, and continue to visualize a critical mass of people greeting strangers with a cheerful "Happy Monday" and friendly smile, to spread peace and goodwill everywhere. I visualize people feeling good in tending to others. I decry (actually despise) the sports dictum: "no pain, no gain." I realize the good we can do comes through God's gifts, Jesus's examples, and the Holy Spirit's inspiration. At the same time, it is just fine that we feel good about ourselves when we reach out to others. My heart aches for those with low self-esteem that result in viewing themselves as inept, worthless, fearful of taking risks, and trying new things.

4) Spiritual Discoveries

God is not a stranger apart from ourselves, but rather is at the very center of our being. Jesus said, "When I am raised to life again, you will know that I am in my Father, and you are in me, and I am in you."

In my old age, finally, I'm coming to trust that Christ Jesus is the Holy One of God, the outpouring of the Holy Spirit, the physical presence of God in others and actually in me. Hence, we are all other Christs. I trust that in the humanity of Jesus lies the glory of us all, that He came to this earth to reveal to us that the transcendent God of history dwells in each of us *as us*. By becoming aware that we are all other Christs, we are the operative expressions of divinity itself. "Do you not know," Jesus asked his disciples, "that the Kingdom of God resides in you?" We are co-creators and co-redeemers.

Jesus came to establish this new order of living by which He lives in each one of us. I'm just now finally getting it—*better late than never*! It is the new kingdom Jesus brought into the world, designed to change everything. It transforms individuals and the world, and is a call to personal salvation and social transformation.

I trust Jesus came to reveal this marvelous event to us, so that we would cease killing each other, for to kill one another in war, capital punishment, or through abortion, is to crucify Christ again.

If I don't trust that Jesus is alive today, all I have is a list of *His* teachings similar to those of Mohammad, Moses, Buddha, and others—inspiring words from spiritual leaders who lived a long time ago.

With a living teacher, life for me is not a waiting game between Christ's first and second coming. Life is to live with trust that Christ is truly here and has never left us. It is the conscious awareness of God's presence within us that enables humankind to experience a new mutual bond with Divinity and with one another. We humans are able to reach out beyond our many mutual limitations and transgressions while offering each other the space needed for one's personal search.

Observing people in the various nations where I've had the privilege to visit and live, I've come to appreciate the diversity of different nationalities, skin colors, histories, religions, and sexual orientations.

Undeniably, we hurt each other. We realize that our limitations and transgressions are a part of us, and we can't ignore them. We are aware of our many failures when we've failed to behave like Jesus. The psychologist Gustav Jung calls this "our shadow." While distinct, my shadow cannot be separate from me. My limitations and transgressions are part of my oneness.

Can we then move on to focus our time and energy on being what God wants us to be, namely, Christ Jesus in us, and *not* focus on our weaknesses and failures? We transform into blessings the genuine hurts to ourselves and others by trusting that God brings good out of evil. God is calling us to focus on Christ in us and others because God needs us to do so. I never used to imagine God needing anything or God changing. Yet, is it not possible for God also to continue to evolve? Maybe changing, rather than unchanging, is God's perfection.

Further, cannot God need our love and cooperation because God wills it? Totally anthropomorphic perception, I realize. It is where my heart is at this moment in my spiritual journey—until it changes.

Spiritually, my life is not about "suffering" and "sacrificing" as I once understood it to be, although barely practiced. My spiritual life isn't a perpetual Lent, "no pain, no gain," as I had been instructed. Christ died on the cross for us to show us how to live and die. Once is enough. If need be, we die like Christ, forgiving persecutors, who know not what they do—but that isn't God's design. God's will, I believe, is that we live in peace, rejoice, and not be fearful because we have no enemies. Jesus kept reminding His disciples of this. Life is not about a better tomorrow; it's about a better here and now. We, as other Christs, get to make it happen with God's grace. Another marvelous challenge and miracle.

I'm now in a place where life is what happens *in* us, not *to* us. My hope is that I and a critical mass of other human beings will stop focusing on ourselves as sinners. Of course, we are sinners, and I'm deeply aware personally that I've done things I regret, stupid beyond reason—but *such past acts are over*. I pray to get over *them* and beyond *them*. I seek to experience salvation here and in eternity as a joyful communion. God forgives me and us continually. So let us rejoice and make merry. We are a resurrected people.

Religion, then, I have discovered, is only tangentially about morality. Religion at its core is about relationships. It's about reestablishing, through awareness, an intimate relationship with the Triune God in and through and with Jesus the Christ. Everything else is secondary.

Because I'm intent to love God above everything else, I love what God is about. And I trust God, motivated by love, is about creating a universe with human beings who love God, ourselves, and all others—no exceptions. The measure of my love for God is my love for God's creation, human beings most especially, but also everything else: animals, plants, nature in all its beauty. Nothing is excluded. For "how can I love God, whom I cannot see, if I don't love all of God's works, which I can see?"

Working for Social Justice

The more aware I become that Christ is in me and in everyone else, and aware that I participate in the oneness of humankind, the more motivated I become to work for social justice.

Social justice, says Jim Wallis, editor of *Sojourners* magazine, "involves right relationships between human beings and God, between human beings themselves and as communities, and between human beings and material creation." And this awareness is a gift from God, a manifestation of the Kingdom of God on earth.

The greatest challenge, I perceive, is my lack of awareness that I need to change my mind and heart and discard the information I received as part of my upbringing.

"I'm not a do-gooder working out my own personal challenges under the guise of helping others, but rather I'm more like a reformed alcoholic who has experienced the liberating power of God's justice and mercy."

– Jim Wallis, Christian writer, political activist,
and founder of *Sojourner* magazine.

As Wallis said, "I'm called to seek justice for the poor, not as the wise to the ignorant or the strong to the weak, but as the poor to the poor, the loved to the loved. My action comes from the consciousness of the Christ-life in me and in all others; it's communal."

Because we cannot change the world by ourselves, we are called, not to wring our hands, but rather to use them, to do community organizing. Our efforts cannot focus only on what's wrong; that focus would be negatively judgmental. Our actions need to emphasize a vision of what constitutes the common good.

Thus, I envision humankind laughing, eating, drinking, telling stories and jokes, and embracing each other, friends and strangers alike. No enemies. Our values are freedom, opportunity, and equality under the law for every one of every race, color, creed, culture, and gender. Courage and service abound, together with empathy and compassion. Indian guru, Ramana Maharshi in being asked, "How should we treat each other?" responded, "There are no others."

"If we have no peace, it is because we have forgotten that we belong to each other."

– Saint Mother Teresa of Calcutta

Further, I visualize structures, systems, and policies designed for implementation of this transformation:

- Economic reform in which there is social mobility for people in all sectors of the economic class structure, most of all for people who are at the bottom—an economy in which prosperity is shared and the poor protected.

- Walls preventing entrance of immigrants come tumbling down, never to be replaced.

- An emphasis on jobs that not only offer fair wages for

348

genuine contributions to the common good, but also offer the opportunity to share in decision-making, protection of the environment, and a concern for future generations' needs.

- Structures designed not for profit but for the promotion of human flourishing, happiness, and wellbeing, with a change from a stockholder model to a stakeholder model of corporate governance. Worries about survival dissipate and interest in solidarity increases.

The issue of government is neither large nor small. The issue is quality. Transparency, accountability, and service are the characteristics of quality government. And we ourselves are responsible for it; as Abraham Lincoln said, we believe in a government "of the people, by the people, and for the people."

Hence, I have come full circle to the realization that to be a spiritual priest I need to be political. Jim Wallis points out that the Reverend Martin Luther King, Jr., ...

> "wasn't content to just ask American Christians not to personally practice discrimination against black people; he understood that the nation needed a civil rights law and a voting rights act to stop racial discrimination and fulfill real democracy for all Americans, including for people of color. The scriptures reveal a God of justice, not merely a God of charity... The most common subjects of the prophets' reproaches are kings, rulers, judges, employers—the rich and powerful in charge of the world's governments, courts, economics, systems, and structures.... When those who are in charge mistreat the poor and vulnerable, say the scriptures, it is not just unkind but also wrong and unjust... The scriptures show great concern for the widow and the orphan, the poor and the oppressed, the victims of courts or

unscrupulous employers, debtors whose debts need
to be forgiven, and strangers in the land who need to
be welcomed."

I hear Pope Francis saying "Amen" to that.

So, I have come to trust that the Christ in me needs to look
out for and love Christ in others, individuals and persons who create or fail to create structures, systems and policies which enhance
the lives of other Christs, even those I may never meet or know.
Recognizing and trusting Christ in others and in myself has been
a slow and growing transformation. I'm grateful for it, and I'm
deeply challenged by the depth of Christ's call to discipleship.

Now, many years later I would add this: With author and nun,
Joan Chittister, I believe the Jesus that truly rose from the dead in
Jerusalem also rises in us, if we invite Him. If that happens, we
begin to live a new and transformed life altogether different. For
one thing, one is no longer afraid of death. One can also live with
paradoxes and more easily think in non-dualistic terms. The benefits are huge.

For example, *dualism* thinks in terms of either/or, resulting in
right or wrong, black or white conclusions. *Non-dualism* thinks in
terms of both/and. Consequently, a non-dualistic thinker can be
both pro-choice and pro-life when it comes to the issue of abortion. How so? By believing in and working for single payer, universal healthcare. Then, pregnant women are assured of being able
to rear their born children in the same manner that the majority of
Americans are able to do so. That is no small issue when one con-
siders the cost of having a child and caring for them.

The reason abortion has continued to cause such conflict is because
of dualistic thinking—and people believing that they have the truth.
Whoever disagrees is therefore automatically wrong/mistaken.

In addition, non-dualitic thinkers could more easily view the
birth of a child as a precious gift from God and rejoice, no matter
what other circumstances might exist.

Finally, I don't consider this summation the "end" of my life or the end of my relationship with you, my reader. Death, even when it happens to me, is just a turn in the road, as my friend Judy Cauley expresses in her poem that follows. My message continues my walking on with my life, an intimate presence, one accompanying the reader in love.

Coming Forth

I am not walking out,
just walking on,
a yet more intimate presence,
one-with-you in love,
only love, always love,
lighting the way,
accompanying you.
I am coming forth...
appearing new,
walking you home.

– Judy Cauley, St. Joseph Sister

INDEX

A

Saul Alinski 335
Peter Arnett 158

B

Joan Baez 81, 84, 86
Tran Ngoc Bau 7-9, 15, 121, 139,
    145-7, 151-2,
Monsignor William Baumgartner
    201
Fr. Daniel Berrigan 86, 95, 99, 224
Mme. Nguyen Thi Binh 218
Archbishop Nguyen Van Binh 139
Archbishop Leo Binz 25, 53, 62, 67,
    70, 85
Dr. Jim Breitenbucher 108
Archbishop Timothy Broglio 326-7
Ambassador Elsworth Bunker 2,
    9-13
Dr. Leo Buscaglia 78
Bishop Charles Buswell 149

C

Lieutenant William L. Calley 142
Sister Judy Cauley 60, 351
Madame Cam 166
Archbishop Dom Helder Camara
    184
Bill Carlson 101, 108, 332

Fr. Marion Casey 41
Deputy Mayor Le Qhang Chanh 224
Lt. Norris Charles (wife Olga) 161
Anna Chennault 144-5
Sister Joan Chittister 78, 350
Professor Noam Chomsky 305-6
Rev. William Sloanc Coffin 158,
    161-2, 175-6, 182
Fr. George Coleman 93
Dr. Don Conroy 39, 59, 70, 81, 191,
Rachel Corrie 267, 271-2, 280, 283,
    287-9, 298
Fr. Charles E. Coughlin 30, 33, 38,
    40, 49
Fr. Donald Cozzins 318

D

Bob Dalton 1, 226, 228, 233-4
Dorothy Day 41, 48-9, 327
Luu Van Dat 219
Nguyen Dinh Dau 313
Fr. John Dear 319-20, 323
Fr. John Dee xxv, 1-2, 12, 16, 19. 21,
    23-7, 149-50
Jim DeHarpporte 234, 237
David Dellinger 157
John Denver 75, 107-8
Fr. Peter Doherty 263
Ngo Cong Duc 139-40, 153, 223

E

Professor Saul Eisen 126
Major Edward Elias 161
Daniel Ellsberg 148
Bishop George R. Evans 149

F

Darrell Fasching xiv
Fred Fleming 40
Monsignor John Foster 327
Tom Fox 120, 138-9, 224, 313
Professor Frank Friedlander 121

G

Fr. George Garrelts 70-1, 93, 191
Lt. Mark Gartley (mother Minnie)
   161, 175
Bui Tran Giang 221
Professor Bob Graham 210
Graham Green 137
Dick Gregory 76
John Howard Griffin 76
Fr. James E. Groppi 115
Bishop Thomas Gumbleton 149

H

Marianne Hamilton 105, 157-8, 191,
   213
Dr. Dale Hammerschmidt 90
John Hart 159, 161, 181, 186
Archbishop Bernard Hebda 319
Dr. Carolyn Lukensmeyer Hirsch
   119
Jerri Hirsch 309-10
Dr. Leonard Hirsch xxv, 1, 150-2,
   218
Venerable Thich Thieu Hoa, the
   Elder 15
Fr. Lan Quang Hoc 170

Gerard Manley Hopkins 27
Fr. Bill Hunt 63, 112, 202
Nguyen Huy 218
Tran Quang Huy 220
Mr. Nguyen Van Huynh 214, 216

I/J

Fr. Al Janicke 91
Professor Diana Johnstone 104

K

Fr. Jim Kaston 93
Bill Keatts 323
Fr. Quenton Kennedy 40,
Mr. Khanh 177
Cardinal Archbishop of Hanoi, Trinh
   Nhu Khua 178
Fr. Frank Kittock 40
Fr. Maximilian Kolbe 25
Kris Kristofferson 111
Frank Kroncke xiii-xiv, 99-100
Dr. Warren and Patty Kump 61

L

Nguyen Tran Le 218
Kurt Lewin 92
Bach Lien 233-35, 238-40, 242
Mme. Vu Thi Kim Lien 218
Nguyen Chi Linh 219
Mme. Thuy Linh 222
Sid Loh 231, 238

M

Bob MacMurdo 310
President Neal Malicky 243
Abraham Maslow 79, 80, 343
Huyhn Tan Mam 223
Senator Eugene McCarthy 26, 88,
   90, 105

Dr. Lois McGovern 92
Senator George McGovern 157, 183
Thomas Merton 48, 55, 65, 102, 204
Ron Meshbesher 101-2
Fr. Huynh Cong Minh 310
George Mische 87
President Monsignor Terry Murphy 202
Fr. Manuel Musallam 266, 272-3

N/O

Nancy Nelson ix, 108, 331
Mother Ngo 172
Ho Ngoc Nhuan 223
Nguyen Dy Nien 220

P

Cyril Paul 74
Pope John Paul II 64-5, 97, 125, 196, 273
Mr. Phan Tuan Phuc 214, 216
Alan Pogue 307-8

Q

Fida Qishta 280
Mr. Trong Quat 161

R

Fr. John Reardon 93
Fr. Jim Remes 4
Fr. Frank Reynolds 343
Archbishop John Roach 202-3
Kenneth Roberts 39
Mike Rodriguez 307
Psychologist Carl Rogers 21, 150, 155
Monsignor Owen J. Rowan 57, 59, 61
Fr. Eric Rutton 321-3
Fr. John A. Ryan 49

S

Rasalyn Sampson 323
Fr. Gregory Schaeffer 208
Bishop Fulton J. Sheen 30, 49
Fr. Don Schnitzius 57-8
Lou Schon 323
Prime Minister Thaksin Shinawatra of Thailand 251-2, 260
Paul Simon 79
Patriarch Irenaios Skopelitis 263
Fr. Henry Sledz 51, 53-6
Professor Suresh Srivastva 156
Fr. Tom Stransky 123
Fr. Charlie Sullivan 307
Fr. Bernie Survil 318, 326
Dr. Suda Suwannapirom 249

T

Charles Callan Tansil 40
Mother Teresa 61-5, 72, 119, 125-33, 224, 273, 348
Bach Lien Thai 233-4
President Thieu / General Nguyen Van Thieu 10, 13, 121, 144-7, 174, 227, 314
Warrant Officer Hugh Thompson 142
Mrs. Nguyen Thi Tinh 214, 217
Dr. Patrick Doan Van Toai 121, 226-8, 233, 246
Nguyen Tran 218, 232, 309
Mr. Tri 169, 177, 179, 183
Nguyen Thao and her sister Nguyen Trang 309
Mr. Nguyen Chon Trung 240
Fr. Phan Khac Tu 232-4
Mr. Viet Tung 170-1

U

U.S. Ambassador Leonard S. Unger
134

V

Professor Gabriel Vahanian93
Mr. Pham Van Kham 166
Mordechai Vanunu 301-2
Dr. Ed Vargo 252
Dean Dr. Vinai 246-8
Dr. John Vinton 92, 102-3, 113-4
Dr. Jeff Voorhees 102, 119, 155-6,
    181, 213

W

Rev. Jim Wallis 347-9
Sister Liz Walters 281
Cora Weiss 157, 182, 185
Fr. Bob Willis xxv, 1, 4, 9, 11-2,
    15-6, 20-4, 150-5, 213
Professor Don Wolf 103, 156, 193,
    251

XYZ

Dr. Nguyen Tran Xuong 232-3, 240,
    242
Dr. Howard Zinn 86

ROBERT D. REED PUBLISHERS ORDER FORM

Call in your order for fast service and quantity discounts!
(541) 347- 9882

Or order online at www.rdrpublishers.com *using Paypal.*
OR order by mail: Make a copy of this form; enclose payment information:

Robert D. Reed Publishers, P.O. Box 1992, Bandon, OR 97411
Fax: (541) 347-9883

Send indicated books to:

Name: _____

Address: _____

City: _____ State: _____ Zip: _____

Phone: _____ Cell: _____

E-Mail: _____

Payment by check /_/ or credit card /_/ *(All major credit cards are accepted.)*

Name on card: _____

Card Number: _____

Exp. Date _____ 3-Digit number on back of card: _____

Quantity		Total	
_____	*Maverick Priest* (Fr. Harry Bury)	$17.95	_____
_____	*Love and War* (Harmsen & Welles)	$17.95	_____
_____	*The Physically Fit Messiah* (Cal Samra)	$14.95	_____
_____	*In Pursuit of Health and Longevity* (Cal Samra)	$14.95	_____
_____	*I Can Still Do It!* (Karen Trolan)	$12.95	_____
_____	*House Calls* (Patch Adams, MD)	$11.95	_____
_____	*Unraveling Reality (*Ishi Nobu)	$16.00	_____
_____	*Invisible* (Frances T. Pilch)	$11.95	_____
_____	*ReInhabiting the Village* (Jamaica Stevens)	$34.95	_____
_____	*Math Jokes 4 Mathy Folks* (Patrick Vennebush)	$11.95	_____
_____	Other books from website: _____		_____

Total Number of Books _____ Total Amount _____

Note: Shipping $3.95 1st book + $1 for each additional book
FREE Shipping on orders over $25.00

Shipping _____
THE TOTAL _____

Thank you for your order.